W9-ADN-938

J. W. von Goethe
Wilhelm Meister's Theatrical Calling

Johann Wolfgang von Goethe

Wilhelm Meister's Theatrical Calling

Translated
and with an Introduction by

John R. Russell

CAMDEN HOUSE

PT
2027
.W5
R87
1995
May 1996

Published by Camden House, Inc.
Drawer 2025
Columbia, SC 29202 USA

Printed on acid-free paper.
Binding materials are chosen for strength and
durability.

ISBN 1–57113–018–7

Library of Congress Cataloging-in-Publication Data

Goethe, Johann Wolfgang von, 1749-1832.
  [Wilhelm Meisters theatralische Sendung. English]
  Wilhelm Meister's theatrical calling / Johann Wolfgang von Goethe ;
translated and with an introduction by John Russell.
    p. cm. -- (Studies in German literature, linguistics, and culture)
  Includes bibliographical references and index.
  ISBN 1-57113-018-7 (alk. paper)
  I. Russell, John Raymond. II. Title. III. Series: Studies in
  German literature, linguistics, and culture
  (Unnumbered)
PT2027.W5R87 1995
833'.6--dc20   94-43843
                                                              CIP

Contents

Acknowledgments

I would like to thank my editor, Professor James Hardin, not only for having suffered through my eccentricities, but, much more importantly, for having pointed out the surprising lack of any modern English translation of this important work by Goethe.

For this translation I used the recent "Munich" edition, that is, *Johann Wolfgang Goethe. Sämmtliche Werke nach Epochen seines Schaffens*. Band 2.2 Das erste Weimarer Jahrzehnt. München: Carl Hanser Verlag. 1987 as well as *Johann Wolfgang Goethe. Sämtliche Werke*. I. Abteilung, Band 9. Frankfurt am Main: Deutscher Klassiker Verlag. 1992. I am indebted to the editors of these volumes for much of the material contained in my footnotes. Also, having known the work previously only from Professor Maync's publication of the manuscript, I was gratefully reassured to learn that it indeed contains a number of scribal or auctorial lapses.

Finally, I wish to thank Professor Thomas Kerth, who gave my first draft of the book a welcome critical reading, and Professor Gerda Jordan, who was of considerable help in polishing the final version.

Introduction

WHEN IN 1910 a pupil showed his teacher a manuscript that had been in his family for some years, the latter, Gustav Billeter, was able to thrill the world of German letters with the announcement of the discovery of a presumably suppressed and subsequently lost early version of Goethe's *Wilhelm Meisters Lehrjahre* (Wilhelm Meister's Apprenticeship), published in 1796. That the earlier work had existed was known from numerous allusions to it in Goethe's correspondence and that of his friends, indicating that its various "Books" had been written over the years between 1776-1785. From one such reference the discovery was given the name *Wilhelm Meisters theatralische Sendung* (Wilhelm Meister's Theatrical Calling). While Billeter had presented only some passages from the work in his announcement, it was printed in its entirety in the following year under the direction of Professor Harry Maync of Zurich, who also oversaw the historical-critical printing in the definitive Weimar edition of Goethe's writings.

That the work had been preserved in Zurich was the consequence of a friendship Goethe had formed with a Frau Barbara Schulthess of that city. Having corresponded with her earlier at the suggestion of his friend Johann Kaspar Lavater, Goethe made her acquaintance during his first visit to Switzerland in 1775. When she learned of his work on a new novel, she requested that she might see a copy of his efforts and he accommodated her. Following a practice of the day, she — together with her daughter of the same name — made a copy of each batch of manuscripts before returning it. It is these copies that the Zurich pupil fortuitously presented to his teacher.

The *Calling* is a chronologically linear narration of how a young boy's fascination with marionettes develops over the years into a young man's decision to join the best theatrical troupe of the day. We are given a detailed description of Wilhelm's middle class home and family, as well as the family business and the town he lives in until he sets off into the greater world, ostensibly in pursuit of business matters. On this journey his experience is broadened to include much of life as it was lived in eighteenth century Germany, from the meanest inns, to factories, the salons of the well-to-do urban middle class, and even the palaces of the aristocracy. A particularly realistic picture is given of the hardships involved in travel at that time due to the roads, the vehicles, inexperienced coachmen, and even brigandry amidst the chaos of war. The roles of the elements and darkness are also not forgotten so that the present day reader can readily appreciate the delight of Wilhelm's troupe when, at the end of a rain-drenched trip on foot and in wagons, they finally catch sight of their destination, a castle with every room illuminated!

During the course of the eighteenth century the significance of the middle class increased to the point where it reshaped the governments and societies of Western Europe. We find a realistic reflection of these times in the work's concern with money matters that perhaps reaches its high point with the brother-in-law's lauding the glories of double entry bookkeeping. Although Wilhelm moves from the world of his family to that of the theater, the move is from family business to theater business: no matter how much the stage-struck hero may rhapsodize about the theater as art, the problems of achieving commercial success or even survival remain at least in the background and are often uncomfortably at center stage.

The title given the recovered work is quite apt in stressing the importance of theater in it. Wilhelm is, to be sure, the central figure around whom all action develops, yet theater *per se* remains the core of the work. The reader is led through a progression of what amounts to the evolution of the theater. Childish play acting leads to the children's attempt at staging a play. Wilhelm is no sooner in the greater world than he encounters a group of miners who engage in street theater intended to praise their trade — and to garner a few gratuities. Upon arriving at his initial destination, he witnesses a pageant honoring the local factory owner and patron of theatrical art. From star-crossed lovers he learns firsthand of the disrespect in which the theater and actors are held. Meeting them soon again after they have joined a troupe, he is introduced by its director to many of the problems that can be encountered when creating a world of illusion. Though Wilhelm keeps telling himself he will soon return to the pursuit of his business obligations, he remains with the troupe when by chance it is invited to perform for a period at a castle where the seventeenth century tradition of court theater is still very much alive. After experiencing at first hand the tumult of war, Wilhelm finally reaches the large port city where he is exposed to modern, that is, urban, middle-class theater.

Another realistic aspect of the work is its unstated subtext of the struggle of the middle class in eighteenth century Germany to establish a cultural identity. Although it is a commonplace that the Enlightenment had little influence in the welter of German states, this is perhaps true only in the sphere of politics and government. It was of tremendous importance in other areas such as education, religion, and the arts, and there is nothing exceptional about a character such as Werner, whom we meet first exploring the nature of drama and whom we soon see singing a paean to commerce. With the spread of literacy there developed a desire for a national literature, that is, an indigenous and original one in German. The theater became a natural center of interest for the bourgeoisie. Just as the middle class had not been anticipated in the medieval social order, it found little of its world reflected in the traditional division of drama into comedy, then usually interpreted as burlesque and performed by itinerant troupes moving from fair to fair, and tragedy, performed for the aristocracy in their court theaters.

The struggle to train professional actors and find permanent work-places for them is depicted quite clearly in the *Calling*, where two of the characters are patterned after prominent figures in the development of theater in eighteenth century Germany. Madame de Retti is a reflection of Karoline Neuber (1690-1760), who, along with her husband, led the first established troupe in Germany, in Leipzig, from the late 1730s and is best remembered for banning Hanswurst, the traditional burlesque comic, from her stage. Similarly, Serlo is drawn loosely after Friedrich Ludwig Schröder (1744–1816), who led what was probably the best troupe in Germany in the last part of the century in Hamburg — surely Wilhelm's port city. Schröder is remembered as being largely responsible for creating in Germany the great respect for Shakespeare and his works which has continued down to our own day.

Parallel to the progression of the various forms of the drama, there runs throughout the *Calling* a discussion of the very nature of this literary form. That this examination signifies more than Wilhelm or the author demonstrating his own acuity is seen from the number of contemporary references cited (and the footnotes they elicit). Among the more important of these are those referring, if not by name, to Johann Christoph Gottsched (1700–1766), a professor in Leipzig who attempted to educate the Germans in what constituted good writing. To illustrate his precepts, he worked with Frau Neuber's troupe and published the highly influential anthology *Die deutsche Schaubühne* (The German Stage), introducing new German works or translations from abroad. His efforts at reform, however, did not progress much further than trying to impose the rules of French Classicism on the emerging German theater. Some of his disciples broke away to continue the fight for a national theater by producing two rival periodicals known collectively as the *Bremer Beiträge* (Contributions from Bremen). Just as it became clear that the application of Reason alone was not the solution for all problems, so did it become obvious that the application of rules was no guarantee of a successful play. Ultimately a much freer concept of what was permissible in the drama won out, a victory metaphorically depicted in our work by Wilhelm's abandoning Racine for Shakespeare.

When Wilhelm, standing between Philine, his Comic Muse, and Aurelie, her tragic counterpart, finally agrees to join Serlo's troupe, the reader can feel that he has reached his goal, yet at the same time he is well aware that, despite its length, the *Calling* is an unfinished work. Among themes remaining unresolved are the search for Mariane, Mignon's very uncertain health, the identity of the radiant beauty who insured Wilhelm's recovery, and, not least of all, the business affairs which sent him on his journey.

It is known that Goethe planned the work to extend to twelve books or approximately twice the length of our text. He did begin writing Book Seven, but no trace of this has survived. His efforts obviously were interrupted by his decision to undertake a journey to Italy during 1786–1788, a watershed experience for him that brought his life and art to full maturity. When he returned to his duties at Weimar, he viewed the world with different eyes, one result of which was a fundamental reworking of Wilhelm's story which gave us and the printing press the *Apprenticeship* rather than the *Calling*.

We will never know precisely why Goethe decided to rewrite this material, but one can make reasonable conjectures. Having made the theater the core of the earlier work, Goethe had to a certain extent run through his material: various dramatic theories had been presented in detail as had the evolution of the subgenres of drama. (The one notable exception to the latter is the omission of opera, which is given but a nod in the *Calling*, but this is not surprising: music is singularly absent among Goethe's profound examinations of so many aspects of the world about him.)

A more probable reason for Goethe's discontent with the earlier work is its principal character, Wilhelm. The reader does not have to exercise any great insight to note that its hero shows next to no development. Despite the many trials and tribulations he endures in a rich variety of encounters experienced on his journey, he remains unbelievably naïve about the real world, as each of his Muses in turn explains to him. He is not a despondent do-nothing like his literary predecessor Werther, for his accomplishments as both playwright and actor are highly praised. But he is not yet a Faust: he remains diffident about the theater and his place in it even while choosing the world of illusion over the real world of active achievement.

There is little point in attempting to detail here the many changes Goethe made in reworking the *Calling* into the *Apprenticeship* but a few can indicate how he managed to write two so different works using much of the same material in both. The essential difference is that the later work is finished and that in it, the principal emphasis is on the development of the hero himself, although the medium for this development remains the theater. Much of Wilhelm's early life was eliminated as were the samples from Goethe's early poetry. Most of the poems preserved were revised, as was the order of their appearance within the new text. The chronologically linear narration of the earlier work was also abandoned. Suffice it to say that the student of narrative technique can scarcely find a more rewarding task than comparing the two.

The *Calling* has suffered a somewhat uncertain fate since its discovery some eighty years after Goethe's death and well after his reputation as Germany's greatest man of letters was not only established but also solidified. When the work was published, objections were raised concerning the propriety of publishing a draft fragment of a text that Goethe had chosen to suppress. Most critics who have evaluated it subsequently, however, have found it to be a work quite capable and worthy of standing on its own. Typical of this view are the comments of Hugo von Hofmannsthal, who wrote in 1931,

> *Wilhelm Meister's Theatrical Calling* — even though it is a fragmentary book — if we possessed only this torso of a book, only that which brought us the figures of Wilhelm, Mignon, Philine, and Aurelie, it would be a significant, substantial, incomparable book. In it we would have from the hand of our greatest poet an unfinished novel, one not unrelated to the great foreign novels of the eighteenth century and yet with elements in it that lift it above all its predecessors.

Remarks on the Translation

I DECIDED TO attempt a translation of Goethe's *Sendung* even though I knew an earlier one existed: *Wilhelm Meister's Theatrical Mission,* introduction by Harry Mayne [sic], trans. Gregory A. Page (London: William Heinemann, 1913. xxxiv + 342 pp.). I assumed that however good this earlier work might have been, it would probably be seriously dated for today's reader. A first attempt was made and then reworked. Only after this revision did I locate a copy of the 1913 translation, with which I compared my own.

It was a great relief to discover that my effort had not been redundant. Page's translation is generally an accurate one although it suffers from poor editing, which need not be detailed here. Suffice it to point out that the Introduction is said to be by Harry Mayne [sic]; if Professor Maync did authorize the use of his observations, he was poorly rewarded. More important, the translation is difficult for today's reader since it is couched in language all too reflective of the aestheticism of the Edwardian literary world. This style is difficult even in expository prose and can become painful when used in conversations that are presumably conducted in colloquial speech.

A second, unnecessary difficulty with Page's translation is its lack of notes. To be sure, an ideal translation would be one without footnotes, but the greater the temporal chasm between author and translator, the more difficult this becomes. One might possibly assume that at the beginning of the present century the typical English-speaking reader was still sufficiently well-versed in the Classical tradition to understand Goethe's many allusions to the literature and mythology of Antiquity, but no such assumption is defensible today. The other principal cause for the profusion of footnotes in the present offering is Goethe's frequent references to the literature of his day. Professor Maync's Introduction does indeed touch on some of these points, but he was a Germanist addressing an audience comprised not only of German speakers but also, in good part, of Germanists, rather than one whose knowledge of the German literary tradition is more modest.

Having pointed out what I found to be weaknesses in the Page translation, I hasten to acknowledge how valuable it proved in pointing out where I had missed a word or sentence and in suggesting revisions for my final text. Since only four (short) sentences were identical in the two translations, the earlier work served as an instant thesaurus, and I gratefully adopted a goodly number of words and phrases from Page as being more felicitous than my own choices. At the dozen or so points where the translations were in obvious conflict, I naturally returned to the original to determine which of us had sinned; if memory serves, we shared the onus more or less equally.

Another aid in translating this particular work was the fact that it is a manuscript copy, rather than a holograph, of what was probably still regarded by the author as a draft. Accordingly, I felt relatively free to insert or otherwise alter punctuation, something particularly true in the case of quotation marks since the manuscript uses none and usually, though not always, has simply a dash to indicate a change of speaker. In like manner, I felt little compunction in breaking overly complex sentences and page-long paragraphs in which the subject at hand obviously changes.

One device used by Goethe was abandoned: To underline the androgynous nature of Mignon, he uses masculine, feminine, and neuter pronouns and adjectives in referring to her. This is confusing enough in German; it would be much more so in English. Conversely, two obvious auctorial lapses were retained as tidbits for the attentive reader: The Lieutenant of Constabulary is also the Lieutenant of Artillery in Book I; Hochdorf and Hochstädt are the same community in Book III.

German terms of address were retained, as were Goethe's spellings of the many names derived from French or Italian. Similarly, I made no attempt to find equivalents for the various coinages mentioned here such as Pfennige, Groschen, Taler, Dukaten, and Louisdor; their relative significance is fortunately clear from the contexts in which they appear.

Book 1

Chapter 1

IT WAS A few days before Christmas Eve, 174*, when Benedikt Mei-ster, a citizen and merchant in M**, a middle-sized imperial city,[1] left his customary circle of friends for home around eight in the evening. Contrary to custom, the tarot game[2] had ended rather early and he was not entirely happy to be returning so punctually to his own four walls, which his wife did not make exactly a paradise for him. There was still some time before the evening repast and his wife did not usually fill such an interval with pleasantries, as a consequence of which he preferred not to come to table until the soup was already somewhat overcooked.

He was walking slowly and reflecting on the position of mayor, which he had filled for the last year, and on its affairs and its small advantages, when in passing he saw his mother's brightly lit window. After the old woman had settled a sum on her son and turned her shop over to him, she had withdrawn to a small cottage, where with only a maid she lived quite comfortably from her ample annuities, occasionally doing something nice for her children and grandchildren, but keeping the best for them until after her death, when, she hoped, they might be more prudent than she had been able to observe during her lifetime. Meister had been drawn mysteriously to the house, where, after he had knocked, the maid hurriedly and secretively opened the door and conducted him up the stairs.

When he stepped through the parlor door, he found his mother at a large table busily removing and covering things. To his "Good Evening" she answered, "Your visit isn't entirely timely, but since you're here, you might as well know. See what I'm doing," she said and lifted the napkins that were spread across the bed and at the same time removed a fur coat she had hastily thrown over a table. The man now caught sight of a number of small, colorfully costumed mario-

---

[1] A number of German cities, such as Nuremberg and Frankfurt, were subject directly to the Holy Roman Emperor rather than to a local prince.

[2] Tarot was still a popular card game in the eighteenth century, its colorful deck not yet abandoned to fortune telling.

nettes lying alongside one another in neat order with flexible wires attached to their heads and which seemed only to be waiting for the animation that would stir them out of their inactivity.

"What's all this?" said Meister.

"A Merry Christmas for your children!" the old lady answered. "I hope they delight them as much as getting them ready has me."

He examined them for a while, seemingly with care, in order not to annoy her at the very outset by appearing to regard her work as useless. "Dear Mother," he finally said, "children are children. You've gone to too much work and in the end I don't see what good will come of it."

"Just be still," said the old woman as she straightened the marionettes' clothing which had become somewhat mussed. "Don't make a fuss. They'll enjoy them. It's always been my custom and I'm not going to change, as you know. When you were small, you were fascinated by them and paraded around throughout the holidays carrying your toys and sweets. Now your children are also going to be just as happy. I'm their grandmother and know my duty."

"I don't want to spoil it for you, Mother," said Meister. "I was just thinking, what difference does it make to the children whether one gives them something today or tomorrow. If they need something, I give it to them. Why do we need Christmas for that? There are people who let their children go about in rags while they save for that one day."

"Benedikt," said the old woman, "I've dressed up puppets for them and arranged a show for them; children must have plays and puppets. It was that way in your youth; you got many a penny from me to see Doctor Faust and the Moorish ballet.[3] I don't know what you're doing with your children and why they shouldn't have the same things you did."

"Which one is this?" said Meister picking up a marionette.

"Don't tangle the wires!" said the old woman. "It's more work than you think to get them just right. Look, that's King Saul. You mustn't think that I've been wasting my money. As far as the fabrics are concerned, I had them all in my sewing box, and I can surely afford the little bit of imitation silver and gold on them."

"The puppets are quite nice," said Meister.

"I think so, too," smiled the old woman, "and yet they don't cost much. I had Merks, the old crippled sculptor, who has owed me the interest on his house for so long, carve out the hands, feet, and faces

---

[3] Two skits performed by the traveling puppet shows which were commonly a part of German fairs.

for me. I won't get the money from him anyway, and I can't throw him out; he's been there since the days of my late husband, and he was always punctual in his payments until his unfortunate second marriage."

"This one in black velvet and the gold crown, that's Saul?" asked Meister. "Who are the others?"

"You should know that," said the mother. "This one here is Jonathan; he's in yellow and red because he's young and flighty, and I've given him a turban. That one up there is Samuel; he caused me the most trouble with his little breastplate. Look at his ephod;[4] that's a watered taffeta I wore before I was married."

"Good night," said Meister, "it's just striking eight."

"But look at David before you go!" said the old woman. "Oh, he's beautiful; he's carved to perfection and has red hair. See how small he is and pretty."

"Well, then where's Goliath?" said Meister. "He's surely there somewhere."

"He's not ready yet," said the old woman. "That's going to be a masterpiece once it's all finished. The Lieutenant of the Constabulary and his brother are making the theater for me; and in the back are shepherds and shepherdesses, Moors and Mooresses, and dwarfs for the dance. It's going to be quite pretty! Just let me do what I want, and don't say anything at home, and see to it that Wilhelm doesn't come running over here. He's going to be delighted, for I still remember how I sent him to the marionette show at the last fair, how he told me all about it, and how well he understood it."

"You're going to too much trouble," said Meister as he reached for the doorknob.

"If we hadn't gone to trouble for our children, how would you have grown up?" said the grandmother.

The maid took a candle and lighted his way down the stairs.

---

[4] The breastplate was a piece of embroidered cloth with twelve jewels representing the tribes of Israel. In ancient times Hebrew high priests wore it on the ephod, an embroidered outer garment.

Chapter 2

Christmas Eve approached in all its festivity. The children ran about
all day and stood at the window, fearing night would never come. Finally they were called, and they entered the parlor where in great astonishment each was shown to his well-lit portion. Each had taken
possession of his share and after gazing at it for a while was about to
take it into a corner and under his protection, when an unforeseen
drama opened before their eyes. A door that led to a side room
opened, but not, as usual, for the purpose of running back and forth.
The entrance was filled by an unexpected splendor: a green rug,
hanging down over a table, completely covered the bottom part of the
opening; from there rose up a portal that was closed by a magic curtain; and what remained of the space at the top of the door was covered by a piece of dark green material that closed it off completely. At
first they all stood at a distance, and as their curiosity grew to see
what glittering thing might be hidden behind the curtain, each was directed to his small chair and kindly told to wait patiently. Wilhelm
was the only one who remained at a respectful distance and had to
be spoken to twice and even three times by his grandmother before
he, too, took his seat. So now everyone was seated and quiet, when
at the sound of a whistle the curtain rose, revealing a view into the
temple painted in bright red. The high priest Samuel appeared with
Jonathan, and their alternating voices completely captivated their
young audience. Finally Saul entered, greatly perturbed at the impertinence with which the burly fellow had defied him and his people.
How happy then our Wilhelm was who listened to every word and
missed nothing as the diminutive, ruddy-cheeked son of Jesse stepped
forth with his crook, shepherd's bag, and sling and spoke: "Most
powerful king and sovereign lord! Let no one lose courage at this. If
Your Majesty will permit me, I will go and battle the mighty giant."
The act came to an end. The other children were all agog, but Wilhelm alone was waiting for what was to follow and was thinking
about it; he was impatient to see the great giant and how it all would
turn out.

The curtain rose again. David was promising the carcass of the
monster to the fowls of the sky and the beasts of the field. The Philis-
tine scorned him and stamped much with both feet, finally falling like
a log and giving the whole affair a splendid conclusion. Later the vir-
gins sang "Saul has slain his thousands, but David has slain tens of
thousands" and the head of the giant was borne before the small victor, who in return received the king's fair daughter as his bride. Yet it

annoyed Wilhelm even amidst all this joy that this lucky prince was the size of a dwarf, for following her conception of the tall Goliath and small David, his dear grandmother had omitted nothing to make both true to character. The rapt attention of the other children continued unabated; Wilhelm, however, fell into reflection, because of which he saw the ballet of the Moors, shepherds, and dwarfs flit before him but only as if in shadow. The curtain fell, the door closed, and the entire small party stumbled about as though tipsy and needing to go to bed. But Wilhelm, who as a member of the group also had to go, lay alone, uncertainly pondering what he had seen, unsatisfied amidst his pleasure, full of hope, longing, and premonitions.

Chapter 3

The following day everything had simply disappeared, the magical veil was lifted, and one again could walk freely from the one room into the next, from which on the preceding evening such adventure had radiated. The others ran up and down with their playthings. Wilhelm, however, prowled here and there as though he were seeking a lost love, as if he found it almost impossible that there should be only two door-posts where yesterday there had been so much magic. He asked his mother if she might have it played for him again and received from her a harsh answer because she could take no pleasure in the fun which the grandmother created for her grandchildren, since this seemed to her a reproach for her own lack of motherly qualities. I am sorry I must say it, yet it is true that this woman who had by her husband five children — two sons and three daughters, of whom Wilhelm was the oldest — in her later years developed a passion for a base person, of which her husband was aware and could not bear, and now slovenliness, irritation, and quarreling crept into the house. Had the husband not been a solid, dutiful citizen and his mother a right-thinking, proper lady, an odious divorce suit would have disgraced the family.

In all this the poor children suffered most, for just as any helpless creature flees to its mother whenever the father is angry, things were twice as bad here from the other side, for in her discontent the mother was usually in a bad humor, and if she was not, then at least she complained about the old man and took pleasure in finding an opportunity where she could expose his severity, his roughness, his bad behavior. That sometimes hurt Wilhelm. He only wanted protection from his father or consolation whenever he had treated him badly; but he could not bear for someone to belittle him, for someone to misinterpret his complaints as evidence against a man whom in his heart he loved quite dearly. As a result, he became alienated from his mother and thus was in a poor way, because his father was also a hard man. Hence nothing remained for him save to withdraw into himself, a fate of great consequence in children and old people.

Chapter 4

Wilhelm had gone on in his childish way for a period, sometimes reliving in his memory that happy Christmas Eve, always enjoying seeing pictures, and reading fairy tales and heroic adventures. His grandmother, who certainly did not want to have gone to so much trouble in vain, upon the long-planned visit of some neighbors' children, had the marionette theater reerected and the play performed again.

If Wilhelm had had the joy of surprise and amazement the first time, then on the second he had the delight of attentiveness and discovery. His interest now was how it all was done. Already the first time he had assured himself that the puppets did not speak nor move of themselves; that did not bother him. But why was it all so pretty and why did it nevertheless seem as if they were talking and moving by themselves, why was it so delightful to watch, and where might the lights and the people be? Those were the questions that disturbed him more and more, as he wished more and more to be simultaneously among the enchanted and the enchanters, secretly to have a hand in the play and at the same time to be an observer and enjoy the pleasure which he and the other children felt. The piece was almost over and had reached the final dance when he slyly attempted to approach the protective screen. Scarcely had the curtain fallen and no one was watching when he heard from the noises within that people were busy cleaning up. So he lifted the lower rug and peered through the table legs.

A maid noticed him from without and pulled him back, yet he had seen this much, that people were packing friends and foes, Saul and Goliath, Moors and dwarfs into a single chest, and this was fresh food for his half-satisfied curiosity. Just as at a certain time children become aware of the difference between the sexes and their glances beneath the surfaces which hide these secrets produce wondrous stirrings in their natures, so it was for Wilhelm with this discovery: he was more tranquil and more disturbed than before; it seemed to him that he had learned something, and he sensed from this that he knew nothing at all.

Chapter 5

In a well-run and orderly home the children have a sense much like rats and mice may have: they are alert to all cracks and holes where they can get to a forbidden tidbit which they enjoy with a covert, delicious fear, and I believe this is a major part of the child's delight. Wilhelm noticed much more quickly than his any of his siblings whenever some key was left in a lock. He bore great respect within his heart for the locked doors he had to pass for weeks and months and into which he only occasionally was permitted to cast a glance whenever his mother opened the sanctuary to fetch something; nonetheless he was all the quicker to profit from any opportunity the housekeeper's neglect occasionally granted him.

Among all the doors, as one can quickly guess, that of the pantry was the one toward which his senses were most keenly directed. Few joys of anticipation in this life equaled the sensation when his mother occasionally summoned him to help her carry something out, and he then had a few dried plums, thanks either to her generosity or to his cunning. The welter of piled-up treasures in their abundance captivated his imagination, and even the unpleasant odor of the intermingled fragrances of the various things there — soap, candles, lemons, and all sorts of old and new canisters — had such a delicious effect upon him that whenever he was in its vicinity and even at a distance of a few paces, he always delighted in its momentarily revealed emanations.

One Sunday morning when his mother had been hurried by the church bells and the whole house lay in a deep Sabbath stillness, this remarkable key remained hanging in its lock. Scarcely had Wilhelm noticed it when he walked softly two or three times back and forth before it, finally advanced in appropriate silence, opened the door and with one step found himself in the proximity of so many long-coveted delights. He surveyed chests, sacks, boxes, canisters, and jars with a quick, probing glance, determining what he should choose and take. Finally he reached for the much-loved dried plums, provided himself with a few dried apples, contentedly added a jar of orange compote, and started to ease his way backwards when his eye was struck by some boxes standing together, out of one of which a few wires with hooks on their ends hung down through the poorly closed lid. Full of anticipation he attacked it and with what divine sensation discovered that in it, neatly packed, lay his world of heroes and delights. He wanted to pick up and look at the topmost, to pull out those on the bottom, but quite soon he tangled the fine wires, and fell into confusion and fearfulness, especially when he heard the cook stirring in the adjacent kitchen. He packed everything together as well as he could, closed the chest, and took only a small, handwritten book which contained the play of David and Goliath and which had been lying on top. With this booty he quietly withdrew to a room in the attic.

From that time on he devoted all his secret, private hours to reading his play over and over, to learning it by heart, and to imagining in his thoughts how splendid it would be if he could bring the appropriate figures to life with his fingers. In so doing he himself turned into David and Goliath, performing both for himself in turn.

In passing I can't leave without comment what a magical effect attics, barns, and secret rooms customarily have on children; there, free from the duress of their mentors, they can enjoy being alone, a feeling that they slowly lose in later years, though it sometimes returns when these sites of disordered utility have to serve as a secret place for writing love letters. In such places and under such circumstances Wilhelm made the play totally a part of himself, assumed all the roles, and learned them by heart except that he customarily put himself in the place of the principal heroes and let the others run about in his mind like hangers-on. Thus the noble speeches of David with which he challenged the arrogant giant Goliath lay in his mind day and night. He often murmured them to himself, and no one paid any attention except that his father, who noticed it now and then, and praised to himself the good memory of the boy who had been able to retain so much from such brief exposure.

Chapter 6

On an evening when the grandmother had summoned Wilhelm to her home, he was sitting in great silence beside her, fashioning all sorts of figures from sheets of wax. Finally he even produced a David and a Goliath and let them harangue one another quite splendidly. In the end Goliath received such a sharp blow that his wax feet loosened from the table and he lay there at full length. His head was immediately separated from his torso, by means of a needle mounted in wax it was put into the hand of the little terror, and also a hymn of gratitude was then sung. The old woman sat quite entranced, listened with astonishment to her grandson, and when he was done, there came praise and questions as to where he had acquired this skill. He did possess some talent for lying but also a sure feeling for when he didn't need to lie. He admitted to his grandmother that he had taken possession of the booklet but begged her fervently to protect him and not betray him because he would take care of it and not lose it. The old woman gave him her promise and to her promise she added something for him and actually for herself: that she wanted to persuade his father to permit his son to perform the great drama at some sort of children's gathering in the presence of the Lieutenant of Artillery. So she ordered Wilhelm to say nothing further of the affair.

A few days later she began her negotiations and encountered some difficulties. Principal among these was that her son had been put into a most disagreeable mood by the continuing bad behavior of his wife. All the worries of the business rested on him, and his wife, instead of recognizing that and trying to be helpful, was the first to harass him in his misfortune, to misinterpret his actions, to exaggerate his mistakes, and to fail to recognize that which was good about him. With his inborn bourgeois sense of industry, this produced an uncertain feeling of struggling and working in vain such as the Damned in Hell are said to have. And had it not been for his children, a glance at whom not seldom restored his spirit and the conviction that he was working for something in this world, it would not have been possible for him to endure it. In such a mood a person quite loses all sense for childish pleasures, which are actually not the father's, but the mother's concern to think up and bring about: if she is a monster, then very little comfort remains for a family in what should be its happiest years. In this case the grandmother provided that comfort. She did manage to arrange things so that for this purpose two rooms on the fourth floor were provided which contained nothing but some wardrobes. In the one room the spectators were to sit, and the other was for the actors with, as usual, the view into the theater filling the opening of the door.

The old man had permitted the grandmother to arrange all that. He himself seemed simply to ignore it on purpose, for he had a principle that one shouldn't let children notice how much they are loved: they would take liberties. One has to appear stern amid their pleasures and sometimes even spoil these so that they not fall into arrogance.

Chapter 7

The Lieutenant of Artillery, who was a godson of the grandmother, was now ordered to set up the theater and to take care of the other things. Wilhelm noticed it, for he came into the house on various occasions that week at unaccustomed times. His curiosity only grew since he sensed rightly that he wasn't permitted to take any part in it before Saturday. Finally the coveted Saturday arrived. At five in the evening the Lieutenant of Artillery came and took Wilhelm upstairs with him. Trembling with joy he entered and caught sight of the marionettes hanging down at both sides of the frame in the order in which they were to appear. He examined them carefully and then climbed onto the foot board which raised him above the theater so that he hovered above his little world. Not without awe did he peer down between the boards, because the memory of what a splendid effect it produced in the audience and the feeling of wonder over the mysteries he was a part of still held him. They held a rehearsal and it went splendidly.

It was the same the following day when a party of children had been invited, except that in the heat of the action Wilhelm dropped his Jonathan and was compelled to reach down with his hand and retrieve him. This greatly disturbed the illusion, caused great laughter, and annoyed him beyond description. But this slip seemed most welcome to the father, who inwardly felt the greatest satisfaction in seeing his young son so capable but deliberately didn't show it; when the performance was ended, he immediately stressed the mistakes and said it would have been quite nice if only this and that hadn't gone wrong. That annoyed our prince deeply; he was sad throughout the evening, but on the following morning he had already slept it off and he grew happy in the thought that, except for the accident, he had performed splendidly. And this wasn't vanity since, except for the Lieutenant, he had no model against which to measure himself. The former had proven accomplished at switching between a coarse and a natural voice, but on the other hand had declaimed affectedly and woodenly, whereas with Wilhelm one had detected a good, true, and courageous soul in the principal roles, as, for example, in David's challenging of Goliath and the modesty with which he appeared before the King following the victory.

Chapter 8

Suffice it to say, the theater remained standing, and since the lovely springtime had arrived and one could survive without a fire, Wilhelm spent his free and play periods lying in the room and letting the puppets perform bravely in turn. Often he invited his siblings and playmates; even more often, however, he was alone. His imagination and his vitality brooded over the small world which was soon to acquire a different shape. After only a few performances of the first piece for which the theater and its actors had been fashioned, it no longer brought him joy. Among his father's books he had found *The German Stage*[5] and various translated Italian operas to which he devoted himself; in each case he immediately redefined the characters and performed the piece. Now King Saul had to play Chaumigrem, Cato and Darius,[6] although it should be noted that the plays were never performed completely; rather it was usually their fifth acts, those involving a fatal thrust.

It was also inevitable that the opera with its many changes and adventures attracted him more. In them he found stormy seas, gods who descended from the clouds, and — what made him especially happy — lightning and thunder. He sought help from cardboard, paint and paper, and he was even able to produce a splendid night; his lightning was frightful to behold, only the thunder was not always successful, but that wasn't all that important. Also he found more opportunity in the operas to introduce his David and Goliath, something not permitted in the classical drama. Every day he felt closer to his small world where he enjoyed such a variety of pleasures, and I can't fail to note that the smells which the puppets had absorbed from the pantry played no small part in this.

The theater was now in good shape and the talent he had had since childhood for using a compass and for cutting out and painting cardboard now served him well although it bothered him all the more that his figures often kept him from presenting important scenes. His sisters who often dressed and undressed their dolls gave him the idea of gradually acquiring removable clothing for his heroes. So he removed the bits of cloth from their bodies, reassembled them as well as he could, saved up some money, bought new ribbon and spangles, begged many a scrap of taffeta, and gradually acquired a new wardrobe for the theater, in which especially hoop skirts for the ladies were not forgotten.

Now he was actually outfitted for even the grandest play, and one would have thought that there would truly be some serious acting. But things developed for him as they tend to fairly often with children: they conceive great plans, make grand preparations and maybe even some attempts, and then everything is dropped. With Wilhelm it

---

[5] *Die deutsche Schaubühne*, an anthology published from 1740-1746 by J. C. Gottsched in his efforts to create a modern German-language theater. It contained thirty-eight plays, both German originals and translations of works by contemporary French and Danish dramatists.

[6] Figures drawn from Gottsched's anthology: Chaumigrem from F. M. v. Grimm's *Banise*, Cato from Gottsched's *Der sterbende Cato*, and Darius from F. L. Pitschel's drama of that name.

went in just this fashion; for him the greatest pleasure lay in invention and imagination. This or that play interested him on account of a certain scene, for which he immediately would make up a new costume. In this process the costumes originally worn had become scattered and misplaced so that not even the original play could be properly performed any more.

Because of infirmity and advanced age his grandmother kept to her bed, and no one in the house paid any attention to the theater, so it soon ended up in great disorder. Wilhelm abandoned himself to his imagination: he was forever rehearsing and making preparations without bringing anything to completion; he built a thousand castles in the sky and didn't notice that he still had not laid the foundation for the first one.

Chapter 9

As his circle of acquaintances began to grow, the other diversions of childhood intruded on his lonely, quiet pleasure. Among them he was by turn now a huntsman, a soldier, a cavalryman, as the character of their games demanded, but here he always had an advantage over the others in that he was able skillfully to fashion for them the necessary equipment. Thus the swords were for the most part from his factory; he decorated and gilded the sleighs, and from a secret instinct and an old attachment he soon transformed their militia into the style of Antiquity. Helmets were prepared with paper plumes, shields and even armor were made, efforts at which the household servants who possessed some tailoring skills and the seamstresses broke many a needle. Now he saw a portion of his young comrades nicely costumed before him; the others, less important, were gradually outfitted, but less lavishly. A quite respectable company was assembled; they marched in the courtyards and gardens, smiting one another's shields and heads quite commendably. There was many a disagreement which Wilhelm soon was able to resolve.

This game, which amused the others greatly, had been played but a few times when it no longer satisfied Wilhelm. The sight of so many armored figures was bound to arouse in him the thoughts of knighthood which had filled his head for some time since he had taken to reading old novels. The flood was unleashed by *Jerusalem Liberated*[7]

---

[7] *La Gerusalemme liberata* (Parma, 1581) by Torquato Tasso (1544-1595). *Gottfried oder Das befreite Jerusalem*, the German translation by Johann Friedrich Koppe, appeared in Leipzig, 1742. Principal figures in it are: Tan-

which had come into his hands in Koppe's translation. He couldn't read the poem in its entirety, but there were passages which he knew by heart and their images hovered before his eyes. He was especially captivated by Clorinda in all her doings. Her forceful femininity, the serene intensity of her being had more influence on the spirit of love which was beginning to bud within the youth than did the wiles of Arminda, although he did not despise her garden. But hundreds upon hundreds of times, as he stood at his window in the evening and looked into the garden and the summer sun sank behind the hills, casting a hazy glow on the horizon, the stars appeared, and night came on from every corner and hollow, and the resonant sound of the frogs pierced the solemn stillness from afar, he recited to himself the story of her sad death. No matter how much he sided with the Christians, he stood by her in setting fire to the great tower. With all his heart he hated Argant and begrudged him the company of such an angel. And when Tancred discovers her by night, their combat begins beneath its bleak cloak, and they duel mightily, he never could utter the words:

> Clorinda's cup is full, she's near her final breath,
> At last the hour has come when she's to meet her death.

without tears coming to his eyes which then overflowed as the hapless lover plunges the sword into her breast, removes the helmet from the sinking woman, and, trembling, fetches water for her baptism. Our Wilhelm's heart overflowed when in the enchanted forest Tancred's sword violates the tree, blood flows after the blow, a voice strikes his heart saying that he is reopening Clorinda's wound, and he seems destined by fate to destroy in ignorance that which he loves. The story took such control over his imagination that what he had read of the poem mysteriously shaped itself into a whole in his soul, overpowered him, and, without understanding how, he began to think seriously of presenting it as a play. He wanted to act Tancred and Rinaldo himself and for this end he found ready at hand two sets of armor which he had made earlier. The one, a coat of mail made of dark gray paper, was to adorn the earnest Tancred, the other of gold and silver paper was for the radiant Rinaldo.

cred, a mature hero of the Crusaders; Rinaldo, a youthful hero of the Crusaders; Clorinda, the beloved of Tancred, who fights the Crusaders and is converted to Christianity only shortly before her death; Armida, a seductress who seeks to draw Rinaldo from his goal; Argant, Rinaldo's counterpart among the heathens; and Gottfried, leader of the Crusaders.

With all the vividness of his imagination he related everything to his comrades, who were delighted with it, yet couldn't quite grasp how they were to arrive at the point where it was to be performed and performed by them. Wilhelm easily dispelled their doubts. He immediately lay claim to a few rooms in the house of a nearby play-mate without taking into account that the latter's old aunt would never give them up. It went similarly with the theater, of which he had no definite conception save that it would have to be on a plat-form, the wings consisting of folding screens, with a large cloth for the background. But he hadn't considered where all that was to come from. For the forest they found a good solution: they persuaded a former servant in one of the houses who had become a head forester to have young birches and firs sent to them. These were indeed deliv-ered to them, but now they were in a dilemma as to how they should perform the piece before they withered. The situation was critical: they lacked space, a theater, curtains. The folding screens were the only thing they had.

In their perplexity they approached a cousin to whom they gave a detailed description of the splendor that was to be created. He didn't know how to bring it all together, but he was helpful to them. In a small room he gathered together what tables he could find in the house and in the neighborhood. He erected the flats and made a rear prospect out of green curtains. The trees, too, were soon standing in ranks. The candles were lit, the girls and boys had gathered, it was to begin, the entire host of heroes had assembled when, for the first time, it occurred to each that he didn't know what he had to say. In the fervor of invention when Wilhelm was preoccupied by his con-cept, he had forgotten that everyone would certainly have to know what he had to say and at what point, and in their excitement at ap-pearing on the stage, it also hadn't occurred to the others. They be-lieved they would easily represent heroes, easily be able to act and speak like the characters into whose world Wilhelm's gift had put them.

They all stood there amazed, asked one another what was to come first, and Wilhelm, who had conceived himself as being in the fore as Tancred, stepped out alone and began to recite some verses from the epic. But this turned all to soon into narration and he finally appeared in the third person in his own speech. When Gottfried, whose turn it was to speak, refused to come out, he had to withdraw amidst great laughter from his audience, a calamity that would fester in his soul more deeply than some subsequent disappointments. It had failed.

The audience was sitting there and wanted to see something. They were costumed, Wilhelm pulled himself together and decided summarily to perform David and Goliath. Some of the group had performed the marionette play with him earlier, all of them had seen it often, the roles were assigned, everyone promised to do his best, and one small, droll boy painted himself a black beard so that if a break should occur, he as Hanswurst[8] could fill it with some slapstick. Wilhelm regarded this unkindly as being contrary to the seriousness of the play, but this time he had to allow it. Yet he swore to himself that if he ever recovered from this embarrassment, he would never again attempt a play without having considered it well beforehand.

Chapter 10

Wilhelm now came into the years when the body begins to develop and when one often cannot understand why a clever and bright child seems to have become dull and inattentive. He now read much and always found his greatest satisfaction in plays, and whatever he read of novels he could not help transforming in his mind into plays. He was under the delusion that whatever delighted in the story would have to be much more effective when performed. If in school he had to read a sketch about some historical or political event, he always depicted carefully for himself where a person was stabbed in a particular manner or poisoned, because, to his thinking, this qualified quite splendidly for a fifth act. In his compositions, however, he could not account for the four preceding ones because he had never read them in a play.

His comrades, who had acquired a taste for acting, sometimes induced him to assign roles, and he, who had a very lively imagination and could imagine himself in every part, believed he also could act all of them. Thus he frequently took those least suited for him and, if at all possible, several roles. It is a trait of childhood to be able to make everything out of anything, to not be misled by the most obvious cases of mistaken identity.

So our boys played on, each fancying himself competent. At first they performed only all-male plays, of which there are not many; in others they dressed some of their number with the means at hand; and finally they included their sisters in their activity. In some homes it was regarded as a useful pursuit and parties were invited to it. An

[8] The principal clown in German low comedy, evolved from the harlequin of the Italian *commedia dell'arte*. The figure was still popular in spite of its having been banished symbolically from the theater in Leipzig at the beginning of the quest for a "national," i.e., German-language theater.

old bachelor among their relatives, who claimed to be knowledgeable, intervened and taught them how they should carry themselves,
deliver their lines, and leave the stage. Wilhelm was usually quite dissatisfied with this instruction since he thought himself capable of doing it better than the man who was directing.

Quite soon they considered doing a tragedy. They had often
heard it said and believed themselves that it was easier to prepare and
perform a tragedy than a comedy. Also they were generally happier
with the former than the latter because here the stale, the tasteless,
and the unnatural quite quickly became apparent, while with the former they saw themselves as noble beings, and there was nothing
which contradicted the bombast, affectation, and exaggeration of their
tragic acting, especially since they had noted in everyday life that
many insignificant persons believe they can give themselves importance by adopting an inflexible carriage and by grimacing oddly.

Boys and girls weren't together long in this play when Nature began to stir and the group began to divide into various little love affairs, where usually a comedy was then played within the comedy.
The happy couples almost squeezed one another's fingers off behind
the scenery and floated in bliss when, quite made up and beribboned,
they appeared twice as beautiful and ideal to one another. Opposite
them the unhappy rivals were almost consumed by envy and in childish spite and malice ruined or caused others to ruin this or that passage.

On such occasions Wilhelm's directorial skills shone. During rehearsals he sought to resolve spats such as this peaceably, was flexible, and overlooked many things as long as the actors were trying and
knew their roles by heart. But on the day of the performance he was
humorless, and as soon as he stood behind the curtain in half-boots,
royal cloak, and diadem, nothing profane or foolish was permitted to
occur, and woe unto the person who chanced to cross him in a Nero-
nic mood. The offending party was intimidated to return to his duty
by so grim a look and so much dignity of gesture and sternness of
voice that for the moment at least calm was restored.

The more plays they performed and the more important these
were, the broader their group became, all the more difficult did the
office of director become for Wilhelm, which he, as founder, occupied
with the support of all. Whenever a play was proposed and selected,
there was considerable discontent until the roles had been assigned.
Everyone laid claim to the main one, to the lovers and the other leads,
so that Wilhelm, who was concerned only with presenting a play, often stepped back and magnanimously took a lesser one, except that
he couldn't bring himself to play the confidant. Moreover, when now

this person or that grew annoying at the rehearsals and perhaps out of childish spite resigned his part shortly before the scheduled day of the performance, he had every opportunity to exercise his patience, his indulgence, his gift for persuasion. And he carried it off. His drive, his perseverance, his love for the good cause, which was fed by the most acceptable form of egotism, the loyalty with which the best among the group were bound to him, these all made everything easier for him. And why shouldn't he realize his plans, a person who knew no other interest once the topic had been raised, who could be distracted by nothing, who instead set out toward his proposed goal as directly as possible and in high spirits, and who through his friendliness and generosity lured his companions down his chosen path?

Good fortune came to the aid of Wilhelm's natural inclinations in that none of the girls to whom in good time he felt an inclination could join the theatrical group. His love for the theater remained quite pure and he could look on dispassionately when one of the others wished to set his princess upon the throne. This impartiality increased the trust of his group, who often were satisfied at his judgment which they grew accustomed to consulting in irreconcilable cases.

Chapter 11

Boyhood is, I believe, less endearing than childhood because it is an intermediate, half-way state. Childishness still clings to them and they to the childish, but with their first reservations they have lost their loving amiability, their mind is turned forward, they envision the youth, the man before them; and because their path leads in that direction anyway, their imagination hastens ahead, their wishes exceed their bounds, they imitate, they imagine what they cannot and are not supposed to be. It is just the same with the inner condition of their bodies, as their outer. And it went likewise for the theater of our young friends. They longer they played, the greater the efforts they made: as they gradually grasped a point here and there, the more boring their play became. The amusing character of their original naiveté disappeared when they often, without knowing it, gave splendid parodies of the plays. It developed into a stilted, vain mediocrity that was all the more unfortunate because they could tell themselves and, indeed, they often heard from their audience that they had improved by far.

A troupe of actors who visited their city at this time brought the greatest ruination for them. The German stage in that day was experiencing a crisis: It had thrown away its baby's shoes before they were worn out and consequently now had to go barefoot. Among these

actors there was much that was natural and good but which was suf-
focating under the burden of affectation, acquired grimaces, and
self-conceit. And just as everything insincere can be imitated most
easily because it impresses us most strongly, so our amateurs had very
soon plucked exotic plumes from these crows with which to adorn
themselves. Gait, posture, and speaking voice were imperceptibly
imitated, and they subsequently regarded it as a great honor if one of
their spectators was so kind as to say that he considered them the
equal of this or that actor.

Chapter 12

With advancing years and unvarying aggravation at home, the elder
Meister placed his only hope in Wilhelm, whose splendid talents at
times provided him a cheerful moment; only he wished the boy might
apply them better and devote himself soon and completely to the
business. Also on various points he had cause to be satisfied with his
son, who had quickly learned French and Italian; in Latin he knew
which case to use; he conducted the correspondence with great facility except that occasionally, and especially in the foreign languages, a
theatrical expression crept in. He was also learning English, and at the
store he was beyond reproach. First, he was never bored because in
slow periods he always immediately brought out from under the
counter a book or a play script. Secondly, his cheerfulness and good
demeanor attracted many people: he knew when to grant a point, and
never grew irritated at the ladies' interminable decision making, but
instead was helpful with good advice and conscientiously tried to dis-
suade people who, after all their deliberations, finally made the poorest choice.

The girls who had seen him in the theater usually appeared a few
days afterwards to see how he looked by daylight. And usually they
agreed that although he was not as handsome as by candlelight,
made-up, and from a distance, yet he still pleased them quite well.
For it is certain that the theater endows actors with a certain glamour
that does not disappear entirely even in everyday life. Their imagination continued to search for the handsome image they remembered,
and even though they initially went away unhappy, they kept returning — something to which the diversity of the business gave opportunity — until they finally found satisfaction or even preferred this
refreshing, genuine fellow to the painted, artificial prince viewed from
afar.

With all these good qualities he still lacked the true spirit of the
businessman. The love for figures and especially the love for fractions,

which are customarily so important, eluded him as did attentiveness to small advantages and a feeling for the great importance of money. Often and with great sorrow the old man noticed that his son could never become good at figures nor a perfect proprietor even though he was rather good at his calculations and wasted nothing.

Wilhelm's spirit had long since risen above these base needs, especially since he lacked nothing in his father's house, and he was too ebullient and honest to keep his contempt for business from showing through occasionally, even to his father. He regarded it as an oppressive burden on his soul, as a glue that constrained the wings of his spirit, as ropes which restrained the flight of his soul for which he felt he was developing naturally. Occasionally, following some such statement, a quarrel developed between father and son, at the end of which the old man was usually angry, the young man upset, and the matter in no way improved, since each party seemed to grow more certain of his views. Wilhelm, who loved his father but also did not like to be assailed, withdrew further into himself. His emotions, which grew warmer and stronger, and his imagination, which heightened, became fixed upon the theater, which should surprise no one. Confined in a town, trapped in middle-class life, depressed in his home, with no eye for nature, no freedom for his heart. As the routine days of the week crept past, he had to go along with them; the foolish boredom of Sundays and holidays only made him more ill at ease. And whatever he chanced to see of the free world when taking a walk never became a part of him: he was a visitor within majestic nature and she treated him as a visitor.

And what was he supposed to do with his abundance of love, of friendship, of premonitions of great deeds? Did not the stage have to become an asylum for him where, in comfort and no matter what the weather, he could gaze in wonder at the world in a nutshell, at his emotions and his future deeds, the figures of his friends and brothers, of heroes and the radiant splendors of nature, all as if in a mirror? In short, if one fully understands how all unnatural feeling for nature comes into focus here in the theater, it should amaze no one that he, like so many others, was captivated by it.

Chapter 13

Various vicissitudes scattered the company which had worked to give life to the small theater. Yet Wilhelm remained its root which sometimes sent up new shoots. It didn't take long until he assembled a group, a piece or two was performed until the usual theater arguments again broke it up. Wilhelm was the happiest recruiter and advocate. Wherever he went, his theatrical world followed him; whenever boredom appeared at a party, he was asked to deliver a monologue. He did so, and the applause he received was coupled with everyone's secret wish to be able to do likewise. Whenever his store of monologues was exhausted, someone had to step up and read the second role; this caused people to learn scenes for two, thereby interesting more people, and the piece took shape.

The more animated Wilhelm's emotions became, the more most of the plays began to displease him. He had read through the enormous stock of German and French plays and had moved further away from those years when one devours everything in print, when one is not easily pleased by mediocre works yet lets everything pass for the sake perhaps of a few passages or an emotional conclusion. He now sought out the stormiest, most delicate or violent scenes, and because he had heard much about graphic presentation, he sought to accompany his delivery with all sorts of gestures, which did not go badly because he was well built and lithe of limb and by nature possessed a noble dignity. Yet it was unavoidable that the expression usually appeared somewhat forced and frightened and embarrassed the audience more than it pleased them. In addition, it must not be forgotten that in idle hours the stabbing, falling down dead, and collapsing in despair were rehearsed most energetically. He also brought things to the point where scarcely another actor presented the ascending scale of the thirty-two passions more forcefully in a single monologue.[9]

Chapter 14

In this restless period of natural artistic endeavors, fate determined that love should bind him to the theater with even stronger bonds. Up till now his small infatuations had been like preludes to a grand musical work where in diverse keys one tone changes to another without producing a definite melody, having no purpose other than making the ear more sensitive for what is to follow and, unnoticed, to lead the listener to the portal where the splendor of the whole is to be revealed all at once. Most people experience love in this manner, and whenever fate loves someone, it leads him thus to happiness and unhappiness.

[9] Goethe treats ironically not only Wilhelm's youthful ardor but also his attempts at categorizing human emotions. The high number here is perhaps derived from the points of the compass, since in the eighteenth century the emotions were frequently metaphorically compared to the winds propelling a ship.

A theatrical troupe came to their town several times a year, and Wilhelm attended performances as often as he could while keeping parental annoyance at an acceptable level. He had noticed among the performers a girl who had occasionally caught his attention because more so than the others she had something in her tone of voice that sometimes moved him deeply, especially whenever she was lamenting or saying something amusingly kind-hearted. She did not always please him, and frequently when he did not like her, he placed the blame on her roles, and once again her small, delicate face and her full bosom spoke powerfully in her behalf. He envied every servant who was permitted to take liberties with her in the play. In his eyes the others seldom acted well. The plays seemed to be presented for her sake, and he considered him who was permitted to throw his arms around her and as a brother or spouse embrace her in joyful reunion to be a god. Indeed, it went so far that whenever she had even a minor role in a piece, he, who normally observed a performance with the keen eyes of an artist and connoisseur, was lifted into true, childlike illusion and sometimes started as if from a dream when a boring act or a scene poorly performed by the others awoke him quite rudely.

So it went on for a while without his making her acquaintance. His middle-class reserve kept him from approaching her whenever he came backstage. And whenever he happened to see her again, a new vein seemed to move in him. He always made a clumsy bow whenever he came to stand not far from her behind the flats, or bumped into something, or singed his coat while respectfully moving aside.

She also looked at him sometimes with such a meaningful look that he had to believe she noticed him, and it made him extremely happy even though she hadn't paid the slightest attention to him. For in the theater and in the *haut monde* we become accustomed to directing our eyes meaningfully toward objects often without noticing them at all, and for a woman who knows from experience that her eyes in various ways can have the effect of exciting and animating others, it becomes second nature for her to play cat and mouse with people without noticing them.

Chapter 15

One evening during this time when Wilhelm was treating some strangers to a glass of wine in a tavern, he made the acquaintance of two actors. They found him so well informed about the theater and possessed of such a good understanding of the actor's art they believed they had found in him the right man to whom they could hon-

orably display their mastery in various roles. Thus they invited him to
visit them in the near future when they promised to read various
things for him. With difficulty he hid his joy when they casually added
that Mme. B** would probably be a member of the party. I'm calling
her Madame here and remember having previously introduced her as
a girl. In order to avoid any misunderstanding, I am revealing now
that she had entered into a marriage of conscience with a person
without conscience. He shortly thereafter left the troupe, and she was
in almost all respects again a Miss. She retained her maiden name and
was variously regarded as unmarried, married, and widowed. To Wilhelm it was important to regard her as the last, and he found it indeed
the best justified.

When he saw her, embarrassment and a pounding heart made him
more outgoing and more pleasant; he was very courteous to her and,
even without his otherwise good demeanor, that alone would have
drawn her attention to him. They began with what was to be performed next, spoke about new plays, about how the German stage
would soon equal the French, that it was a sin to perform only works
in translation upon it, that important gentlemen were becoming interested in it, and about the status of the actor, that day by day it was
becoming more honorable and more respectable.

In presenting this last point, Wilhelm outdid them all. "It is a disgraceful prejudice," he exclaimed, "that people vilify a profession that
they have so many reasons to honor. If the preacher who proclaims
the word of God is therefore the worthiest person in the land, then
one can certainly deem as worthy the actor who brings the voice of
nature to our hearts, who with cheerfulness, seriousness, and suffering
dares various attacks upon the hard hearts of men in order to purge
their darkly hidden feelings and to elicit the divine harmony of relat-
edness and love among one another. Where is there a refuge from
boredom like the theater; where does society come together more
pleasantly; where better must men admit they are brothers than when,
all hanging onto the figure, the voice of a single person, they are all
borne aloft in one emotion? What are paintings and statues compared
to the living flesh of my flesh, compared to this other self which suffers, is happy, and immediately touches every sympathetic nerve
within me? And where can one expect more virtue: in the burdened
businessman who scrapes together his living from his fearfully shabby
business, or in him whose art, which provides him bread, simultaneously penetrates the noblest, greatest feelings of humanity, who every
day studies and presents virtue and vice in its nakedness, and who
must feel beauty and ugliness most deeply before he can bring others
to feel them? I do believe that with some this distinction is obscured

by a life on the road marked by poverty and stress, but for just this reason, how cruel it is to reject out of narrow-minded pride the others who are striving toward that which is better."

He continued for a while quite animatedly so that all stood in great astonishment, and although from time to time something occurred to them that did not seem to agree with his defense, they were nonetheless thoroughly satisfied, and when he concluded, they assured him it was true that they were treated unjustly. Mme. B** also added this and that, but soon she was able to turn the conversation to Wilhelm's splendid manner of delivery and paid him the compliment of saying he must have done quite a bit of acting already. Although this came somewhat unexpectedly since he felt he had been neither acting nor declaiming, but openly pouring out his heart, he immediately took up the word and, regarding this as a transition to a different conversation, assured them honestly that he had always had a great love for the theater but unfortunately could never get enough. The others assured him that for an amateur, it was already a great deal if he performed this or that role more or less adequately, but much study was required to be of the theater, as the phrase runs, which is the province of the actor. This did not totally please Wilhelm, who imagined he possessed what they called art, but he let it pass.

Now each offered to deliver a monologue for Wilhelm. The one who in the grip of tragedy knew neither his father nor his brother and did not spare the child in the womb came forward; with the praised monologue and the conversation with the spirits from *Richard the Third*,[10] he brought sweat to his brow and fear to his guest. The others, in consideration of the purpose, came forth partly with comical passages, partly with sentimental ones, and each did his utmost to impress the young connoisseur more than the others had.

He was as attentive as he could be, given the double handicap of the proximity of his beloved and his mulling over the monologue he was going to recite. First he praised everything as a whole and then especially each passage where they had asked him whether he had paid attention to this or that expression. This was in him neither falsity nor myopia; rather the wish to find much good led him to deem much good and even if he suspected strongly that it was not quite right, he nevertheless let it pass out of generosity, cast blame on himself or his mood, or simply thought no more about it.

Mme. B** and Wilhelm now could not agree who should perform first. Finally in their conversation it developed that he had played

[10] *Richard der Dritte*, by Christian Felix Weiße (1759).

Mellefont[11] and she Miss Sara; also one of those present knew the role of Norton more or less by heart. Thus they quickly agreed to perform together. Wilhelm adopted as much discomforting gloom as he was able; Sara hovered in gentle lament and reported her frightful dream quite fearfully. In doing so she also knew how to make it unclear whether she was being nice to the hero of the piece or to the actor, as a result of which Wilhelm was so enchanted by her acting that he regarded her the first actress of Germany.

After their sample was ended, all exchanged praise and satisfaction. Wilhelm had delivered admirably some passages where his emotions sufficed; also the admiration of the spectators would have been mixed with envy had they not been able to tell themselves that in all the passages where he had dared to encroach upon their art, he had remained far behind them. They stayed together for a while; Wilhelm accompanied Madame to her home, where in order to join his family punctually at dinner, he unfortunately had to decline her invitation to come upstairs, but he retained this offer. That night and the following day her image appeared to him so often that he was quite distracted and clumsy in his work. In the evening, when he closed the store, an invisible hand grabbed him by the nape of his neck; he felt himself propelled forward and, as if in a dream, he found himself sitting on the settee at the side of his adored one.

Chapter 16

A girl who attracts a new admirer to join the several she already has resembles a fire when a new piece of wood is put upon it. She is quick to flatter the darling newcomer, busily reaching to him and around so that he soon glows in full splendor. Her eagerness seems directed only towards pleasing him, yet with every move she reaches more deeply within him, devouring his innermost marrow. Soon this piece too will lie on the ground like its abandoned rivals and, glowing from within, will burn out in smoke-stained sorrow.

At first Mme. B** did not know what to make of Wilhelm. The first days of their acquaintance passed in relative volubility until this faded and he lapsed into an ecstatic silence in which we in the presence of

[11] Like the following two parts, a principal role in Lessing's *Miss Sara Sampson* (1757).

the object of our love can derive inexpressible bliss even from boredom itself. His goodness, devotion, naiveté, innocence, complacency, adoration, and affection embarrassed her in the beginning. In her early years she had all too soon seen the childish delights of love driven away from her. She was conscious of the many humiliations she had had to experience in the arms of one man or another. Also currently she was giving herself up to the secret pleasures of a rich and indescribably boring, spoiled ninny, and, being by nature a good soul, she never felt quite right when Wilhelm with a true heart held and kissed her hand. Whenever he peered into her eyes with the total, pure look of youthful love, she could not endure his gaze; she was afraid that he might sense her experiences in her own. In confusion, she cast down her eyes, and the happy Wilhelm believed he was finding a portent, a dear confession of love, and his senses vibrated like the strings on a psalter. Fortunate youth! Happy days of love's first urgings! Then a human being resembles a child who is delighted for hours by an echo, can sustain the burden of conversation by himself, and is quite well pleased with the exchange if the invisible partner repeats only the last syllables of his own words.

For some time Mariane found help in the following manner. She had loved, was capable of loving, and in Wilhelm's presence, as if before a strange creature, she had a feeling which resembled awe. By being now natural, now theatrical, she knew how to put herself into the mood in which he was; her droll manner assisted her greatly, and it wasn't long until she came to know him. In his presence she felt herself a better person; she recalled the few happy, pure hours of her youth; and the entire love with which Wilhelm embraced her, the high value that this good soul placed on her, and her own affection for him soon erased, particularly in his presence, all repugnant feelings of her unworthiness. Her other lover was out of town, and in her mind she put aside her relationship with him just as one drives guilt out of the sphere of active memory into that of historical perception.

He saw her just as often as he could, which, of course, seems seldom to one in love. To be sure, he sometimes did have free evenings, he neglected his friends and otherwise found some time, but then she was usually busy at the theater and to avoid encountering angry faces from father and mother, he could stay out no later than eight or, at the most, eight-thirty, when the play was usually over. She, however, knew how to arrange things: he was expected if he did not see her name on the playbill, or she had herself driven home during the ballet and he was able to stay until the rattling of coaches compelled him to part from his happiness.

From the parterre he almost could not endure to look at her, it so grabbed him by the throat. He went backstage, behind the scenery. The magic of the theater was gone, but the magic of love remained. He could stand for hours alongside the greasy illuminating cart, let the fumes from the tallow lamps attack his nose, and look out toward her. A glance from her made him tremble, and amidst the scaffolding of boards and laths he would imagine a paradise for himself. The stuffed lambs, muslin waterfalls, cardboard rose shrubs, and the facades depicting straw huts aroused in him the most delightful images he had ever read in the poets of the pastoral world. Even the scrawny, tallish, full-breasted dancers did not always repulse him because they were standing on a stage with his one and only. And thus it is certain that Love, which has to animate even rose gardens and myrtle groves and moonlight first, can also bring life to wood and paper shavings. Love is so strong a spice it can render the dullest and foulest broths tasty.

So strong a spice was indeed needed to make acceptable and consequently pleasant the state in which he usually found her disordered household and occasionally herself. Having been raised in a proper middle-class home, order and neatness were the element he breathed, and his sensitive imagination had always imposingly decorated his room, which he regarded as his small realm. His bed curtains were drawn back in great folds by tassels, like the awning of a throne. At some expense he had procured a carpet for the middle of his room and a fine rug for his table. He placed and arranged his books and equipment almost without thinking so that they usually formed an attractive grouping. He wore his cap as though it were a turban and had had the sleeves of his bathrobe shortened in the Turkish style on the excuse that they bothered him when he was writing. And when in the evening he was quite alone and no longer feared interruption, he wore a silk sash about his torso. Also it is said that indeed he sometimes thrust into his belt a dagger he had appropriated from an old armory and marched up and down with it. He is even said to have absolved his prayers in no manner other than kneeling on the carpet.

This fastuous side of his character and conduct, by the way, did very little harm to his natural character; indeed, whoever paid close attention would find this trait in many children and young people. But what am I saying! It is traditional in this world that one can scarcely imagine majesty other than in a splendid robe with a train, that the dignity of the estate, the nobility of the deed can be made visible and exemplary for man only in pompous representation. One cannot make them feel that greatness and nobility are the purest and truest expressions of that which is natural and that they therefore cannot be made visible or imitated.

How fortunate Wilhelm thus in his heart deemed the actor whom he saw in possession of a majestic wardrobe and constantly exhibiting noble conduct, whose soul represented a mirror of the most glorious and splendid things the world had brought forth in the way of attitudes and emotions. He conceived of his domestic life as a series of worthy deeds and occupations, among which his appearance in the theater was simply the highest peak, just as is the gleam of the silver which, long stirred by the smelting fire, finally appears shining out of its rainbow of colors as one single mass before the eyes of the worker.

At first it gave him pause whenever he was with his beloved and through the happy fog that cloaked him he glimpsed tables, chairs, and the floor. The remnants of a transient, casual, and false finery lay scattered among one another in the confusion of haste, like the glittering scales just scraped from a fish. The tools of human cleanliness — combs, soap, towels, and ointments — were likewise visible along with traces of their use. Books and shoes, dirty laundry and silk flowers, cases, hairpins, cosmetic jars and ribbons, sheet music, and straw hats; nothing refused to associate with its neighbor, all were united by the common element of powder and dust.

But since Wilhelm usually did not know where he was when he saw her, since everything she touched was part of her, so everything became dear to him and ultimately he even found in this unkempt, disorderly housekeeping a charm which his heart had never revealed to him in his own pompous neatness. It seemed to him whenever he moved a corset to get to the piano, whenever he placed her skirts on the bed in order to find a seat, whenever with unembarrassed candor she did not seek to hide from him many a natural trait that strangers customarily strive hard to hide from one another — it seemed to him, I tell you, as though he were drawing closer to her, as if a union between them were being strengthened by invisible bonds.

Harder to digest was the behavior of the other actors whom he sometimes met at her place and whom he became acquainted with through her. Busy in their idleness, they usually made a great fuss about extremely petty matters, what sort of clothes they would wear, from which side they wanted to enter, how long the play would run, complaints about the injustice of the director in failing to recognize their talents, that someone had not known his role yesterday, that such and such a piece was unplayable, the German theater was improving daily and the actor was becoming more and more respected. Such were the conversations among the theatrical. From everyday life came topics such as coffee houses and wine gardens, gambling, some comrade in debtor's prison, what some actor was receiving per month with another troupe, a quarrel among a couple of sharp-tongued women that divided the group into two parties, and things of this sort. The conclusion was always the audience and its attention and satisfaction, and the great, important influence of the theater on the creation of a nation and the world.

Wilhelm did not know how he should interpret that properly; he did not manage to form a clear understanding of these contradictions since his love left him little time for any other consideration.

Chapter 17

It happens quite rarely that two young, equally innocent souls set out on the path of love hand in hand, wander along harmlessly, lost in its serpentine paths, and see themselves led unexpectedly to places from which they felt themselves far removed. For just as Nature almost without exception has subordinated inexperience to experience, thus it is here, too. One party will always play the role of the friend who, knowing the area, wants to initiate the newcomer into its beauties. Silently he guides him imperceptibly here or there, at this or that prospect abandons him to his rapture without betraying the great things still ahead, lets him laboriously and unnecessarily climb and descend in order to show him a pleasant view from its most effective side. The second party — whether or not he notices the deceit — thanks his guide for his kind efforts.

As modest as Wilhelm was and completely believing in Mariane's virtue, his caresses increased imperceptibly with each day, and she, without denying him possession of that which he presumed, simply detained him for a while at each stage where otherwise his love and respect would bid him rest. Her embarrassment, the feeble resistance with which she opposed his kisses, the deep reflection into which she often fell all transported him into such enraptured passion that he clung to her with every fiber of his being. In his arms Mariane first became acquainted with the happiness of love to which she had been a stranger, and the affection with which he pressed her to his bosom, his gratitude at simply being at her side, permeated her, and daily her spirits were more rejuvenated.

Often she now wished seriously to herself to be free of that liaison which we mentioned before, the thought of which grew more repugnant to her with each day. But how to get free? We all know how difficult it is to risk a decisive step, that thousands would rather drag their lives miserably toward each new day in fading fortune! And now a girl in such circumstances! She had quite soon inquired casually about his wealth and his situation and then saw clearly that she could hope for no reward for that which she wished to sacrifice to his love. He had already spent on Mariane all the interest earned from the capital which his grandmother had set upon her grandchildren during their parents' lifetime.

She considered her situation back and forth, and when she saw no way out, she again abandoned herself for a while to going ahead, to life and love. Day by day, however, there faded increasingly the casualness, the animation, the humor with which in the beginning of their passion they had sought to bind each other firmly and which had spiced each caress. Formerly they joked in small scenes from this or that piece, made fun of one another with badinage from some author, and when the aroused male embraced her and punished her with a kiss, and through such a blissful catastrophe they made the past into a lie, these were the highest moments of love. Now, however, when they outdid one another in these delights, it had an effect upon Wilhelm's head as though he were tipsy from beer; he grew dull and irritable in his yearning so that he fell into all manner of petty jealousies and teasing. For this we probably must forgive him, for he was in a worse way than a person pursuing a phantom since he held in his arms and touched with his lips that which he was not supposed to enjoy, from which he was not supposed to derive satisfaction.

Mariane, who perceived his torment, would probably have shared with him in many a moment the happiness which he so ardently desired. She felt within herself that he was worthy of far more than she could give him, but his confusion and his love obscured his advantage. Her silence, her uneasiness, her tears, her fugitive embraces — sweetest music of surrendering love — put him beside himself in repressed suffering and at her feet until finally both of them in dreamlike moments of transport became lost in the joys of love that fate reserves for humans in order to compensate them in a small way for so much stress and suffering, want and affliction, waiting, dreaming, hoping, and yearning.

Chapter 18

Wilhelm, whose happiness was now complete, gave himself over entirely to the raptures of love. If previously he had been bound to Mariane by desire and hope, now he was by the most blissful satisfaction from which he seemed again and again to drink with renewed thirst. Thinking of Mariane seized him ever more strongly in her briefest absence, for if she formerly had been necessary for him, now she was indispensable since he was tied to her with all the bonds of humanity. In the purity of his soul, he found that she was half, no, more than half, of his being. He was grateful and absolutely devoted.

Mariane, too, could deceive herself for a time; she shared with him the sensation of his intense happiness. Alas, if only the cold hand of reproach had not sometimes grabbed her heart! She was not safe from it even at Wilhelm's bosom, even beneath the wings of his love. And she was to be pitied when she was quite alone again and descended from the clouds to which his passion had borne her, down to recognition of her position. For imprudence was her help as long as she lived in abject confusion, deceiving herself about her position, or probably not recognizing it; the incidents to which she was exposed seemed isolated. Pleasure and irritation alternated, her humiliation was tempered by vanity, and privation often was compensated by momentary surfeit. She could cite need and habit as law and justification, and for the time being all unpleasant feelings could be cast off from hour to hour, from day to day. Now, however, the poor girl had felt herself at moments lifted up into a better world, had looked down, as if from above, from light and joy into the abject wasteland of her life. She had felt what a miserable creature a woman is who does not instill love and respect simultaneously with desire, and found herself both inwardly and outwardly where she had started from. She now had nothing at all that could lift her; wherever she looked and searched in her thoughts, there was emptiness, and her heart had no mooring.

Completely the opposite, Wilhelm soared. For him, too, a new world had opened, but one full of happy prospects. When the abundance of first joys abated somewhat, what had darkly disturbed him before now presented itself clearly before his soul: She is yours! She has given herself to you! She, the beloved, desired, adored creature has in loyalty and faith given herself to you, but not to an ingrate. Wherever he stood or walked, he talked to himself, his heart overflowed continually, and in a profusion of splendid phrases he recited to himself the noblest thoughts. He believed he had heard the clear call of destiny, which, through Mariane, was offering him its help in tearing himself away from his tedious, stagnant, bourgeois life, something he had long desired. The discord between his parents weighed upon his heart. To be a daily witness to such misfortune gnaws at one's heart, which either consumes itself or hardens, and goes to ruin whichever it does. In addition, one of his friends, a very settled person, asked for his sister's hand and thus could assist his father and take his place in the business.

The thought of leaving his father's house and his family seemed easy to him and did not even enter his calculations. He was young and new in the world, and his eagerness to race through its expanses towards happiness and gratification was heightened by love. His calling to the theater was now clear to him; the high goal he had set himself seemed nearer and nearer as he struggled toward it at Mariane's side. And it was inevitable that in happy moments he caught sight of the emergence of the perfect actor and creator of a great German theater, for which he had heard so many people sigh — and never without some pleasant application to himself. Everything which until now had slumbered in the innermost recesses of his soul came alive, and from its varied ideas and the rich palette of love he created a misty painting in which the shapes tended to melt into one another but also gave an all the more pleasant effect to the whole.

Meanwhile our pair went on living for a while with quite different pressures of the heart. Since they were never bored when together, they scarcely noticed how quickly the days flew by and let one after the other pass without reaching a decision which might have clarified or determined their fate.

Chapter 19

Wilhelm's friend and presumed brother-in-law was one of those people definitely set in their existence, who are usually called cold because under provocation they do not light up either quickly or visibly. Also his relationship with Wilhelm was a running argument through which their affection grew ever firmer. Each was called to accounts by the other. Werner to his credit seemed from time to time to apply a rein and halter to Wilhelm's impressive but unfortunately occasionally desultory talents. And Wilhelm often sensed a magnificent triumph whenever he carried his cautious friend along in a moment of passion. Thus the two played off each other, and they became accustomed to meeting daily simply because neither had anything in common with the other, they did not understand one another, nor could the one make himself understood by the other. But because they were both good people, they walked beside and with one another toward a single goal and could never understand why neither could bring the other to his own position.

Werner noticed that Wilhelm's visits were growing less frequent, that he would restlessly break off discussions of his favorite subjects, that he no longer immersed himself in vivid imagining of unusual ideas, which is, to be sure, always a sign of an untrammeled, self-sufficient heart which can find solace in the company of a friend. Werner, who was very precise, looked for a fault in his own conduct until some coffee house gossip put him on the right track and some of Wilhelm's exuberant indiscretions increased his certainty. He undertook a closer investigation and discovered quite soon to his horror that Wilhelm had attached himself to an actress, to a woman who was seducing him, taking his money, and, moreover, was being kept by the most unworthy rival. He made every effort to inform himself accurately about everything, and when he had done so, he launched his attack on Wilhelm. He presented everything in great detail, at first casually, then with the most urgent seriousness of well-meant truth. He left no detail unclear and let his friend taste all the bitterness with which composed people are often so generous toward lovers. But he fell from the sky when Wilhelm with some emotion, yet with great assurance replied, "You don't know the girl! I know that appearances are against her, but I am as sure of her fidelity and virtue as I am of my own love!"

Werner remained firm, offered to provide proof and witnesses. Wilhelm rejected them and soon departed in sullen shock like someone whose decayed but firmly rooted tooth a clumsy dentist has tried to pull in vain. With comforting indignation Wilhelm cast all suspicion out of his mind. The entire beautiful image of Mariane that hovered before his soul had for a few moments been shoved aside and besmirched by Werner's account. It did not take long until Wilhelm had completely cleaned it up, put it to rights, and when he saw her for a moment that evening, it began to gleam and glisten anew.

Werner considered day and night how he could straighten out his friend through persuasion and representations and made various attempts which, however, were politely evaded. At this he became sad and could not understand how the best convictions presented in total sincerity could not be powerful enough to impress Wilhelm's good and admirable heart.

During this period, the elder Meister took to his bed in illness. Wilhelm's work consumed his days, worry about his father his evenings; thus only the night was left to him for his beloved. This was agreeable to her, and he found a door which led from a woodshed into a narrow lane and was very convenient for slipping out of the house by dark.

The strange ambience of the night, the empty lanes which were customarily filled with commerce, the flickering night lights in his acquaintances' windows, and the sense of secrecy all heightened the adventure, and he crept almost every night to his beloved, wrapped in his greatcoat and with all the Lindors and Leanders[12] in his bosom.

[12] Names commonly given to the lover in French dramas and operettas of that day.

Chapter 20

In the meantime Mariane, who became ever fonder of him, was in a pitiable state. The generosity of her rich lover had not been interrupted by his absence, and now in sending some muslin for a negligee he had announced his impending arrival.

She had often been in a state of confusion and could stare into the fate of the coming day as if into a gloomy eternity. But this time she was pushed from too many sides. Two lovers concurrently, which under other circumstances might have worked, became more difficult here. In the loyalty of his heart Wilhelm had related to her in precise detail the suspicions which someone had wanted to bring against her, so she knew he was at least aware. The other man was arrogant and ill-bred in his bearing, and she was in a position where, in order to be sure of one of them, she did not wish to spoil things with either. Wilhelm's tenderness had triumphed over her prudence, and she sensed that the undesired pleasure of becoming a mother was approaching.

She had revealed this to an old theater seamstress, who was a reliable confidante in such cases and who, after some gruesome suggestions that made Mariane shudder, gave her the advice that if it really was to be, she would do better to place the blame on the rich lover rather than the poor one and to not let Wilhelm notice anything at all. As to the rest, she should place complete trust in her to handle the matter cleverly.

It was this old woman who had restrained Mariane from a solemn union with Wilhelm; she regarded him as a small fry which a prudent fisherman throws back into the water. "What do you want with him?" she often said. "His parents won't allow him to marry you, and to elope with him would be an unforgivable folly. He doesn't have anything, and what good's a husband about your neck who's in love with you. And on top of all that, our director's a man who loses his sense of humor as soon as an affair becomes a scandal. He's zealous for the reputation of his troupe, as he calls it, and rather than have someone say that one of his actresses has debauched some handsome young man of the town, he would chase her off on the day it became public. And where to go then? A roving actor is a more miserable creature than even a wandering apprentice.[13] Instead, if you can hold him, you'll come back again in perhaps a year's time. His father will have

[13] Under the guild system, once an apprentice learned the fundamentals of his trade, he became a journeyman, i.e., was sent out penniless to prove he could earn a living and to learn the tricks of the trade as practiced in other regions.

died meantime, and an old love can always be resumed with advantage."

The theater seamstress was a child of this world; she was right up to a certain point and was felt to be right in Mariane's heart, up to a certain point, for the latter had no idea of how she might part from Wilhelm. But prudence has a somewhat commanding character so that we follow it even against our inclinations.

Wilhelm did not understand Mariane's behavior at all. He, who regarded her as his wife, called her nothing but his "little woman," often through his caresses wanted to lead her to a closer declaration, a definition of their relationship. He felt her always avoid the point of marriage, where the girls usually meet one more than half way. Yet he again grew tactful and suspected that she was exercising quite different tact. He was on the point of declaring himself, and always left the way he had come, thinking it over and quarreling with himself for yet another day. He was always ready to take the leap, and never moved at all.

Through all this, however, his ideas became ever more confirmed, his vague prospects, his confused hopes turned into plans. During his father's illness he had imperceptibly expedited the marriage of his elder sister with Werner. It was agreed upon and only the necessary formalities were holding it up for a while. In his mind he had already made his recovering father completely well again, had substituted his brother-in-law into his place in the business and the affairs of the family, and he seemed to himself sometimes to be experimentally removing his feet from their heavily locked chains like an artful thief or a magician sometimes does when imprisoned, in order to convince himself that freedom is possible and nearer than shortsighted people imagine.

Thus whenever in a free nocturnal hour he strolled across a square, casting off all pressures and raising his hands up to the sky, he felt everything to be beneath and behind him and himself to be free. Now hastening to the embraces of his beloved in the furtive night, and again imagining himself on the brightly illuminated theater scaffolding in the embrace of his beloved and thus in that of nature and artifice, admired and envied, so that for him the long way through the city to her house was one moment, uninterrupted save here and there by the call of a night watchman.

And when Mariane received him with naturalness and artifice, mastering her secret worries and affirming her delight, when in his arms she unexpectedly dedicated the white negligee, in which she truly looked quite angelic, when satiated from pleasure, what was he to do other than sweep her along with him into the happy future? And she, who now seemed never to share his feelings, was silent and embarrassed at his loving question as to whether he might regard himself as a father! He found an interpretation for it, to be sure, and a good one. Throughout this period he offered the surfeit of his emotion and his good nature to straighten things out and bridge the gaps, except that he never was able to feel quite right in doing so.

Chapter 21

The director of our acting group had already threatened at various times to leave the town. Although it was not too small and did have its well-to-do citizens and even idle rich, he nonetheless could never turn a profit except at fair time. For many the drama of jack, queen, king and ace was more interesting; the other friends of the theater hesitated at the half Gulden or availed themselves of free tickets. They had no intention at all of subscribing; thus art had to go begging, as is the custom in this world, since one can hardly conceive of fun as something for nothing. To be sure, the threat was often only a bluff, which, however, moved the public to come again and Wilhelm to make more urgent arrangements.

Werner was now actually participating in the affairs of the business, and Wilhelm, who had never left the town of his birth, persuaded Werner, who had been to a number of other places, that such a trip was most important for an inexperienced person. They had agreed on a certain sum of money which Werner was to provide and be repaid over time; and even if Wilhelm regarded this deception as totally justified and was convinced that his parents and relatives in the future would bless him for it, the thought of the first moment when they learned of it was a stone against which his imagination sometimes painfully bumped.

Finally, the group seemed seriously no longer to want to extend their stay. Norman, Wilhelm's rival, hastened his trip in order to enjoy Mariane's love a few days more, and Wilhelm finally resolved to possess her forever and to tie himself inseparably to the theater.

Werner, whom he now urged to expedite the means for the proposed trip, suspected nothing wrong, for prudence never anticipates the extraordinary. He thought it was good that it was working out and that Wilhelm was leaving a place that necessarily reminded him so often of an unfitting love, soon after the object thereof had departed.

In recent days Wilhelm had become more secretive in his ways. This let the other conclude that he had changed for the better, kept him from further restrictions, and gave him all the alacrity Wilhelm could desire.

On the other hand it was welcome news to Mariane when Wilhelm asked her permission not to see her for a few days. It gave her breathing space to gain composure for welcoming her impetuous Norman, to whom her heart did not go out.

Wilhelm now sat by himself at home rummaging through his papers and examining his possessions for what could be useful to him on his voyage into the world. Everything that had earlier satisfied his taste in books and things was now put aside. Only works of good taste, poets and critics, were included among the elect. Since in recent times he had profited very little from the latter, his desire for them now increased when, blushing, he leafed through them and found them still uncut since coming from the bookbinder. He had acquired them in the complete conviction of how necessary such works were, but had never gotten started in his study of them.

One part of the time he also used to compose a long letter to Mariane. He needed to write in order to express completely and fully how he felt in his heart, for although he could deliver a memorized role straightforwardly in the theater and in everyday life often went on at length about opinions and whimsies, it nonetheless often stuck in his throat when he was expected to impart his feelings vividly. He could never find grand enough words to express what he felt, and when he used an excess of words he still found that it didn't coincide with what was within him. Writing helped him out of this difficulty, for just as we tend to give the absent beloved a more splendid appearance, we also find nothing wrong with a heightened expression of our feelings that would be denied by the present, which is so hostile to everything romantic. The letter which he wrote Mariane was the following:

Chapter 22

Beneath the dear cloak of night which so often has sheltered me within your arms, I sit and think and write to you, and whatever I contemplate and pursue is for your sake. Oh Mariane! For me, the happiest among men, it is as with a bridegroom, who, filled with premonition of what a new world will develop within him and through him, stands thoughtful at the sanctified threshold, longing before the mysterious curtains whence the sweetness of love murmurs toward him. I have forced myself not to see you for a few days. This was easy in the hope of its reward: To be with you forever! Completely yours! Dearest, you don't know what I want, yet you could know it. With sweet professions of a love that dares say nothing because it wants to have everything, how often have I probed your heart in search of a mutual desire for an eternal union. You certainly understood me, for in your heart the same desire must be budding. You have perceived me with every kiss, in every moment of nestling comfort; and now your evasions, your modesty — how I love you, my darling! What another woman seeks to elicit through artifice, the decision that a girl usually seeks to make ripe while the sun shines, you evade and, in seeming indifference, close the already half-opened heart of your beloved.

I understand you! What a wretch I would have to be if I failed to recognize from these signs the pure, unselfish love which thinks first of me! Don't say a thing! We belong to one another and neither of us can forsake or lose a thing if we live for one another. Accept this hand, and these superfluous pledges. We have tasted all the joys of love, but there is new bliss in the confirmation of the thought of its enduring. Don't ask "How?" Don't worry! Fate will provide for love, and all the more so when it is unassuming. My heart has long since left my parents' house. It is with you, just as my spirit hovers over the stage. Oh, my beloved! Is there possibly another human being who has been allowed to unite his wishes so?

What now keeps sleep from coming over my eyes, what ties me to my papers, what rises and falls within me like dawn and dusk: your love and my happiness. I can scarcely keep myself from arising and racing to you, and am restraining myself in order not to take foolish, risky steps like some nitwit. I am acquainted with Director S**, and my journey will take me directly to him. A year ago he often repeated the wish that his people had some of my enthusiasm and my joy in the theater, and he will certainly welcome me. There's no future with your troupe. Also S** is so far from here that in the beginning my activities won't become known. I'll find casual lodgings there right away, look about, get acquainted with people, and then come for you. Mariane, you see how I can constrain myself in order to have you for certain! To not see you for so long, to know that you are alone in the wide world — something I don't dare say aloud. And then again your love, which safeguards me from everything!

And I beg you, don't deny me this one thing before we part: Give me your hand before a priest, and I will depart in peace. It is only a ceremony for the two of us, but what a beautiful ceremony: the blessing of Heaven joined to the blessing of this earth! It can be done easily and secretly at the nearby nobleman's estate. I have enough money for both of us for the beginning; we will share and before it's gone, Heaven will help us further. Yes, dearest! I am not worried at all. Whatever is begun in such elation must have a happy ending. I have never doubted that a man can survive in this world if he is serious, and I feel I am strong enough to earn a living for two, for several. They say the world is ungrateful; I haven't yet found it to be ungrateful to those who understand how to do something for it.

My whole soul lights up at the thought of finally appearing on the stage and of declaiming to men's hearts what they have yearned so long to hear. How many thousands of times it has made my soul wince, I who am so captivated by the majesty of the theater, when I've seen the most miserable actors imagine they could deliver a noble sentiment to our hearts. It is worse than the forced artificiality of a falsetto, a sin the way it's customarily delivered by the ineptitude of these coarse fellows.

The theater has often had a fight with the church, and neither has anything to blame the other for. One might wish that in both places there stood only the noblest of men, so that God and Nature would always be glorified. These aren't dreams, my love: as I've been able to feel by your heart that you are in love and meant for me, I shall seize this shining thought and say — no, I won't say it, but I shall hope that great beauty, that vision of the superhuman in human form so desired by all, will descend upon us. I am just as certain of this as of the joys granted me at your bosom, which are always called divine by men because in these moments they are lifted above themselves.

I cannot close; I've already said so much and don't know whether I've told you everything that concerns you, for there are no words for the tumult always raging within my heart.

Take this note for now, my love. I've read it through and find I ought to begin anew, but for the meantime you have everything that you need to know and what the plans are when I shall soon return to your bosom with the elation of sweet love. I find I resemble a prisoner who is filing away his chains while listening. I shall wish a good night for my parents in their unsuspecting sleep and soon a longer good night — Fare well! For now I shall close, I have nodded two or three times, it is deep in the night.

Chapter 23

Since spring was already approaching, the day seemed not to want to draw to a close as he yearned his way toward Mariane's, the letter neatly folded in his pocket. Finally he stole to her dwelling and could scarcely imagine being in her arms again after so long an absence. But her heart was as if cut to shreds, agonizingly warring with itself at each of his embraces. His plan was simply to make a date for that night, to press the letter into her hand on leaving, and to enjoy her delight upon his return late in the night. Yet before he was aware of it, he grew quite languid in the coveted proximity of his beloved. She was ill and couldn't say where; she was very ill at ease and could not agree to his suggestion that he return that night. He, who from relatively long familiarity was accustomed to honor such cautionary signals, retreated quietly and it seemed to him that the time was not right for delivering his letter. He kept it with him, since various gestures from her suggested that he leave quietly. In the intoxication of his impending love, he gathered up a scarf he found lying on her dresser, stuck it into his pocket, and grudgingly left her lips and her doorway.

He stole home, could not bear it there long, changed clothes, and again sought the open air. In the street he heard a pleasant serenade from clarinets, French horns, and bassoons, which swelled completely through him. These were traveling musicians of whom he had heard people speak. He approached them and, for a bit of money, took them with him to Mariane's residence. There were trees nearby which had ornamented the square for years. He situated his singers beneath them. He himself rested further away, abandoning himself completely to the hovering tones which murmured about him in the refreshing night. Stretched out beneath the fair stars, his existence seemed to him a golden dream. She is also hearing these flutes, he said to his heart; she knows whose thoughts, whose love is making the night euphonious. Even at a distance we are bound together by these melodies, as we are at any distance by even the subtlest tuning of love. Oh, two loving hearts are like two magnetic compasses: what moves in the one must also move the other along, for it is but one which moves both, *one* force which flows through them. Can a person in her arms imagine the possibility of parting from her? And yet, I shall be far from her, will seek a refuge for our love, and shall always have her with me. When away from her, lost in thoughts of her, how often has it happened that I touched a book, a dress, or something and believed I felt her hand, so completely was I enveloped by her presence. And to recall those moments which flee the light of day as they do the eye of the cold observer, to enjoy which the gods abandon their untroubled existence of soaring bliss! To remember! As though memory existed for the euphoria of the intoxicating drink that flogs all composure from our senses and their heavenly constraints — and her figure!

He became lost in memories, his composure passed over into desire. He embraced a tree, cooling his hot cheek on its bark, and the winds of the night greedily inhaled the breath which burst forth passionately from his pure bosom. He looked for the scarf which he had taken from her earlier; it was forgotten, still in his other clothing. His lips yearned, his limbs trembled in desire.

The music stopped, and it seemed to him as though he had fallen from the element which had borne his emotions up to now. His uneasiness increased since his feelings were no longer fed and placated by the gentle music. He wandered about and was carried towards Mariane's residence. He sat down upon its threshold, he grew quieter. He kissed the brass ring of the knocker at her door and sat quietly for a while. How he imagined her in sweet dreams, behind her drapes in the white negligee with the red ribbon about her head! And then he imagined himself so close to her that it seemed to him she must be dreaming of him. His thoughts were as gentle as the spirits of the twilight; tranquillity and desire alternated within him while love, with trembling hand, played thousandfold upon the strings of his soul. It was as though the music of the spheres had halted quietly above him in order to eavesdrop on the gentle songs of his heart.

Had he had with him the house key with which he usually opened Mariane's door, he would not have held back; he would have pressed forward into the temple of love. He walked unsteadily beneath the trees as if dreaming, gradually moving away. Several times he started to turn off toward home but he returned again and again. Finally, as he gained control of himself and looked back once more from the corner, it seemed to him as though Mariane's door opened and a black figure emerged from it. He was too far away to see clearly, but before he pulled himself together to look again, the apparition disappeared into the night, only he thought he saw it far in the distance, passing a white house. He stood and squinted, and before he collected himself to run after it, it had become lost among the many lanes. To his eyes and his heart he felt like a person for whom a bolt of lightning illuminates some corner and who subsequently with blinded eyes seeks its previous shapes, the connection of its paths in the darkness.

And just as a midnight ghost that creates monstrous fright can be explained to a child in subsequent moments of composure, and just as doubt can always expand and contract in the soul, so it was for him as he leaned against a cornerstone, not heeding the light gray of morning and the crowing of the roosters. The commotion of the early tradesmen finally drove him home through his secret entrance.

By the time he arrived he had all but banished this phantom from his soul with the most cogent arguments, yet the beautiful mood of the night, which he now looked back upon as a phantom, was also gone. To comfort his heart and to set a seal upon his restored faith, he withdrew the scarf from the pocket of the jacket worn earlier. The rustling of a note which fell out of it withdrew the cloth from his kiss; he picked it up and read:

As much as I love you, little fool, what was wrong with you yester-day? I'm coming to you tonight. I believe that you are sorry to be leaving here, but be patient; I'll also be coming to the *** fair. Listen, don't wear that dark green and brown jacket for me again; you look like the witch of Endor in it. Didn't I send you a white negligee so that I can hold a white lambkin in my arms? Always send your notes to me via the old slut; the Devil himself chose her as our Iris.[14]

---

[14] In Greek mythology, the servant of Hera and frequent bearer of her secret messages.

Book 2

Chapter 1

WILHELM HAD NOW begun to recover and Werner, as he had become accustomed to doing during the worse phases of his friend's illness, still came by regularly every evening. By telling stories, reading aloud, and also simply through his presence the latter sought to divert him from the secret thoughts in which the unfortunate person found a delight in reliving his misfortune and eating away at himself.

Once, when Wilhelm awoke at dusk from his slumber and parted the curtains of his bed in order to get up, he discovered Werner, who, in order not to disturb him, had sat down at the window with a book. Following a "Good Evening!" the patient asked "Why don't you have a light brought? What are you reading?"

"I found a volume of Corneille[15] on the table and had just opened it to his essay on the three unities. I've heard so much talk about them and was eager to read what this famous author decided about them."

"Well, he probably didn't decide anything," responded Wilhelm. "His text seems to me more a defense against all too strict legislation than a law itself which would be a guide for his followers."

"I also soon noticed that I had been wrong," said Werner, "when I thought that from these pages I could plant a yardstick in my soul with which I would be able to judge plays in the future."

"Even if there are rules by which to judge the works of writers," Wilhelm rejoined, "they may not be so easy to apply as are length and weight or the four processes of arithmetic."

"I don't understand that," said the other, "for if a rule is correct and established, then one must be able to see easily whether the author has observed it or not."

Wilhelm was silent.

But I notice that to satisfy my readers, I shall have to connect my narrative to the end of the previous Book.

---

[15] Pierre Corneille (1606-1684), French dramatist. The work referred to is his "Discours sur le poème dramatique" (1663, German 1750).

When the plague or malignant fevers of a similar sort attack, they rage more quickly and more violently in a healthy, sound body. Thus when misfortune overcame poor Wilhelm, in one moment all his entrails were aflame. Just as when fireworks accidentally catch fire while still being set up, within his bosom happiness and hope, lust and joy, reality and dream suddenly collapsed upon one another. In the moments of such devastating fate the observer usually freezes, and for him whom it strikes, it is a blessing if he loses his senses.

Periods of loud, ever recurring, unbearable suffering followed. Yet these might also be regarded as a blessing of Nature, for in such hours Wilhelm still had not yet entirely lost his beloved. His sufferings were untiringly renewed by attempts to hold onto the happiness that was escaping from his soul, to recapture the possibility of it in his imagination. One cannot call a body completely dead as long as decomposition endures, for the forces that seek in vain to pursue their old functions now work on its destruction, and only when these too are exhausted, when the entity is decomposed into indifferent dust and bones, then arises the pitiably empty feeling of death, to be comforted only by the spirit of the one living in Eternity.

In such a new, completely loving soul there was much to kill, to tear apart, to destroy, and the recuperative strength which resides in youth did give nourishment and increased strength even to the violence of his suffering. The blow was too tellingly lethal. Werner, now by necessity his confidant, enthusiastically reached for fire and sword in order to attack the hated passion, the monster, at its core. The opportunity was so felicitous, the evidence so close at hand, he pursued it with such vigor and ferocity, step by step, not granting his friend the slightest comfort of the slightest momentary deceit and destroying every hiding-place, so that Nature, which did not want to let her darling go to ruin, attacked him with disease in order to grant him breathing space from the other side.

A virulent fever with its consequences, the medicines and the debility, the efforts of his friends about his bed, the proximity and love of his family, which only becomes truly appreciable in times of need and distress, were so many distractions in his changed condition and a meager entertainment. Only when he became better, that is to say, when his strength was exhausted, did he look down in horror into the complete abyss of his desolate misery, a sensation as if one were looking down into the hollow crater of a burned-out volcano. From then on he made the bitterest accusations against himself, that after suffering so great a loss he was capable of enjoying a single painless, tranquil, or indifferent moment. He despised his own heart and yearned for the solace of tears and torment. To reawaken these within him, he reproduced in his memory all the scenes of his past happiness. Depicting them with utmost vividness, he struggled his way back into them, and when he had worked his way up to the highest point possible, when the sunshine of past days seemed again to stir his limbs and lift his bosom, he looked back into the frightful abyss, contemplated the fall with pleasure, hurled himself down, and wrested from Nature the bitterest suffering. And thus he repeatedly tore himself apart. For youth, which is so rich in hidden strengths, does not know how wasteful it is when it adds so much willful suffering to the pain that a loss incites, as though it wanted thereby first to bestow a genuine value upon that which was lost.

He was so convinced that this loss was the first, last, and only one he could experience in his life that he spurned every consolation which sought to represent his suffering as finite. He hated every joyful, otherwise sympathetic impulse *per se* and cultivated instead that stagnating, creeping, involuted emotion which secretly gnaws away at the core of life. Faint, feverish emotions, echoes of his illness, crept into his innermost structure and were supported by a false diet of body and soul. He fled people, kept to his room, which never seemed warm enough to him.

Coffee,[16] which he had not known before, insinuated itself as a medicine, then became his favorite drink, taken at first once a day and then twice and soon was indispensable. This disagreeable and commonly prevalent poison of the body and the purse affected him most dangerously. His fantasy was filled with dark, unstable images with which his imagination became accustomed to presenting a restless drama which would have chosen Dante's *Inferno* as a worthy arena. The transient, deceitful mood which this traitorous liquid provides is too stimulating that a person, having felt it, would want to give it up. The lassitude and dullness which follow its use are so desolate that one is driven to revive the former condition through new indulgence.

Tea, a worthy, though distant relative of the destructive bean, was also usually offered in the evening as a good companion , one able to enliven domestic routine. Because wine was consumed — not always in moderation — whenever good friends had been invited, and conversation flows best in such a medium, there arose from this and other connections an ugly discontent throughout his whole being. He was lashed by false moods, his thoughts were confused and exaggerated, he was all but unrecognizable compared to his former self.

[16] The effect of drinking coffee was still debated in Europe, a century after its introduction there. Goethe opposed it throughout his life.

Unfortunately this condition, which is almost as indescribable as it is unbearable, will be well understood by many who, like our friend, regard themselves as extraordinary physical and moral phenomena and ascribe those lacerating emotions which disturb them to the force of their hearts and the strength of their spirits; yet with a bit more discipline in their diets and a bit more of Nature in their pleasures they would become quite decent and quite natural human beings to the satisfaction of themselves and their families. Indeed, my friends, permit me to say to you: you often seem to me like small, gentle streams into which boys carry rocks in order to make them ripple.

The vestiges of that first illness still lay stubbornly in Wilhelm's veins. Because of his style of living, Nature could not be led into its normal path. He despised any diversion or activity. In his dressing-gown, slippers, and night cap he found ease of mind and ultimately happiness in a pipe of tobacco. Almost nothing more was needed to transform this well-educated, orderly, free human being into the condition of those persons who, often without imagination and inner calling, agonize over their misunderstood books like cobblers upon their stools.

And he would have perished, too, had he not been saved by the strength of his nature which again was striving toward that which is upright, and pure. The more tightly his physical fetters were drawn, the more his inner strength struggled until it broke loose at the first opportunity and ransacked his entire body. Any hope of subduing it was in vain. With the wisdom of a knowledgeable disciplinarian it took vigorous action, seizing each disorder by its roots, turning everything topsy-turvy, throwing out what was too coarse and consuming the somewhat refined. Merciless in its irresistible workings, it several times brought our friend to the Gates of Death.

But its cure was also thoroughgoing: everything alien and false was driven out, and in its innermost relationships his well-formed body was restored for its future fate. True, his strength then recovered so slowly that one could often believe that it was again fading. In the most dangerous moments he had simply renounced all life which seemed to lie behind him; he had been freed from this world, and the peace which came from this feeling was a favorable climate from which the convalescent derived a subdued vitality. Gratefully he now accepted from the wellspring of life that which in the fury of his condition he had cast aside and trod upon. And thus for a second time he was led like a child back into life, and at the first return of cheerfulness, like a child he attacked his previous playthings.

What attracted him first were theater books. With much pleasure he again read one after the other the best works, which here and there appeared to him in a new light.

Werner had been leafing through one such volume during the midday nap of his friend, as we mentioned at the beginning of this Chapter.

Chapter 2

Werner could not bear it when Wilhelm let a conversation drop and withdrew into himself for a while. He never felt it was to be interpreted as contempt when upon such occasions his friend's heart gently closed and his searching soul withdrew to realms whither it wished to take no prudent companion. Werner, for his part, regarded friendly conversation as existing for mutual instruction, for explaining his doubts, and, each convinced by the other, for reaching agreement.

Wilhelm on the other hand seemed to have noticed here and there that the human spirit constitutes an individual entity that could never unite with another although they could touch at a greater or lesser number of points. He had to attain this insight quickly, for a creature that is evolving has little in common with those fully developed, even those of his own kind. And what hovered before him as the truth hung from so many threads, was so concise, so full of visions, and to be sensed only vaguely, that he was almost never in a position to move forward in a conversation and to say quite plainly and clearly what he wanted.

As a youth he had had an extraordinary love for grand, splendid words and sayings; he adorned his spirit with them as with a precious garment, and he was happy at this as if they belonged to him, childish at this superficial splendor. As a consequence, when the youth started feeling from within and his spirit began to work and stir, he scorned words, for he regarded that which was welling up within him as inexpressible. Nor could he capture it in words; it all stretched out to such an extent that he could not confine it within the narrow, fearful bonds of specific expression, especially when someone contradicted him. To share that which filled his soul with a willing listener provided him the greatest pleasure, as we have seen in earlier examples and shall see again.

He was not at all suited, on the other hand, for dialogue; he had no talent for putting himself into the minds of others. Often when the thread of his thoughts was broken by the attacks of an opponent, for the sake of clarity he would introduce points, comparisons, anecdotes, and quotations that had no apparent connection whatever with the subject under discussion. Thus the opposition carried the day, and even when he had defended himself vigorously and, to put an end to things, he finally sought to help himself through paradoxes and invocations to Heaven and Earth, he was usually outvoted and laughed at. From this he gradually became accustomed to struggling silently toward the sun which would bring his wings to maturity and let them spread. Especially in the recent period, since the grand knot to which he had tied everything was rent asunder, he had trouble finding himself in anything.

Werner gently sought to pick up the thread of the dropped conversation. "If you don't object and I'm not to read something aloud, then explain to me to some extent what the three unities mean and what one is supposed to think about them."

"My head is not entirely clear," said Wilhelm, "otherwise I would gladly fulfill your request. But I'll confess to you, the more I consider it, the more I become convinced it's dangerous to select a road into the land of drama that approaches from this direction."

"Just give me some idea of it," said Werner. "Do you reject these rules and these three unities entirely?"

"If you only knew," said Wilhelm, "how you confuse the concepts in your words. I don't draw back from any rule that is derived from the observation of nature and from the character of a thing. I also do not disdain these so-called unities, partly because they are a necessary component of a play, partly because they serve to adorn it. I simply regard as inept the method with which we are presented these otherwise good and useful precepts, because it shackles our thoughts and prevents us from recognizing the true relationships. If someone divided man into soul, body, hair, and clothes, the foolishness of such a way of teaching would soon strike you, even though you couldn't deny that all these components are found in yourself. The former is not much better and just as unphilosophical if one examines it more closely. A tally where things of completely different values are entered one after the other.

"Taken in its higher sense, the unity of action determines the success not only of the drama, but of every literary work, and it seems indispensable to me. How many important points we must discuss in light of it before we come to time and place, concerning which so much is to be said and because of which one has to be tolerant in viewing almost all writers. Indeed, if we ultimately have to have unities, why only three and not a dozen? The unity of manners, of taste, of language, of character *per se*, of costumes, of staging, and of illumination, if you will. For what does unity mean if it's to indicate anything other than inner completeness, harmony with itself, propriety, and probability.

"How variously this word has been used up till now as a technical term! With each of the so-called unities it signifies something different. Unity of action means partly simplicity of plot, partly the clever and close connection of several plots. Unity of place means monotony, inflexibility, or limitation of the scene. Unity of time means a brief, comprehensible, to a certain degree probable amount thereof. Thus you'll have to agree with me that these things shouldn't have been laid out this way alongside one another or one after the other. Therefore in my study of the drama I cast these old formulae completely out of my mind in order to find a more natural and proper approach. In doing this I've been more careful than ever to look up what thoughtful men have written about it. I've even recently read a translation of Aristotle's *Poetics.*"

"Share some of it with me," interjected Werner.

"I truly don't yet know what to say about the total work," said Wilhelm. "A person would surely have to have read several of his writings in order to become more familiar with his style and above all be better educated about Antiquity than am I. Meanwhile I did write down several excellent passages from it and have arranged them in my fashion, examined them, and commented upon them."

"I can't possibly give up my wish," Werner added, "to have a detailed and specific yardstick by which to measure the value of a work."

"You're making a mistake," responded Wilhelm, "if you imagine a person can simply put such a yardstick into another person's hand. One has to consider an object for a long time and become thoroughly acquainted with it; only then does one correctly understand the nature of the opinions that knowledgeable and learned people have thought about it. And just as the poet precedes the critic, we, too, must see, read, and hear much before we start to think of passing judgment. And that doesn't take into account that if someone is not a member of the guild, he will do best to abandon himself to his natural feelings and not ponder for a long time whether the author or actor delights him."

"That's what I've always maintained," said Werner, "but recently someone babbled away at me for too long and confused me. Thus, for example, I emerged with pleasure from *The Merry Cobbler, or The Devil to Pay*[17] and saw everyone had enjoyed it greatly. Certain per-

---

[17] C. F. Weiße reworked Charles Coffey's *The Devil to Pay* as *Die verwandelten Weiber, oder Der Teufel ist los* ("The Women Transformed or The Devil

sons who are regarded as knowledgeable took offense with me at that, made fun of my bad taste, and explicated the correctness of their views to me at full length. No one cares to stand there as though he had been slapped, especially when one has a pair of eyes in his head just like anyone else."

Wilhelm responded, "it's harder than you think to be fair. I want to tell you how I'm conducting my research, for I don't see any other way of making my point. I've been searching for a long time ,and especially since my illness has left me time for reading, to find out what's the essence of the drama and what are only incidental features. To be sure, this needs more time than I've been able to find, for one would have to know the history of drama from its origins, the theatrical traditions of all nations, and the majority of their works. One would have to investigate where they must agree with one another to be good works and in what ways they can differ. The good Ambassadorial Adviser R**, whom you also liked so well, first brought me to these thoughts. But I see this is not something for me. I wanted to start with the French theater. I took up Corneille and scarcely had I read a few works, there was a great ferment in my head and an irresistible urge to immediately compose a play in his manner."

"But you surely wrote it down," said Werner. "Do let me see some of it! You've always been so secretive about this. If my wife hadn't told me, I wouldn't have known at all that you've written so many different things."

"Perhaps one day an hour will come when I'll be foolish enough to give you an accounting of the early days of my efforts. I'm sure that for a thousand writers and others concerned with talent and the arts things have gone as they did for me. A burst of youthful imitation leads the kindred spirit along well-defined paths, the great models inspire us, the beginnings are easy, playfully we enter a path whose difficulty and length we notice only when we've already covered a part of it. Habit and inclination bid us to stick with it, usually with inner reluctance and the gnawing feeling that we remain far behind those whom we thought to surpass. Just bring out Corneille, the part with Cinna,[18] and read me a few scenes from it."

Werner did so, but since he rendered the French verses poorly, Wilhelm finally seized the book and read with such passion and

to Pay"). He later wrote a continuation, *Der lustige Schuster oder Der zweite Teil vom Teufel ist los* ("The Merry Cobbler or The Second Part of The Devil to Pay"). They were performed in 1752 and 1759.

[18] Corneille's tragedy *Cinna* (1643).

spiritual exaltation that Werner finally exclaimed, "Splendid! Extraordinary!"

"Tell me," Wilhelm continued, "isn't it the same with you? Don't these situations have to affect mightily the souls of all men? Yet taken as a whole, so singular, so simple and beautiful! It is so grand but seems so natural, one takes part completely and yet doesn't dare to imagine himself in the situation; one is and remains an observer and waits to see how exalted beings will conduct themselves. Indeed, if the author has the strength and imagination, is capable of presenting vividly what we at best can only conceive of and imagine, if we see our demigods take each important step firmly and resolutely, with the conduct of each remaining resolute and inviolate in their frightful situation, how satisfied we are and how gratefully do we return when these dilemmas, these mixed feelings are presented to our hearts with such loving dread, agreeable even when they are fearful. If someone is simply grasping for something new or wishes to open his breast in empathy, he'll always find satisfaction in such a work, it seems to me. I beg you to read the work through! Do read it!"

"You've made me very curious about it and about his others. Are they equal to this one?"

"Just as a man can never be entirely like another, nor entirely unlike."

"His fellow countrymen called him The Great, although some, if I'm not wrong, questioned this epithet."

"I won't dare to decide which he deserves as a poet. I admire what is above me, I don't judge it. This much I do know: He surely had a great heart. A deep, inner independence is the basis of all his characters; strength of spirit in all situations is what he depicts best. Granted that in his youthful works it sometimes appears as braggadocio and in his old age dries into hardness, that still remains a noble soul whose utterances benefit us."

"Should one be so certain in drawing conclusions about the author from his work? In a play it's no great art to be noble and magnanimous, to give away a kingdom, to renounce a loved one, to risk one's life and do things of that kind which in everyday life, I'd wager, a king would shrink from just like the next person. On the stage a person can allow his princes to be as heroic as he likes."

"One can't be truly heroic on the stage any more than anywhere else if one doesn't possess this great quality. When he is treating lofty themes, a writer with a small, petty soul will always look for greatness in the wrong place, he immediately becomes exaggerated and foolish, and not a person will credit him for it. On the other hand, the truly noble always commands our applause and admiration. Just as horrible emotions move us to fear and sad fates to pity, so falsity makes us contemptuous, arrogant misuse of power incites our hatred, and thus it goes with each of the many emotions which stir us singly or in conjunction! Certainly whoever possesses the high sense of humanity and whom Nature has made a poet so that he can produce this effect vividly will move and profoundly stir the human soul throughout the ages."

Werner now sought to change the conversation, which he felt was becoming too animated for Wilhelm's physical condition, and hoped in conclusion to lay hands on some of our young poet's own works, but try as he might, it was impossible on this evening to penetrate his secrets. Too full of the image of Corneille and, if one wishes, the ideal of Corneille he had created for himself, he regarded his own works as scribblings from a school exercise, which, when the pupil had filled his notebook, were usually cut up for curling papers. He sensed a void that his feelings did not permit him to leap across. A strange situation for a writer, indeed for any human being. Nature has made us so happy with ourselves that we do not easily regard another person, his accomplishments, and possessions without returning to ourselves to enjoy with most pleasant anticipation our own, and be they ever so little. Generous Mother, how wisely and lovingly you have furnished in simple plenty the small, confined household within each of us.

Werner finally rose since he noticed his friend had overexerted himself in the heat of the conversation. He saved it for another time.

Chapter 3

On one of the following days he surprised Wilhelm, who was busy sorting a number of papers, some of which he concealed upon Werner's arrival. These were letters from Mariane and notes referring to her. "If you have some of your writings at hand," said the newcomer, "show them to me."

"If you'll call the baby by its proper name and not call them writings, I'll probably consent to making myself ridiculous."

Meanwhile he raked the scattered papers together and was glad to put them aside in so pleasant a manner, for he was often troubled by the thought Werner might insist that all remaining reminders of Mariane be removed and the remaining letters, which he might well suspect to exist, be sacrificed to the fire. Thus he brought out a packet, which, when unbound, broke down into many individual thick and thin notebooks, folios and sheets.

"Alas," Wilhelm thought to himself as he pulled on the cord, "how I had hoped not to see you again! How changed is my fate since I tied you together!" He had put this collection aside with the other things he intended to take with him on his flight. "Don't touch anything!" he cried when his inquisitive friend started to reach for them. "Don't disturb the order of anything. You probably can't imagine it, but these papers are arranged in chronological order."

"That's a good idea. One can see all the better how you've developed."

"I'm only afraid in the future the nuances will interest neither me nor anyone else. First of all, I must prepare you to find many outlines, many individual scenes, and the beginnings of pieces, with almost nothing finished."

"Strange! Did things also go for you as for many young writers of whom I have heard?"

"Oh, if only they would for all writers! We wouldn't have the opportunity to see so many short works which remain unfinished even though they're ended. Not everyone would be excited by a childish impulse to cling excessively to the feeling of being able to produce similar foolishness in great quantities. Our literature wouldn't resemble a tavern where the lowest person bathes in satisfaction because he can always find his equal who'll drink with him. So first of all, here are some acts and scenes in the style of Plautus."

"Of Plautus? How did you choose him?"

"We were studying him with the schoolmaster, for I was also supposed to learn a little Latin. He was the first dramatist I ever read and so he was imitated on the spot. I've already told you on another occasion of our puppet plays, our epic-dramatic impromptus which lacked nothing save the dialogue."

"Read me something."

"God forbid, it's horrible! You can just imagine: There is a cantankerous, old miser who is cheated, a servant who cheats, a young man in love who doesn't know what to do. You can guess the old man isn't old, the young man isn't young, the servant doesn't behave like a servant, but that they do and say the most obvious things Plautus has them do and say."

Wilhelm could have added: "In the beginning the apprentice in every art takes from his model only what he sees in it and in so doing is only a few steps removed from many masters who imitate their predecessors and, at best, what they see in Nature. How seldom does someone appear who through his own inner strength glorifies what is true and produces something splendid."

"Meanwhile," continued Wilhelm, "I had to endure that all sorts of figures continued their games in my head. It wasn't by choice: everything I read or heard narrated was immediately repeated within me, and the more I subsequently devoured theatrical works, the more, if I may say so, there arose in my head a theater, where everything took place within its bounds. Here, my friend, you see some examples from the following period!"

"What! Verses! Pastoral names!"

"Alexandrines[19] of every variety and heroic pastoral plays; this was a genre which delighted me to excess. You can see that by the fact that two are completely finished, followed by a horde of unfinished ones."

"You must let me have them, just for fun."

"Gladly, for you'll laugh right heartily at the seriousness with which everything is treated. My principal characters, born of princely lineage, deprived of their rule by strange fates, fleeing and unrecognized, stop at the quiet homes of hospitable shepherds. What a contrast of emotions and characters! What a wealth of images! What a variety of narratives and descriptions! To be sure, this genre is truly made for the author as a child who likes to include everything everywhere. Whatever the tragedy possesses of the elevated and moving, the comedy does of the amusing, the pastoral play of the delightful, you can bring it all together here in one package."

"Shouldn't one be able to create good works in this manner?"

"Yes, indeed, and they do exist, but they weren't mine. A boy who doesn't know himself, who knows nothing of people, who always borrows from the works of the masters whatever pleases him, what will he write about?"

"Where did you take all these things from?"

"Where from? From my imagination, which was like a living warehouse of puppets and silhouettes always moving among one another. Just as card players never tire of fighting one another with a few cards and are delighted by the numerous combinations in which the marked or arbitrarily assigned value of these heroes becomes frightful or, under different circumstances, the hero lies at the feet of the servant, I had my few figures play endlessly in various roles. What in former times had been merely a puppet, theater, or masque was now breathed upon by a gentle spirit; the figures became more beautiful, more charming, and you can imagine it was the spirit of love that here, too, was displaying its animating force."

[19] Hexameter couplets with a caesura after the third stress, the verse form used in classical French dramas.

"I'll find the traces of that in these notebooks?"

"Oh, yes, on every page and of the author, too. I now began to feel my power, to tell myself fairy tales about myself, and now we set off into the wide world. Nothing hindered me from being as handsome, as good, as generous, as passionate, as miserable, as frantic as I wanted to be. I strung the adventures together as I wished and resolved them as it seemed good to me. And since I busied myself purely with verse, I had double or triple pleasure when it was done, except that in viewing the work I usually seemed to myself even cleverer than I had thought when I planned the work. Thus many a passage suffered great revisions and most of my undertakings ended in disaster."

Werner meanwhile had looked into the works and read some of the longer passages. "The verses aren't bad," he said.

"I thought so, too, at the time. Since I had no one who could say a word about them to me, Gottsched's *Stage* was the yardstick by which I measured my plays, and to me their content always seemed more interesting and the verses just as euphonious as his, and thereby I was sure of myself because in my inexperience I regarded all my models as classic."

"Didn't anyone help you with these verses?"

"Who was there? And no one can help you write verses: that was my least concern! From my youth I've always been able to keep on speaking or writing in any meter I heard or read. The mold was secure in my head, if only the material I had to pour into it had been of any use."

"You'll get there if you continue to practice in your idle hours."

"In idle hours," said Wilhelm with a deep sigh.

"Indeed," responded Werner, "You'll always find time since you don't love lavish parties and don't go to the coffee house."

"How wrong you are, dear friend, if you believe that such a project, the conception of which fills the entire soul, can be produced in hours which must be scrimped together and then are interrupted. No, the poet must live entirely for himself, entirely for his beloved object. He who from Heaven is most preciously endowed, who has received from Nature an indestructible wealth, must also live in inward composure with his treasures in the bliss which a rich man seeks in vain to produce, surrounded by amassed possessions. Look at men, how they run after happiness and pleasure, their wishes, their efforts at chasing money and time, and for what? For that which the poet has received from Nature, the enjoyment of the world, the feeling of one's self in others, a harmonious coexistence with many often irreconcilable things. What disturbs men save that they cannot connect their ideas to reality, that enjoyment eludes their grasp, that what they wished for comes too late, and that everything they achieved does not exert the effect upon their hearts that desire permitted them to sense from afar?

"Fate has placed the poet, not unlike a god, above all this. He sees the confusion of passions, families, and empires moving about aimlessly; he sees the insoluble riddles of misunderstandings, often lacking only a one-syllable word for their resolution, causing indescribable and irreparable confusion. He shares the sadness and the joy of each human fate. Where the man of the world drags along all his days in a corrosive melancholy over some loss or runs toward his fate in unrestrained joy, then the sensitive, responsive soul of the poet strides like the sun progressing from night to day, tuning his harp in gentle transitions for joy and sorrow. Native to the soil of his heart, the fair flower of wisdom grows up, and if when the others daydream and are scared out of their senses by frightful visions, he lives the dream of life as a waking person, and the most marvelous things that happen are for him simultaneously past and future. And thus the poet is simultaneously teacher, prophet, a friend of the gods and of men. How can you wish that he befoul himself with a base occupation, he who is built like a bird to fly above the world, to nest in the clouds, and to take his nourishment from buds and fruits, easily hopping from one branch to the other? Should he like a steer pull a plow, like a dog train himself for a certain scent or perhaps even, tied by a chain, protect a farm with his barking?"

Werner had listened with astonishment and, as one can easily imagine, found little reality in these words. He interrupted him, "If only men were made like birds and, without spinning and weaving, could spend a blissful life of enjoyment! If at the approach of winter they could only move so easily into distant regions to avoid deprivation and protect themselves from the cold!

"So lived the poets in times when Nature was more respected, and so they always should live. Self-sufficient in their innermost being, they needed little. The gift of imparting beautiful feelings and splendid images to men in the sweetest, resounding words and melodies had enchanted the world from time immemorial and was a rich inheritance for them. At the courts of the kings and the tables of the rich, before the doors of those in love, one hearkened to them while closing the ear and the soul to all else, just as one deems oneself blessed and stands still in rapture when, from the bushes through which one is wandering, the voice of the nightingale calls forth with striking affect! They found a hospitable world, and their apparently low station only elevated them all the more. The hero listened to their songs, and the conqueror of the world paid homage to a poet because he felt that without him, his awesome existence would simply pass by like a storm wind. The lover wished his desire and the delectation of it to be as thousandfold and as harmonious as the inspired voice of the poet depicted it. Even the rich man in surveying his own possessions, his idols, found them even more precious when illuminated by the glow of this spirit which sensed and heightened the value of everything. Indeed, who, if you will, has fashioned the gods, lifted us up to them, brought them down to us, other than the poets?"

"It's a shame," thought Werner to himself, "my otherwise so reasonable friend raves on so incessantly about this point."

"Yes, my dear man," the other continued, "to devote oneself exclusively to such an existence, what bliss! Just consider how many men believe themselves talented if with a certain ease they can deliver their thoughts in meter decorated with pleasing rhymes, even if one immediately misses in them the spirit which marks the poet. How fearfully thousands desire this distinction and how they work in vain to achieve it."

"I've heard many intelligent people offer the opinion that this or that person could have better spent his time and efforts."

"I believe that many deceive themselves, but that they also deceive themselves in others. Like any other natural instinct, the innate passion for poesy is not to be stifled without destroying its possessor. And just as the clumsy man who is punished usually makes a second mistake in the serious intent of atoning for his past, the poet in trying to avoid poetry truly becomes a poet."

"Have you felt this irresistible urge from childhood on?"

"You can see that from these papers, yet they're but the hundredth part of what I wrote and a thousandth of what I conceived. Unfortunately my desire didn't lead me far, and I regard these relics with sadness and contempt; there's nothing in them of any value."

"Perhaps you're wrong about that."

"Oh, no, I know whereof I speak; I couldn't flatter myself for long except through hope. I hoped the yearning of my heart would bring me nearer to the object of my desire, and I can't describe to you how great that yearning was. My wishes were especially directed toward tragedy whose gravity had an unbelievable appeal for me. I still recall a poem, which must be around somewhere, where the Muse of Tragic Poetry[20] and another female figure, in which I had personified Commerce, argued right boldly with one another for my worthy self. The invention is quite common, and I don't remember whether the verses

---

[20] Melpomene, whose attributes, the mask of tragedy, a crown, and dagger, are soon cited.

were worth anything, but you ought to see it for the sake of the fear and loathing, the love and passion which reign in it. It is childish and tasteless and written without reflection, but it proves all the more what it is intended to prove. How timidly I had depicted the old matron with her skirt tucked into her belt, her keys at her side, her glasses on her nose, always busy, always in motion, quarrelsome and frugal, petty and grouchy! How miserable I described the condition of him who bowed beneath her rod and earned a servile living in the sweat of his brow! And how different the other appeared! What a vision for tormented hearts! Splendidly crafted! To be viewed in her character and conduct as a daughter of freedom. Sense of self gave her dignity without pride; her dress became her, covering every part of her without distortion, and the ample folds of the material repeated, like a thousandfold echo, the charming movements of this divine person.

"What a contrast! And you can readily guess to which side my heart turned. Also nothing was forgotten to distinguish my muse: crown and dagger, chains and masks, as my predecessors had handed them down to me, were also given to her here. Their contest was heated, and you can imagine that the language of the two characters stood in contrast, since at the age of fourteen one is accustomed to painting black and white strongly against one another. The old woman spoke as is appropriate for one who picks up pins, the other like one who bestows kingdoms. The warning threats of the crone were scorned, for I had already turned my back on her promised riches. Disinherited and naked, I surrendered myself to the Muse who threw me her golden veil and covered my nakedness."

"Don't forget to search it out; I'm curious to make the acquaintance of the two ladies. What mad things one has in his head in childhood!"

"May I confess to you, my friend, and won't you find it ridiculous when I tell you those images still pursue me and do so, if I examine my heart, as seriously or even more so than at that time. Ah, who could have predicted to me that the arms of my spirit, with which I was reaching into the infinite and with which I hoped surely to embrace something great, would so soon be shattered? Whoever had predicted this for me would have brought me to despair. Even now, when judgment has been passed on me, now when I've lost her who instead of that divinity was to lead me to my desire, what's left for me save to submit myself to the bitterest sufferings?

"Oh, my brother," he continued, "I don't deny it; she was in my secret plans like the tackle to which a rope ladder is secured. Hopeful amid danger, the adventurer hovers in the air, the iron breaks, and he lies shattered at the foot of his desires. For me, too, there is no longer any consolation, any hope!" As he stood up he called out, "I'd like to tear these unfortunate papers into shreds and fling them into the fire." In his rage he seized a few notebooks, ripped them, and threw them to the floor.

Werner recoiled and could scarcely restrain him with force.

"Let me alone!" said Wilhelm. "What good are these miserable sheets? For me they are no longer one stage in my development, nor an encouragement. Are they to be left to torment me to the end of my life? Are they some day to serve for the mockery of this world instead of arousing its compassion and awe? Woe unto me and my fate! Only now do I understand the lament of the poets, of those sad men who became wise through suffering. Up till now I regarded myself as indestructible, as invulnerable. Now, alas, I see that a grave, early injury can't be outgrown, that it can't be repaired. I feel I must carry it with me to the grave, not leaving me for a single day of my life. The pain which will ultimately kill me and her memory shall remain with me, live and die with me, this memory of the unworthy woman.

"Oh, dear friend, if I am to speak from the heart, the memory of that surely not completely unworthy woman! Her station, her fate have excused her to me a thousand times. I've been too cruel, you've initiated me too mercilessly in your coldness, your hardness has held my deranged senses captive and hindered me from doing for her and for myself what I owed both of us. God knows what condition I have put her into, and only gradually does it strike my conscience in what desperation, to what helplessness I have abandoned her. Wasn't it possible that she could explain her actions? Wasn't it possible? How many misunderstandings can confuse the world, how many circumstances can beg forgiveness for the greatest mistake! How often I see her, sitting alone in the silence, propped on her elbows. 'This is the loyalty, the love,' she says, 'he swore to me! To end the beautiful life which bound us together with this rude blow!' "

He broke into a flood of tears while laying his face on the table and moistening the papers scattered there. Werner stood beside him in great embarrassment. He had not anticipated this sudden shift of emotions. A few times he started to interrupt him, a few times he tried to redirect the conversation, but in vain! He could not fight the flood!

Here, too, their sustained friendship resumed its good service. Werner let the violent attack of suffering pass, began to arrange the papers, collected them, made a mark where they had left off, pocketed a few notebooks, and had Wilhelm promise he would save them and one day continue going through them with him. And thus they parted. Wilhelm sunk in the silent reliving of pain, and the other

shocked by the new outbreak of passion which he long ago had believed mastered and overcome through his own sound advice and
persuasion.

Chapter 4

> You deepest shadows welcome me most kindly,
> Here my breast can find its peace less blindly,
> You silent pond, you tree which I once chose,
> Grant me the peace this sinner no more knows.
>
> You tree trunk, who, whatever men were thinking,
> Have stood here long in confidence unblinking,
> With children roundabout to whom you bowed
> In youth, as we did, too, when storms us cowed,
> Now strengthened well by sturdy, manly vigor,
> You face the weather and the seasons's rigor:
> You, steadfast one, provide me courage, too,
> And teach my breast to face my fate like you.
>
> Oh gentle breeze that makes the still wave dimple,
> That murmurs pleasantly about my brow and temple,
> From bough to bough you fly as fancy bids,
> A single breath from you can move a thousand twigs:
> Oh, with your pinions' silent ministration,
> Can you not bring my bosom consolation?
>
> Alas, no happiness I here shall find,
> I fled the court, the swarm remained behind.
> I left them there, in their well-guarded places,
> To plan their plots while wearing friendly faces,
> I left the retinue of wealth and might,
> The flattery, and splendor's glaring light,
> And thought that here I'd give myself to nature,
> And by myself restore my moral stature;
> Though now completely free, my heart here burns,
> The old torment with doubled force returns.

Accompanied on a beautiful spring day by Wilhelm's sister, now
Werner's wife, our friends had directed their walk to an area which
had always drawn them both since childhood. They had arrived at a
spot where as children they customarily played together and conversed as young people with hopes for the future. The married couple
sat down beneath an ancient oak and were enjoying the beautiful
view. Wilhelm walked up and down, reciting the poem above with

great sincerity to the objects which surrounded him. For almost any occasion he found ready in his head a few or several verses from some play or poem, and when he was alone or if it was appropriate to the company, he did not restrain himself. Then even almost mechanically, through an association of words, he was moved to dig out a part of his supply.

Werner immediately recalled having read this monologue in one of the heroic pastoral plays that his friend had recently entrusted to him. Since that time he had not dared to speak of it because he feared the return of the emotional suffering; now, however, because of the risky words of its conclusion he saw his friend coming very close to being exposed to the danger of his favorite passion. In his haste he knew of no other means of drawing him away from it other than by beginning to talk about the works and seeking to guide his agitated friend into a quiet conversation. He was not wrong and he succeeded, for specific things do not always have a specific effect; changes in the situation and circumstances often transform an object completely.

"I've already enjoyed reading this passage," he said, "in *The Royal Hermit*[21] and I remember a part of it."

"I don't want," responded Wilhelm, "to be guilty either of immodesty or of excessive humility. The passage might be acceptable if only I could justify it and several like it at the places in the text where they stand. A mistake that is easy to succumb to is prolonged exploration of melancholy moods, dwelling on descriptions and comparisons that are actually the death of the drama, which can be judged solely by its ongoing plot. This flaw runs through almost all the works I've written up till now, and even if there might be acceptable passages in them, for this reason they'll always be rejected by the masters of the art."

"As far as I'm concerned," said Werner, "beautiful passages are the nicest thing about an entire work, for they draw your attention and you can profit from them."

"I have nothing against that, if they don't hinder the development of the plot. Rather I'm convinced a good work can have many strong passages, and indeed, if you wish, can consist of splendid passages, even if they aren't all suitable for writing in souvenir-albums. I myself succumbed to that disease that is so prevalent in the public, and for my cure I have not myself, but my excellent friend R** to thank, to whom I showed some of my things. How happy I would have been to profit had he stayed here longer. What, for example, is so outstand-

[21] Variously interpreted to be an early work by Goethe, but most probably an allusion to what was to become his drama *Tasso*, which was begun in 1780, the time when he was writing the present book of the *Calling*.

ing in the piece you mentioned and I was reciting? The desire common among men to be free of confusing situations and to enjoy one's existence to the full beneath harmless trees as this is sometimes granted to us on a summer evening! In how many hundreds of poems has this already been expressed for better or worse? Take away the verses that depict these feelings and that at best would have sufficed for a mediocre elegy, perhaps take away a few similes that might adorn an epic poem, then what remains is either banal and childish or distorted and exaggerated. How can you now expect me in any way to imagine good things about that work?"

"An author, I would note, is rarely an impartial judge of his own creations; he goes first too far, then not far enough. I only wish that the piece were printed or performed; we would see how it would be received."

"God preserve me," Wilhelm started up, "from having the opportunity of ruining the public. I would like that just as little as being ruined by them, and usually that's what happens, as I've noted, from the reciprocal respect and indulgence they display toward one another. If I were to perform publicly, I would hope to please, and even please a wide audience. I've always regarded authors as wrong or very vain who dedicate their works just to the cognoscenti and consign those whom they don't please to the horde of the ignorant. That which is good, to be sure, must first be examined by knowledgeable persons and, if I may put it this way, be given a seal of approval; but if it is to be popular, it must create a general, favorable impression, particularly upon those who cannot judge. And I believe that he who has collected both of these votes for himself, which together, if I may apply the Latin proverb,[22] constitute the voice of God, has attained the highest mark.

"He may regard himself with some satisfaction in that the highborn and the plebeians have united in choosing him. If only one were led earlier to that which is right! For through these and similar mistakes I wasted all the effort I spent on my tragedies, which, as my learned friend made me see, apart from a few passages — and they are anything but new and elevating — generally abound in poorly imitated theatrical passion, their cheeks puffed with commonplace moral precepts, and, as if forgetting themselves in all this, they stumble back and forth on their way, ending not with a conclusion or a denouement, but with a fall and a crash."

---

[22] *vox populi, vox dei.* "The voice of the people is the voice of God."

"You speak as though of a great number. Were there so many? People didn't notice that you were so industrious."

"Wherever I went and whatever I was doing, I was making plans, and if I could find time to myself, I wrote verses. But you won't find more than three or four works completely finished."

"Isn't that enough?"

"There are, however, several quite long fragments and, as I told you, the beginnings of a whole host of others."

His sister, who had taken the hamper and glasses from a maid who brought refreshments and had been arranging them on the grass, also joined in the conversation and, like a person who has been waiting for some time to say what she wanted to say, addressed her husband with some animation: "It is truly too bad he let everything drop. I can assure you they were quite lovely works, and in all my days I've never seen their equal performed. I gladly transcribed them for him and in so doing noted the passages that pleased me best."

"What sort of heroes did you choose?" asked Werner.

"You'll be surprised that I took them from the Bible," replied Wilhelm, "even though it's quite natural."

"From the Bible!" called the former. "That's the last thing I would have expected!"

"And yet," said Wilhelm, "it is quite natural. The first story that captures our youthful attention and causes us astonishment tells us of those Holy Men to whom God deigned to devote special attention. We hear them spoken of as though they were our own ancestors, and the most eminent men of the most eminent nation must become for us the first in the world. We don't examine why their actions are interesting; rather their actions are interesting because they are told about them."

"You said," Werner interjected, "some of these plays were finished; what sort of materials did you treat in them?"

"Let Amelie tell you that," said Wilhelm and smiled. "Perhaps you'll again be astonished when you see the enemies of the people of God appear as the leading characters of my pieces. I can assure you, however, that it was with orthodox intentions, for the Prophets did their duty and told them the unvarnished truth at the outset; frightful dreams and premonitions agitated their pangs of conscience and didn't leave them a peaceful moment, so that they were quite exhausted and worn down by the fifth act."

Amelie let it be known quite clearly that she found it unpleasant when her brother made light of this matter. It had, indeed, once been deadly serious to him, and she still liked them. Her husband begged her to name the heroes for him and to his great surprise he heard the infamous names of Jezebel and Belshazzar. "Oh, oh!" he called out. "A queen hurled from a window! A hand reaching out of the wall! To regard those as theatrical devices calls for considerable courage of the imagination."

"I'm pleased," said Wilhelm, "that what's in poor taste strikes you immediately. It will surprise you even more when I tell you that it was for just this reason I chose these stories. Rest assured, many playwrights work in this manner. In a novel or a story, if something is singular, they immediately think it must be presented as such and that it will also provide enough material for the four preceding acts, even though it's as little suited to the drama as is the fatal leap of my queen and the menacing magic hand."

"How, for Heaven's sake," said the brother-in-law, "did you treat these materials?"

"Perhaps you'll scarcely believe me if I assure you that I handled them completely according to the rules and with full theatrical professionalism."

"You have to read them," interjected his sister, "otherwise he won't tell you honestly."

"First I must admit," Wilhelm continued, without reacting to her comment, "that speculation about some unusual kind of death brought me to the subject of Jezebel. I saw that all my predecessors had gone to the most artificial lengths to concern themselves with daggers, poisons, and other tools of mischief so that almost no new combination remained for their successors. Thus I was struck all the more by the plunge which ended the life of an infamous queen."

Contrary to his custom, Werner erupted in loud laughter and cried, "I don't understand. Was she really supposed to have been thrown down from above as one can see it in the Merian Bible?"[23]

"How can you imagine such a puppet show prank from a seasoned author! No, my work was to be performable before people of the best taste. The scene is a grand hall from which it doesn't move, and in the Fifth Act, where Jezebel seeks to move her conqueror through feigned charms and flatteries, to frighten him through threats, the hero in justified anger comes to a halt amid reproaches and curses and cuts short a well-conducted conversation in rather knightly fashion when he commands the guard to hurl her down. The latter seize her — and the curtain falls."

"Bravo," cried Werner, "that was well conceived!"

---

[23] A Lutheran Bible with illustrations by Matthäus Merian (1593-1650).

"I was only afraid," countered Wilhelm, "that one day in a performance the curtain by accident wouldn't come down, whereby, of course, the whole effect of the tragedy would have dissolved in laughter."

"You'll surely find quite splendid passages in the work," his sister said to her husband, "and the queen is so godless, one hopes that every evil will befall her."

"Isn't it true, Amelie," said Wilhelm, "you were also especially angry at her for laying claims to a young king you wouldn't have spurned yourself?"

"Now about Belshazzar," Werner interjected.

"I'm not going to let you take him from me. There are such beautiful passages in it, all of which I've memorized."

"Give me an idea of it," said Werner."

"My heroes," responded Wilhelm, "were usually young because I found nothing more interesting than the youth which I was experiencing myself, and thus my King Belshazzar was a fine young gentleman."

"Do you still remember," his sister said, "what the stranger whose taste you make so much of said on his walk the morning he had read the work?"

"I'm sure," replied Wilhelm, "he said it out of merciful generosity in order not to destroy me completely. He maintained the young king was well drawn. Actually he's a person of whom there are many in every class. He desires to do good, has a feeling for honesty and virtue, a vague, foreboding awe of the strict god of the Hebrews, a comfortable, traditional subservience to his own gods, is casual concerning his realm, occupied by his passions, keenly interested in festivities and banquets, by preference being entertained, to which his courtiers willingly contribute their talents."

"Well, that doesn't sound so bad," said Werner.

"Just listen to the monologue with which the king begins the Second Act," said Amelie. "I know it by heart."

"Do recite it," replied Wilhelm. "Meanwhile I'll take a stroll on the embankment. I really don't like it when someone recites my things to me."

"How would you feel if they were performed?"

"I don't know, that would take care of itself, but it would embarrass me in any event." And so he went off from them.

"Just imagine," Amelie said when he was gone, "that it's the King's birthday, that in the night the conspirators open the First Act and have just disappeared as the day dawns. The sun comes up, the King, awakened by the sound of drums and trumpets proclaiming the festivities to his city, tears himself from the arms of his beloved and from the terrace surveys the splendor of Babylon. I should also note that in the preceding act one conspirator mentioned with contempt Belshazzar's fear of stormy weather."

Chapter 5

What charming festive day has driven out the night,
Awaking me from sleep? A day of grand delight!
Within her gentle arms sweet Love was me embracing,
Now joy calls to me, with golden hours enticing.
The city jubilates, the fields about resound
In morning's sun-drenched glow, their splendor knows no bound.
Song after song does rise, a thousand throats' expressing
Unto the king their praise and wishing fortune's blessing.
As with one voice they call to me from every side
To be the people's head, and like the gods beside.
Let every hour flow past and bring me such sweet pleasure!
Whatever man can wish is mine and mine to treasure.
May my untroubled fate be tranquil as the sky!
How dare you, cloud, appear? Go hide and flee my eye!
The glory of this feast's to my high self addressed,
And yet a thunder cloud strikes fear within my breast?
Oh human heart so frail, oh spirit lightly captured,
You swell up, and you rise, from flattery enraptured.
A people on its knees can cause your pride to swell,
Their slavishness to you does cast a magic spell.
And when the heavens' might exciting you strikes down,
You, childlike, bow the head that boldly bears the crown.
Oh, providence, as true to me as to your lover,
Come on the morning breeze, about my head to hover!
In your embrace alone do I enjoy, light and free,
What birth did bring and what you offer me.
My spirit spreads about and pushes everywhere
To grab for my great realm an ever greater share,
To march with victor's gait through all the world there be,
And grudgingly to halt on reaching earth's last sea.
But if my heart's soared high, in vain it now must prove:
I hear: You're not the Lord! Acknowledge Him above!
Your slave looks up at you, to him you're regal glory,
Look down upon him now, his lot and yours one story;
A hundred temples may display your golden face,

You'll need but little room in your last resting place.
Do you rule o'er the day? Or joy? Or aggravation?
Yes, time will show you too our common destination.
It's He alone who lives, He'll live beyond time's date,
The sky can Him support but trembles 'neath His weight;
Enshrouded in the storm, He steps out forcefully,
The thunder brings His word, my deafened senses flee.
I hear: You are but dust the wind will blow away,
You are, oh Majesty, the flower I'll mow today.

Amelie had to repeat various verses twice for her husband, who praised them highly and tried to remember them. Following the return of her brother, an argument began anew, one quite similar to that we described in the preceding chapter. His sister spoke of the work with delight. Werner gave her his support before the fact because he assumed the entire work was as successful as the monologue.

Wilhelm had much to criticize about it, and while he spoke he was considering many things and was asserting the result of a number of observations that the others had not made for themselves. Present before his soul were literary works familiar to him to which he compared his own, and, as an artist, he was speaking about the inner forces which drive a work to people who were making their judgments only according to the effect it had on them. It was impossible for him to convince them, especially since, if one were to observe it exactly, all three truly were right.

But he never failed to assert again and again his favorite precept that in the drama the plot, to the extent it advances and can be presented, is the principal concern and that attitudes and emotions must be completely subordinated to this developing plot, and indeed that the characters may reveal themselves only in action and through action. This was conceded, and immediately examples were cited that demonstrated the opposite. Finally he assured them that he despised his works up till now because they were all marked by this flaw. "They are," he said, "like people whom no one values because they talk a great deal and do little."

Amelie was annoyed at this and said jokingly, "Just show us some of the new things you've written since you've become so learned."

"I won't do that," responded Wilhelm, "for I regard what I've developed following my new insights as rather good and, although I know I'm on the right road, I'm still afraid I might not have the strength to continue on it or, without the direction of a skillful master, I might subsequently again go wrong and even more dangerously so. My old works I'll leave to you for praise and criticism; let me brood in secret over my current ones. The public can confuse even the masters; we pupils, driven back and forth by the wind like young, tender, newly planted trees, cannot take root, and run a danger of drying up. Instead, in conclusion, I want to read you some excerpts from a short essay I have here among my things, one my friend sent to me concerning various questions I had posed about dramatic points. Among critics there has been much debate, indeed even fighting, concerning the source of the pleasure people experience from the drama and, in particular, from tragedy. People have been of various opinions concerning its nature and its purpose. You'll hear philosophic musings that seem to begin somewhat obscurely, yet provide many a thought concerning this matter." Wilhelm produced the sheet and read:

> Man is destined by his nature and through the nature of things to varied fates: pleasure and pain, fortune and misfortune in their highest degrees are to him equally remote and equally near. A premonition, if I may call it that, of evil and of good is given to him, which at the same time is most inwardly bound to the strength to assume and to bear life's burdens.
>
> In the course of its days every soul is more or less prepared for that which awaits it so that usually something extraordinary, when it occurs and especially as soon as the first moments of surprise are past, seems familiar and bearable. Although I don't wish to deny that many behave quite poorly when faced with unanticipated good luck or misfortune, we nevertheless find many to whom we otherwise aren't able to ascribe strength of character will accept unexpected good luck with equanimity and being struck by bad luck with composure. We often see men distinguished by nothing extraordinary who endure pain, illness, or loss of their loved ones with quiet perseverance and even approach their own death as something familiar and necessary.
>
> That the premonition of good in all men is connected with the desire to possess it is natural and soon becomes apparent. It is more difficult to notice, however, that man has a lust for evil and a dark yearning for enjoying pain, which is related to other feelings, and cloaked by other symptoms that can divert us from our observations.
>
> It has long been said that the state of indifference is the one which man most seeks to flee. As soon as soul and body have been set at ease by sleep and rest, then both again desire to bestir themselves, to be active, to become stimulated, moved, and thus aware of their existence. The desire to enjoy this stimulus exists in a thousand ways. The simpler man needs a simpler, slighter, weaker one; the educated man one more elaborate, stronger, more often recurring. This desire is so powerful that it seldom remains within the bounds of a man's strength and thus, although even the seemingly moderate person indeed does

not end every day of his life drunk, he nonetheless consumes the entire sum of his existence earlier than it was destined.

Man is inwardly moved by everything unusual which he encounters. An evil which has passed becomes a treasured memory for his entire life. Stories of unusual things happening to others are most welcome, be they preserved from the past or brought to us as novelties from strange parts of our world. But the populace is most strongly affected by everything that occurs before its eyes. A smeared painting or a childish woodcut attracts the unlettered man far more strongly than a detailed description. And how many thousands exist who in the most splendid picture see only the story? The grand pictures of the ballad-singers[24] make a far deeper impression than their songs, although these, too, capture the imagination with strong bonds.

What can make a greater impression on the masses than when directly before them the hero arises as if from the grave, moves before them, reveals his innermost self, suffers, and in the end perishes in the fictional danger? How many thousands are drawn irresistibly to an execution, which they loathe; how the hearts of the crowd tremble for the evildoer, yet how many would return home dissatisfied if he were pardoned and his head remained on his shoulders? The spurting blood which dyes the pale neck of the guilty man sprinkles the imagination of the observers with indelible spots. Years later, the soul, shuddering, looks lasciviously up at the scaffolding, again sees all the frightful circumstances and hesitates to admit to itself that it is savoring the horrifying drama. Those executions that the poet arranges are much more welcome.

The healthy human being can be moved by nothing without at the same time there being set into vibration the strings of his being from which the rapturous harmonies of pleasure flow down upon him. And even frightful, destructive desires, which are frightening even in children and which we seek to drive out through punishment, have secret paths and hiding places through which they cross over into the sweetest delights of all. All of these inner passages and paths are thoroughly shaken by the electricity of drama and especially of tragedy, and a fascination seizes the man; the less intelligent he is, the greater his pleasure becomes.

The concepts which men make of men and things are so obscure, so confused, so incomplete that a foolish case of mistaken identity doesn't distract them in the least. Charles XII[25] is recognized by his boots and his buttoned-up coat, but especially by his bushy hair,

---

[24] Particularly at fairs *Moritatensänger* would use large pictures to elucidate their often gruesome ballads.

[25] Of Sweden, a reference to C. F. Weiße's comic opera *The Hunt* (1770).

Henry IV[26] by his twisted mustache and ruffed collar, and people willingly accept the most contradictory representations of departed royalty. And I will even maintain that the more the theater is cleaned up, though it must certainly become more pleasant for knowledgeable and tasteful people, it will nonetheless lose more and more of its original effect and purpose. It seems to me, if I may use a comparison, to be like a pond that must contain not only clear water, but also a certain portion of mud, seaweed, and insects if fish and water fowl are to exist in it comfortably.

Since I am compelled to put down my pen and look back on what I have written, I see that I am as confused and incomplete as anyone who has dared to treat such a matter. Let these fleeting thoughts only stimulate your own thinking. Perhaps the next time we shall speak of the farce and its respectable daughter, the comedy. In so doing, if we want to get to the bottom of things, we mustn't forget the gypsy and the dancing bear, nor even the dangerous leaps and contortions of wandering daredevils.

Our friends were, each in his fashion, on the point of taking up the heavy burden of this reading, to roll it, and, if possible, to knock off some of its sharp edges (for the reader is usually so constituted that he would like to pick up every object in his hand well rounded to observe it in comfort and subsequently roll it towards his target like a bowling ball) when they were interrupted by a sight which drew the complete attention of all.

Chapter 6

A party of armed men came across the field, whom they immediately recognized by their broad, long coats, by their wide lapels, unshapely hats and heavy weapons, by their candid gait and informal bearing as a detachment of rural militia from the neighboring district. The group came nearer, greeted them, stacked their weapons by the large oak and settled down comfortably on the clearing beside it in order to smoke a pipe of tobacco. Our friends fell into a conversation with a corporal and heard that he had been sent by his superiors to take into custody here on the border a couple of young people who had

---

[26] Of France, an allusion to C. F. Schwan's comedy *Henry IV's Delight in Hunting*.

eloped and who had been arrested by warrant in the next city. The
oak which had aroused such poetic feelings in Wilhelm was actually a
boundary tree. Here they intended to rest and await the arrival of the
captive pair.

Wilhelm was taken aback at this news, but even more when he
heard the young man was an actor and the girl the daughter of a well-
to-do man in the neighboring town. From the rambling story which
the corporal related, so much could be learned: that a half year ago
an acting troupe had visited them but had not been able to sustain itself for long. When they finally departed, an actor stayed behind who
had not wanted to move and who, because he was content to teach
young people French and dancing for a modest sum, had found some
patrons and supporters. In the house of Herr N., where he boarded,
he had become acquainted with the gentleman's daughter from his
first marriage, to whom his second wife paid no special attention. He
had often gone walking with her and had given her elocution lessons
in the garden, about which people had begun to talk. There had been
quarrels about this in the house and one morning the two were
missed. The parents ran to the officials and sought the help of neighboring authorities. Thus they had been apprehended and now were to
be surrendered to them.

Our friends were astonished at this story since the similarity of
fates, albeit with genders reversed, struck them, and their curiosity to
see the mismatched couple was greatly aroused. It wasn't long until
the magistrate's clerk came riding up, conversed with the detachment,
and, upon inquiries from our group, filled out the story with some
further details.

At last in the distance a wagon was seen approaching surrounded
by a civilian guard that was more ludicrous than formidable. Ahead of
it rode an odd looking town clerk who saluted his counterpart beneath the oak at the boundary stone with great gravity and wondrous
gestures, just as perhaps the spirit and the magician might do on dangerous nocturnal operations, the one inside the magic circle, the other
outside.

The attention of the observers, meanwhile, was drawn to the
wagon. The old coach in which the beauty initially had been transported had broken en route. When a peasant's wagon was requisi-
tioned to help, she begged the company of her friend, who, on
account of the special concept of criminality in his case, had been
burdened with chains and had walked alongside her. Thus they were
sitting side by side on some bundles of straw, looking at one another
tenderly, and when he kissed her hands, he moved the rattling chains
with great dignity.

"We are very unfortunate," he called to our party which had approached the wagon, "but we are not as guilty as we seem. Thus do cruel people reward true love, and parents who totally neglect the happiness of their children, tear them with violence out of the arms of the joy that they had found after long, dark days."

The questions put to them by the group were somewhat more prosaic. By the time they were answered, the representatives of the law had absolved their ceremonies, the wagon moved on, and Wilhelm, whom the fate of the lovers interested greatly, asked his married companions to go with him to the courthouse, which lay about half an hour away. They excused themselves with the approach of evening and took their way back to the city; he, however, hastened after his lovers. Since he hoped to renew an old acquaintance with the official before they arrived, he took a footpath and reached the building in good time, where he found everything astir and ready for the arrival of the fugitives.

The clerk, who arrived soon after, related with great joy how everything had gone successfully and that the young people were not far from the town. With more satisfaction he added that he had ordered that the wagon not enter through the city gate and that they should be deposited by the garden which was connected to the official building by a small gate, so that they could be brought in without attracting attention.

Although the dull and unfeeling manner in which the man treated the affair displeased Wilhelm, he could not help but praise him for having used so much foresight in sparing the unfortunate couple. The former accepted the compliment smugly, but actually was rejoicing in his heart because he had played a prank on the citizenry assembled before the building and deprived them of the highly desired spectacle of the public humiliation of a girl who otherwise regarded herself more highly than did others. After this he told another official how splendidly the horse rode that he had acquired only yesterday in a trade with the Jew, and he went on at great length about its good qualities, so that Wilhelm was prevented from inquiring more closely about the affair. Secretly he was very surprised that when expecting such important events, in the midst of the most serious official actions, a person could bring up with great interest such extraneous, unimportant, and — he would have liked to add — foolish things.

Their arrival was announced. The magistrate had no special love for such extraordinary cases because in handling them he usually made one mistake or another and try as he might was usually rewarded by the provincial government with a sharp reprimand. With heavy gait he entered the office, followed by Wilhelm, the clerk, and several respected citizens who had gathered out of curiosity.

First the beauty was brought in, who without arrogance entered very calmly and with self-assurance. The manner in which she had straightened her clothing which couldn't have been in the best condition from her flight and captivity told Wilhelm that she was a girl with self-respect. Without being asked, she began to speak in composure about her situation.

The clerk ordered her to be silent and held his pen poised over his paper. The magistrate composed himself, looked at him, cleared his throat, and asked the poor child, "What is your name and how old are you?"

"I beg you, sir," she replied, "it has to strike me as strange that you ask me about my name and my age since you know very well what my name is and that I am just as old as your eldest son. Whatever you want to know from me and whatever you must know, I will gladly tell you straightforwardly.

"Since my father's second marriage I have not been kept to my best advantage. I could have made a number of fine marriages had my stepmother not frustrated them in fear of an expensive dowry. Then I became acquainted with young Melina, whom I had to love, and since we foresaw the difficulties which stood in the way of our union, we resolved to seek with one another in the wide world the happiness which was denied us at home.

"I took nothing with me save what was my own; indeed, I still have claim to a considerable inheritance from my mother. We did not flee like thieves and robbers, and my husband does not deserve to be dragged around in chains and ropes. The prince is just; he will not approve this severity. If we are punishable, we are not so to this extent."

The old magistrate became doubly and triply embarrassed at this. The prince's flunkies were already buzzing in his head and the girl's eloquent, smooth speech had completely destroyed his plan for the protocol. His discomfort grew even greater when upon repeated routine questioning she would not expand upon her statement, but steadfastly referred to what she had just said.

"I am not a criminal," she said. "They brought me here on bundles of straw to disgrace me. There is a higher justice which shall restore us to honor."

The clerk, who meanwhile was recording her words, whispered to the magistrate that he should just continue, a proper protocol could be prepared later. The old man again took courage and now began with barren words and traditional, dry phrases to inquire about the sweet secrets of love.

The color rose in Wilhelm's face, and the cheeks of the well- behaved criminal were stirred by the charming color of modesty. She grew quiet and stammered until embarrassment finally bolstered her courage. "Be assured," she cried out, "that I would be strong enough to confess the truth, even if I had to speak against myself; should I now stammer and hesitate when it is in my favor? Yes, from the moment when I became aware of his devotion and loyalty I have regarded him as my husband. I have granted him everything that love demands and that a confident heart cannot deny. Now do with me what you will. If I hesitated for a moment in admitting it, then it was out of fear that my admission might have evil consequences for him."

When he heard that, Wilhelm formed a high opinion of the girl's attitudes, while the members of the court viewed her as an insolent wench, and the citizens present thanked God that cases of this sort had not happened in their families or at least had not become publicly known.

In this moment Wilhelm placed his Mariane before the judge's bench, putting even more beautiful words into her mouth, letting her sincerity be even more heartfelt and her confession even more noble. A passionate desire to help the lovers overcame him. He did not conceal it and privately asked the magistrate whether he might put an end to the affair, everything was quite clear and needed no further details.

This helped to the extent that the girl was permitted to step down, but in exchange the young man, after his fetters had been removed outside, was ordered to come in. He seemed more reflective about his fate. His responses were more respectful and more composed, and if he for his part displayed less heroic generosity, he commended himself to Wilhelm rather through the delicacy displayed in his remarks.

An end came to this interrogation, which agreed in everything with the preceding one except that to protect the girl he obstinately denied what she had already admitted. She was finally allowed to reappear, and there developed between the two a scene which completely won our friend's heart to them. What customarily occurs only in novels and plays he now saw in an unpleasant court chamber: the struggle of mutual generosity, the strength of love in misfortune.

"Is it true then," he said to himself, "that modest affection which timorously hides from daylight and men and dares to relax only in isolated loneliness and in deep secret, when dragged forth by a hostile accident then presents itself more courageously, strongly, and bravely than other blustering and swaggering emotions?" He secretly

envied their happiness, and the loss of Mariane revived completely in
his soul. If he could have had her again by so doing, how gladly
would he have put himself in the place of the two lovers and sacrificed himself to unfeeling justice!

Through his mediation the whole procedure concluded rather
quickly. He brought it about that they were both taken into light ar-
rest, and if it had been possible, he would have taken the fair beloved
to her parents that same evening, for he resolved to become an in-
termediary and to assist the happy and respectable union of the two
lovers. He sent a message to his brother-in-law that he would be
away for this evening and the following day. Then with the permission of the magistrate he went to where the young man was being
held in a small room.

Chapter 7

Even during the hearing the thought had occurred to Wilhelm that he
had seen the young man before in some other place. The face
seemed familiar to him; the manner, on the other hand, unknown; he
could not recall the name Melina in any way. When the guard opened
the door of the cell, he stepped in, and peering closely into the
stranger's face called out in sudden inspiration," Why, Herr Pfefferkuchen,[27] is it you whom I've found again? Is it possible I could fail
to recognize you for a whole half hour?"

"Is it you," the other cried, "with whom I had the pleasure of
spending a pleasant evening in M** along with some comrades and
our delightful Mariane? Probably my changed haircut, different clothing, and a different name misled you." Wilhelm was taken aback and
did not know to which of the three or to all together he should attribute his blindness.

If we are allowed a guess concerning his reaction, it was probably
caused by this: The Pfefferkuchen whom he knew was actually a dull,
small, limited person, without the grace of nobility in his movements
and bearing. His manner was as common as his name, and apart from
a strong voice and a certain intensity with which he played emotional
roles, there was nothing which would have distinguished him. This
was the image that had remained with Wilhelm. The Melina, on the
other hand, whom he had encountered in chains, whom he saw before the judge's bench, was put by his circumstances into a quiet melancholy; he moved the others because he himself was moved, and his

[27] Lit. "pepper cake," a spiced cookie commonly baked at Christmastide.

determined conduct at the height of danger elevated his being for a moment and spread a noble dignity about his whole person.

"How did you come to such a completely foreign name?" said Wilhelm.

"It's not so far removed from the previous one," said the former. "Names have a great influence on the imagination of men. Mine gave occasion for mockery and was objectionable to me. Because in various places one says honey cake instead of *Pfefferkuchen*, I translated it as Melina as soon as I had occasion to appear in a strange town for the first time."

"I doubt that anyone will figure out the etymology," responded Wilhelm.

Melina (which name we do not wish to begrudge him) thereupon began to tell his entire story to Wilhelm, and the latter burned with the desire to hear something more about Mariane, concerning whom, as soon as it was at all appropriate, he inquired with discreet questions. "Our troupe lost a great deal with her departure," the other said.

"Did she leave?" replied Wilhelm.

"Yes," said the former, "and in an unpleasant manner. When we left M** that time, we took our way toward the fair at ***. Mariane had been in poor spirits throughout the last days and so she remained in the coach, where I sat beside her for several stations. The usual quarrels which arise in the difficult moving of a troupe did not interest her, she accepted everything, she no longer sang and joked as she did formerly, and the amusing incidents which occur to one person or another couldn't bring a smile to her face. She was often criticized for that, but this too seemed neither to disturb or embarrass her; we couldn't make heads or tails of it. Suddenly in ***, where we had spent the night, we heard a great quarrel between her and the director. As we later learned, the latter had received from the city to which we were going a letter from the relatives of a young man with whom she had had a relationship. The letter was threatening and humiliating for her and the director, who was in great conflict with her about it and who finally brought her to the decision to leave the company. She did in truth go no further, but stayed behind in the inn which we left. Since it was obvious from the letter that the old theater seamstress also knew of the affair, the director, who would have liked to be rid of her long before, took this excuse to discharge her too. So the two women remained alone; many of the company pitied them. I have inquired about her subsequently and learned nothing about her."

Wilhelm grew so pensive at this recital that for quite a while he didn't listen as Melina reverted to his own story, expanding on what had happened to him, and dwelt in particular on his thoughts for the

future. Still and withdrawn into himself, staring fixedly ahead, Wilhelm
stood before him and the former interpreted this trance as thoughtful
attention. How surprised was he then when to his question, "Do you
think I'm doing the right thing and will fare better in this metier?.,"
Wilhelm looked up and without reflection answered, "Oh, yes! I'm
convinced you can choose none better and that your spouse, as far as
I know her, will also be successful in the theater. She has a nice figure, a dignified manner, a pleasing voice, and youth sufficient to find
her way in a new career."

Our friend could not help imagining that the actor and his young
wife would seek out the theater. It seemed to him just as natural and
necessary as it is for a frog to seek water. He had not doubted it for
one moment; on the contrary, he believed he had heard from the
other during his trance that which his own soul was saying. Melina on
the other hand had recited to him exactly the opposite and now said
to him in some surprise, "You must not have understood me, sir, for I
have resolved not to go back to the theater again, but to accept a settled position of whatever nature, if I can find one."

"You are making a mistake," responded Wilhelm. "Without good
cause it is not advisable to alter the life one has chosen and, moreover, I would know no other that offers you so many amenities as does
that of an actor."

"One sees that you never were one," replied Melina.

To this Wilhelm said, "How seldom is man content with the condition in which he finds himself; he always wishes for that of his neighbor, from which the latter likewise yearns to be free."

"Meanwhile there still remains a distinction," replied Melina,
"between the bad and the worse. Experience, not impatience, makes
me act thus. Is there a more pitiable, uncertain, and difficult living in
the world? It would almost be just as good to beg from door to door.
What mustn't one endure from the envy of colleagues, from the parti-
sanship of the director, from the malicious whims of the public! In
truth, one has to have a skin like a bear that is lead about in the company of monkeys and dogs and is whipped in order to dance to the
tune of the bagpipe before children and the rabble."

Wilhelm had all sorts of thoughts for himself which, however, he
didn't want to say to this young man's face. Thus he continued the
conversation with him only in a somewhat distanced manner. The
former opened up all the more honestly and broadly. "If it weren't
necessary," he said, "that the director fall at the feet of every city official in order just to obtain permission to cause a little more money to
circulate during the four weeks of the fair! I often pitied ours, who
was in certain respects a good man even if on other occasions he

gave me cause for displeasure. A good actor always wants more money from him, he can't get rid of the poor ones, and if he wants to try to balance his earnings with his expenses then it's immediately too expensive for the public. The house stands empty, and in order not to be destroyed completely, one has to perform with losses and aggravation. No, sir, since you wish to help us, as you say, I beg you to speak most compellingly with the parents of my beloved! Let them provide for me here, let them give me a petty position as clerk or tax collector and I will deem myself fortunate."

After a few more words were exchanged, Wilhelm departed with the promise to approach the parents early the next day and to see what he could arrange. Scarcely was he alone when he erupted with the following words: "Unfortunate Melina, you who should still be called Pfefferkuchen, not in your condition, but in yourself lies the wretchedness that you cannot master! What person in the world who without inner calling took up a trade, art, or any sort of living could not, would not, like you, have to find his situation unbearable? Whoever is born *with* a talent and *for* a talent finds in it his most beautiful existence. Nothing exists in the world without difficulty; only inner compulsion, desire, and love help us overcome obstacles, break new paths, and lift us out of the narrow circle in which others torment themselves miserably. For you the stage is nothing more than the stage, and the roles what class work is for the schoolchild, and you look upon the audience as they see themselves on workdays. For you it could all be the same to sit behind a desk over ledgers, entering the interest payments the hungry peasants bring. You do not feel the consuming, harmonious whole, which is discovered, grasped, and executed by the spirit alone. You do not sense that within men a better spark lives which, if it receives no fuel, if it is not stirred, becomes more deeply covered by the ashes of daily needs and indifference, yet, and be it ever so late, is almost never extinguished. In your soul you feel no strength to fan it, in your own heart no wealth with which to feed the awakened spark.

"Hunger compels you and want frightens you, discomfort is repugnant to you, and you cannot see that in every class the enemies lurk which can be overcome only with joyfulness and steadfastness. You do well to yearn for the confines of a common position, for how could you fill one which demands spirit and courage? Give such attitudes to a soldier, a statesman, a cleric and with equal justice he'll be able to complain about the wretchedness of his condition. Indeed, haven't there even been people who were so totally devoid of all humanity and feeling for life that they have explained the entire life and essence of mortals as a miserable existence resembling that of dust?

"If the figures of productive men stirred within your soul, if a sympathetic, activating fire warmed your breast, if the mood which comes from our innermost self spread across your whole body, if the sound from your throat and the words from your lips were delightful to hear, if you sensed yourself to be sufficient within your self, then you would surely seek out the place and opportunity to make yourself felt in others."

Amid such words and thoughts our friend had undressed, and with a feeling of heartfelt contentment he climbed into bed and composed for himself an entire novel about what he would do on the coming morning if he were in the place of that unworthy person. These fantasies gently escorted him into the realm of sleep and there, greeted with open arms by their sister dreams, strengthened and reanimated by them, they surrounded the resting head of our friend with a presentiment of heaven.

Early in the morning he was again awake and thinking about his impending negotiations. He quite soon overcame the small embarrassment at approaching total strangers in so important a matter. He came before their house and his heart pounded in anxiety. He stated his message modestly and soon found both more and fewer difficulties than he had anticipated. It had indeed happened, and even if extraordinarily strong and hard people forcefully oppose what is done and cannot be changed and thereby tend to make the matter worse, it has, on the other hand, an undeniable force on the minds of men, and once they truly see that which had seemed impossible, it takes its place alongside the ordinary, as we've already had occasion to note above. Thus it was soon agreed that Herr Melina should marry the daughter. On the other hand, because of her misbehavior she was to receive no dowry and to promise to leave her maternal inheritance for some years with her father at a low rate of interest.

The second point concerning settled employment occasioned greater difficulties. They did not wish to look at the undutiful child, nor did they wish to be constantly reminded by his presence of the union of a vagabond with such a respected family, one even related to a high church official. There was just as little hope that the princely officials would entrust a position to him. Both parents were equally strongly opposed, and Wilhelm could arrange nothing. He spoke very energetically for them, although basically he did not begrudge the return to the theater to this person whom he thought little of and was convinced he was unworthy of such good fortune. Had he been familiar with the secret motives, he would not have taken the trouble at all to convince them, for the father, who gladly would have kept the daughter with him, hated the young man because his wife, before the latter courted the girl, had herself cast an eye on him; she, in turn, could not stand to see in her stepdaughter a successful rival.

I shall not describe in detail the freeing of the two lovers, their reception at home and the end of this story. Enough, after some days Melina and his young bride, who displayed a greater desire to see and be seen by the world, had to depart against their will and seek a place where a company of actors was earning its living.

Chapter 8

Sunday had come and Wilhelm still had not shown up at home. His brother-in-law interpreted this to mean, as was indeed the case, that he had spent the time partly in reconciling the family, partly for his own pleasure. It was a holiday and everyone wanted to go for a walk. Werner had let the father and mother, his wife, the clerks, maids, and servants go, and he remained at home, which was to his liking. Wilhelm's grandfather, who had earned a great deal from business, had built the house, but under the direction of the father it had lost much of its middle-class splendor, which Werner was endeavoring to restore gradually. He walked about and saw how far the workmen had come during the week, and what remained to be done in the coming one. The roof was completely rebuilt, several weak beams had been replaced, new boards had replaced rotted and weathered ones, the mason was working to point the cracked walls, and a painter was smoothing and dignifying them with whitewash. Much had also been done within the house: all rooms and chambers had been whitewashed; instead of the old, smoke-stained, dark wainscoting the walls were painted with new, bright colors or papered.

Suffice it to say, wherever one stepped, one saw the signs of an emerging life which gave hope of a long duration. Werner surveyed all this with great satisfaction and since he found the necessary repairs all but finished, he began to think about the pleasure of completing it little by little as his finances permitted.

In the middle of the house was a sandstone-paved courtyard, which since Werner had taken over again provided a pleasant spot in the summer. What had formerly filled and disfigured it had been removed and each item taken to its place in stables, coach sheds, and attics. In its improved state, it served as a gathering place and strolling area for the family. At its bottom there stood an artificial grotto where formerly a water fountain had been, but its pipes had fallen into disrepair and many of its ornaments broken off. To restore it, Werner had already ordered mother of pearl shells, corals, galena, and the other necessary items and hoped soon to see everything in order again and to drink a glass of wine and smoke a pipe with good friends beside the leaping water on a Sunday.

After he had considered all this, he climbed to the upper part of the house, where between two gables a balcony had been constructed, which he found in very poor condition. Here, too, he was thinking about new tubs filled with orange trees, brightly colored flower pots, and exotic plants with which he hoped to ornament his hanging garden and create a small paradise between the chimneys. As evening came on, he climbed down, visited in passing the cellar, checked the chests of sugar, barrels of coffee, and baskets of indigo, for which he had a particular affection because it was good business. Thereafter he sat down in the office, opened his ledgers, and took delight in this reading matter because the profit obvious from them made his eyes gleam as if he had been reading the most tasteful book.

In the meantime Wilhelm entered, who, quite full of his adventure and the lovely regions he had visited in the company of some friends, talked to his brother-in-law about them with great animation. The former did indeed listen to him with his usual patience; however, this time he himself was so filled with a passion that in response to Wilhelm's questions about what he had been doing, he guided their conversation toward those things that interested him most.

"I was just going through our books," said Werner, "and by the ease with which the state of our capital can be seen, I was admiring once again the great advantages which double entry bookkeeping affords the businessman. It is one of the most elegant inventions of the human mind, and every good manager should introduce it into his business. The order and ease of having everything in front of oneself increases the desire to save and to earn. And just as a man who does business poorly prefers to remain in the dark and doesn't care to add up the sums he owes everyone, nothing is more pleasant on the other hand to the good businessman than being able to see every day the bottom line of his growing fortune. Even an accident, though it surprises him annoyingly, does not shock him, for he knows right away the variety of earned profits he has to put into the balance. I am convinced, my dear brother," he went on, "if you could just once get a true feeling for our business, you would find that one can apply with profit and pleasure many capabilities of the mind in it."

"It is possible," replied Wilhelm, "that I might have acquired some inclination, perhaps even passion for business if from childhood on it hadn't dismayed me in its pettiest form."

"You're right," replied the former, "and the description of business personified in a youthful poem you told me about is splendidly appropriate for the petty shopkeeping in which you were raised, but not to the commerce that you had no opportunity to become acquainted with. Believe me, you would find things to occupy your fiery imagination if in your mind you could envision the armies of enterprising men who, like rivers crisscrossing the world, engage in import and export. Since our mutual interests are so closely connected, I've always hoped they might be our mutual concern. I could not imagine you in a shop measuring things by the yard, weighing them. Let our shop clerks take care of that and instead join me in order, through all kinds of business and speculations, to capture for ourselves a part of the wealth and well-being in their necessary circulation through the world. Cast a glance at all the natural and manufactured products from all parts of the world, see how by turn they've become necessities. How pleasant and creative it is to provide easily and quickly at that moment for anyone who desires whatever is popular, or lacking, or difficult to obtain, and to maintain careful inventory, and to enjoy the profit from each moment of this great circulation. It seems to me that's what will make for great joy in anyone with a good head. But, to be sure, one must first become an apprentice in this guild, something that can scarcely happen in this place. I've thought about this for a long time and it would surely be an advantage for you in any case to undertake a journey."

Wilhelm did not seem disinclined and Werner continued, "Once you've seen a couple of large commercial cities, a couple of ports, then you'll surely be captivated by seeing where everything comes from, where it goes to, and you'll certainly also enjoy seeing it pass through your hands. You'll see the most insignificant product in the context of total trade and thus you'll respect everything because everything increases the flow from which you earn your living."

Werner, who developed his proper understanding in conversations with Wilhelm, had also become accustomed to thinking of his trade and his affairs with a certain uplifting of the soul. And he always believed he was acting more justly than his otherwise reasonable and valued friend, who, so it seemed to him, placed so great a value and the whole weight of his mind on the intangibles of this world. Sometimes he thought there had to be a way to overcome this false enthusiasm and to set so good a person on the right path. In this hope, he continued: "The great people of this world have taken control of the earth and live in splendor and plenty from its fruits. The smallest spot has been defeated and taken captive, all possessions secured, every group is paid little for performing its assigned task and only from the

necessity of sustaining its existence. Where is there a more just occupation, a fairer conquest than in trade? If the princes of this world
have taken command of the roads and the rivers and exact a good
profit from whatever passes through and by, are we not to seize the
opportunity joyfully and through our activity also levy a toll on those
articles which, partly through need, partly through vanity, have become indispensable to men? And I can assure you that if you wanted
to apply your poetic imagination, you could boldly oppose my goddess to your own as an indomitable Nike. True, she prefers the olive
branch to the sword, she knows neither sword nor chains at all, but
she does bestow crowns upon her favorites, who, let it be said without disrespect to your own goddess, gleam with real gold taken from
the source and pearls which her ever industrious servants have
fetched from the depths of the sea."

Although this sally, gentle as it was, annoyed Wilhelm somewhat,
he was too good-natured to respond, and basically he could readily
accept that every person should think the best of his trade as long as
no one challenged that to which he wished to dedicate himself.
Meanwhile he accepted the harangue from the suddenly impassioned
Werner with just the casualness with which the latter customarily accepted his.

"And you," Werner cried out, "you who are so sincerely concerned
about human affairs, what a spectacle it will be for you when you see
bestowed upon men the good fortune that accompanies adventurous
undertakings. What is more exciting than the sight of a ship, arrived
from a successful voyage, or returned early from a rich catch? Not just
relatives, acquaintances and shareholders, but every chance observer
is delighted when he sees the joy with which the captive sailor jumps
onto land even before his vessel has fully reached it, again feeling
free and now enabled to entrust to the loyal earth that which he took
from the treacherous water. We live by profit and loss, and if both
appear to us only as numbers, the one creates a dark fear within us
and the other gives no inner, sincere joy. Fortune is the goddess of
active people, and in order to feel her favor properly, we must live
and observe people who are full of life and feel perceptively."

Werner described more such scenes which tempted and cheered
his friend. For a long time the latter had again felt well enough in
mind and body to undertake something. He was not comfortable at
home; and he had been thinking of all sorts of opportunities for seeing the world and all that there might be to undertake and pursue.
Thus he was very pleased that Werner spoke of a trip and he answered, "If you think that there is money on hand for this expense
and that it might be well spent, then I am very satisfied. Certainly I'd

like to look about a bit, and since you've traveled quite a bit, you'll do best to make a plan for me which I'll gladly follow."

Werner replied, "You'll always find as much as you need, and according to my calculations, your trip will still bring in money."

"It's not all so certain," replied Wilhelm, "I'll learn so much of monetary value."

"Nor do I understand it so," said the former. "On your way you can with the greatest of ease do business that will be profitable for us. I recently extracted from our books the overdue accounts in all the towns and villages where we do business; I'll write down explanatory notes for you, provide you with the papers, and on your way you can easily not only take along your travel money everywhere, but also send me something from time to time, for there are considerable sums among them which I don't want to regard as lost."

"To dun debtors isn't exactly a pleasant occupation," said Wilhelm.

"It's a matter of habit," said Werner, "and one comes to terms with people more quickly than one thinks. I place great store in personal contact: one can discuss things much more readily with his debtors, and easily acquire new customers, the people need to be pushed a bit. We'll have to talk further about this and you'll soon and willingly agree to my thoughts. Your father will readily agree; it was our intention even before your illness. When you come back again you'll have seen everything and become acquainted with the people. Surely you'll end up doing business at my side willingly. You'll look around in the big cities and visit interesting factories and buildings. In the evening you'll find good company, or even a well outfitted theater that I'd surely like you to see." What Werner here brought up at the end was what Wilhelm had thought of first and was the weightiest factor in his considerations. They soon reached an agreement and made all the necessary arrangements.

Book 3

Chapter 1

The composition of a travel party is a kind of marriage, and unfortunately a person often finds himself in one, as with the latter, more from convenience than from unanimity, and the consequences of a frivolously entered union are the same both here and there. Wilhelm had hired a coach to a certain destination and, in order not to bear the expense alone, had located three more passengers who were traveling the same route. Each had his particular interest which he made his sole topic of conversation with the others, hoping thereby to derive some advantage for himself. One was a mining surveyor, the second a wine merchant, the third, though the least self-interested, found nothing of note on the whole trip save horses and girls. Wilhelm was stonily silent in their company; he was especially annoyed by their ill-bred conversations, their coarse and exaggerated demands at the inns, and their constant arguing with the coachman, who drove not one whit faster therefore.

They stopped at noon at an inn where the mining surveyor met some of his people, whom he had ordered here, standing before the door in the midst of a group of peasants.

Every sort of man who wears a uniform impresses the masses and usually knows very well how to profit from this advantage. The miners had brought zithers and were playing and singing while the others stood around them gaping. The party pushed their way through, and the singers doubled their efforts since now they could hope for a good gratuity. After greeting their superior, they presented various pleasant songs with spirited and harsh voices. All at once, when they observed that their performance was pleasing, they expanded their circle and one of them stepped forward with a pick and pretended to be mining while the others performed a piece. It was not long before a peasant stepped out of the group and gave him to understand with threatening gestures that he was to remove himself from the premises. Our party was surprised at this and only recognized it was a miner disguised as the peasant when he opened his mouth and in a kind of recitative inveighed against the other for daring to loiter about his field. The former did not lose his composure, rather he began to inform the country fellow that he had a right to do so and informed him about the basics of mining. The peasant posed all sorts of foolish questions at which the audience laughed heartily. The miner sought to correct him and ultimately demonstrated the advantages which would flow his way if the subterranean treasures of the land were burrowed out. The peasant, who had first threatened the former with blows, was gradually placated and they parted from this argument as good friends and, particularly in the case of the miner, in the most honorable manner of the world.

After they had finished, everyone, and particularly Wilhelm, willingly made a donation. The meal was ready, and since the mountains were near and the trip was proceeding slowly and with difficulty, they decided after eating to proceed on foot to their evening's quarters. The postilion described the way for the party and they soon drifted apart with one group hurrying ahead while the others lagged behind.

Wilhelm was soon alone. With easy gait he strode through hill and dale in the sensation of great pleasure. He saw overhanging cliffs, murmuring streams, overgrown hillsides, and deep valleys for the first time, and yet his earliest youthful dreams had hovered about such regions. At this sight he was now rejuvenated, his soul was cleansed of all the pains he had suffered, and with youthful cheer he recited passages from his first dramas, passages from other poets, especially from *Il pastor fido*,[28] which in these secluded places flooded his memory. He animated the world which lay before him with all the shapes from the past, and every step into the future was for him full of premonition of important deeds and remarkable events.

Several people, following one another, approached him from the rear, passed him with a greeting and hurriedly continued their way into the mountains. They occasionally had spoken to him without his having taken notice of them. Finally a more talkative person joined him and told him the cause of the unusual number of pilgrims. "In Hochdorf," he said, and this was the name of the evening's quarters for our travelers, "a play is being given this evening and everyone in the neighborhood is hastening to see it."

"What!" cried Wilhelm. "Has the art of drama found its way here and erected a temple to itself in these lonely mountains, these impenetrable forests?"

"You'll be even more surprised when you hear who's performing it. There's a large oilcloth factory in the place which employs many people. The manager, living, so to speak, removed from all human

---

[28] (The Faithful Shepherd), a pastoral play by Giovanni Battista Guarini (1538-1612).

society, knows no better employment for his painters and workers than to have them put on plays. He doesn't allow them to play cards and wants to keep them from coarse habits. That's how they spend the long evenings, and today, since it's the old man's birthday, they're holding festivities in his honor."

At the name of the place and of the factory director, it occurred to Wilhelm that this man was also on the list of those from whom he was to seek payment. "You're coming at a bad time," he said to himself, "in that you're reawakening a worry they perhaps had put out of their minds for a moment." This observation ruined the whole rest of the way for him, and he approached the house not without a certain well-intentioned concern. The remainder of the travel party had arrived at the inn earlier and, attracted by the novelty of the play, had obtained entrance, and Wilhelm too was greeted quite cordially by the head of the household. When he gave his name, the old man acted quite surprised and called out, "Oh, sir, are you the son of the good man to whom I owe so much gratitude and to whom I'm also still indebted? Your father has been so patient with me that I would have to be a scoundrel if I didn't pay him faithfully and honestly. You come at just the right time to see that I'm serious about this. For years I've always asked for deferment; however, I've just collected some substantial outstanding debts, thank God, and I've made a distribution of them in which your father has not been forgotten. I still owe him a hundred Dukaten, but two hundred Taler are ready for him, and he'll surely give me credit for the remainder until the next fair."

He called in his wife, who seemed just as delighted to see the young man, assured him he looked like his father, and greatly regretted she could not put him up for the night because of the many visitors. Wilhelm produced his papers and his powers of attorney, the old man led him to his office and paid him the two hundred Taler on the spot in gold. "If it keeps on like this," he thought to himself, "Werner is quite right that it's easier than you think to hold people to their obligations."

The hour of the play was approaching when suddenly the disheartening news was brought that the new pastor, who had arrived only a few months ago, had forbidden the play or rather proclaimed that he could not allow a play in his parish until permission from the authorities was produced. In vain people had told him the official knew only too well about it and had himself been in the plays fairly often. He certainly would have nothing to object to about it, but no one could go there and back in less than three hours. But in vain! The pastor remained adamant, and the entire group was in great distress.

Wilhelm undertook to straighten him out, went to him, and gave a most moving speech. The cleric was implacable when the young spokesman presented a variety of reasons. In vain! He stuck with his opinion and asserted he neither wanted to nor was able to yield. The unhappy ambassador turned back full of anger and irritation, the whole group was beside itself. The actors came up in costume and declared with great discomfort that the lamps and candles were lit and everything was waiting only for the signal to start. People were complaining, stamping their feet, running about, screaming.

When the noise was at its worse, horses drove up before the door and the Chief Forester and some hunters climbed down. He was extremely surprised at the confusion in which he found the house, because of which they almost forgot to extend to him the usual display of respect.[29] When he heard the reason why, he called out: "The padre won't let you perform! Well! Well! I'll whisper a little something into his ear. We're good friends; he'll surely do it as a favor to me." He indeed went to him and soon came back with the permission, they only needed to start. For his part, Wilhelm was curious to know the arguments with which this cavalier had persuaded the cleric; he said to himself, "It seems to me I didn't omit anything a rational person can say on such an occasion, yet I wasn't able to convince him."

The party was now led into the playhouse which was a barn next to the garden. The interior decorations surprised everyone for they were pleasant, although without any distinctive taste. One of the painters who worked at the factory had been a helper at the Dresden opera. Canvas and paints cost little, and their efforts were rewarded by the thing itself. Their presentation, which they had half borrowed from a traveling troupe and half fashioned in their own manner, bad as it was, entertained the audience. The plot, that two lovers want to steal a girl from her guardian and then from one another, elicited all sorts of interesting situations and made the action of the play lively. "I see from this," said Wilhelm to himself, "those Ancients were right who asserted that if a play is full of action, it can please and delight even without moral breeding and depiction of true humanity. These, they say, were the beginnings of their theater, and I almost believe they were also the beginnings of our own. The coarse person is content if he simply sees something happen, the educated person wants to feel, and reflection is pleasant only to the well educated."

He was roused from his silent observations by a cloud of tobacco smoke which grew thicker and thicker. Soon after the start of the

---

[29] As an officer of the court, the Chief Forester expected such ceremony.

work, the Chief Forester had lit his pipe, and gradually several others took this liberty. An even worse entrance was made by this gentleman's large dogs which, to be sure, had been shut out but soon found a way in through a back door. They ran across the stage, bumped into the actors, and by leaping over the orchestra found their master in the parterre.

As an epilog they had patched together a congratulatory tableaux: a poor portrait of the old man was set upon an altar and draped with wreaths; to this they paid their respects in pious poses. The youngest child stepped forth in finery and gave an address in very mediocre verses that moved the whole family to tears and even the Chief Forester, whom it reminded of his children. How powerfully do local circumstances affect the hearts of men, and how moving a solemn occasion can be, even if not done in the best taste!

Chapter 2

After a few days' journey the party came into a middle-sized town where they wanted to rest and each might pursue his own affairs. Here their association came to an end: the driver returned home.

Wilhelm presented his letters of introduction and with varying success sought payment from several persons on his list. Some paid, some gave excuses, some took it ill, and some denied their indebtedness. According to his instructions he was to take legal action against certain gentlemen, therefore he had to seek out a lawyer and engage his services. This last was as distasteful to him as anyone can imagine, yet he was conscientious and wanted to do things properly.

The society into which he moved entertained him no better. Good people who went their ways six days a week, did something good in addition on Sundays and, moreover, spent every evening in a closed circle playing billiards or omber! These were also the festivities with which they hosted him and one can say they did their best at this without doubting for a moment that their guest was as pleased by their company as they were by his.

He still liked it best at his inn, for it was always lively and there were always new diversions that interested him. A large party of rope walkers, acrobats and jugglers, who also had a strongman with them, had arrived with a great number of women and children, and while they were preparing for a public appearance they played one prank after another. Now they were fighting with the innkeeper, now among themselves, and if their quarreling was insufferable, their expression of pleasure was completely unbearable. On the market square he saw a spacious structure erected, the trapezes installed, the posts for the

slack rope secured, and the bucks for the tight rope properly positioned.

The next morning the parade set out that was to inform the city
about the spectacle being prepared for it. At its head a drummer and
the owner on horseback, behind him a dancer on a similar nag with a
child before her, decked out in ribbons and spangles. Following them
two by two came the remaining troupe on foot, the children daringly
posed on their shoulders. Paliasso[30] ran amusingly back and forth
among the converging crowd and played very tangible pranks such as
kissing a girl here or spanking a boy there with his slapstick. He distributed his handbills and aroused in the public an irrepressible crav-
ing to get better acquainted with him this evening. The printed an-
nouncements proclaimed the manifold talents of the troupe, especially
those of a Monsieur Narciss and a Mlle. Landerinette, who as princi-
pals of the production had cleverly withdrawn themselves from the
parade, thereby granting themselves a certain respectability and exciting greater curiosity.

The evening came on, Wilhelm was led into a house where a large
group was assembled, and at the appointed hour the floor was filled
with ordinary people and the windows with persons of some distinction.

With some inanities at which an audience always tends to laugh,
Paliasso focused their attention and put them in high spirits. Some
children through unusual contortions aroused first surprise, then horror, then compassion. The scene was much more pleasant, however,
when the athletic acrobats, first one after another, then all together,
whirled backwards and forwards in the air. Loud applause and
shouting rang from the whole audience. Now something new drew
their attention: the children had to go onto the rope one after the
other, the clumsiest first in order to stretch out the show and to dem-
onstrate the difficulty of their art. Some of the acrobats and a grown
woman presented themselves with some skill, but they were not yet
Monsieur Narciss, nor Mlle. Landerinette.

Finally they, too, emerged from a kind of tent with red drapes and
through their handsome figures and delicate finery fulfilled the spectators' hopes that had been happily nourished up to now. He, a light,
cheerful fellow of medium size, black eyes, and a mass of hair, and
she, no less attractive yet strongly built, took turns on the rope with
easy movements, bold leaps, and unusual poses. Her ease, his daring,
the precision with which they performed their feats increased the

---

[30] The name typically given to the clown of an acrobatic troupe.

general pleasure with each step and leap. The dignity with which they conducted themselves and the obvious attentiveness of the others for them gave them the appearance of lord and master of the entire troupe, a position which everyone had to respect. The enthusiasm of the common people spread to the spectators in the windows; the ladies looked at Narciss, the gentlemen at Landerinette. The people rejoiced, and even the more refined public did not refrain from clapping; one hardly laughed at Paliasso any more. The joy and the magic became so great that everyone forget to steal away when some of the troupe pushed their way through the crowd with pewter plates in order to collect money.

"They did their job well," said Wilhelm to his travel companion who stood in the window next to him.

"Here and there," the other replied, "but that girl is a brave, cheerful thing."

"They did everything well," said Wilhelm. "I admire their skill at making even the lesser stunts significant by gradually introducing them at the right time just as when they began with the simplest or even the clumsiest among their children and proceeded to the most composed and skillful of their virtuosi."

The companion did not share Wilhelm's opinion; rather he assured him it was the unbearably boring stuff of trivialities that served no purpose other than to waste one's time. "They should have done their good tricks one after the other, then they'd have finished their business in a quarter of an hour."

"Do you believe that the public and the people themselves would gain any advantage from that?" Wilhelm said. "Doesn't everyone's want to be entertained for a while and don't they wish to present their acts in the most advantageous light?"

"It's an old routine and a trick of the trade, I've seen them all use it."

"As you wish," said Wilhelm, "but nature and experience have taught them the best rules, and if for the few days they remain here they continue in this way, step by step, and keep as I am convinced their best acts for the finish, then they'll be very effective and make a lot of money. I might wish such ingenuity and good taste for many a writer."

The stranger, who was not served by such abstract conversation, began to enumerate Landerinette's charms while Wilhelm analyzed her specific skills.

Wilhelm had guessed quite rightly, for on the second day the level of their performance was on the rise. The preliminaries, if I may use that term, they eliminated entirely, yet everything proceeded in the same order as on the preceding day. They performed a few more complicated and seemingly more dangerous stunts, Paliasso's jokes remained the same, only they seemed to have a greater effect the more they were repeated. And just as a thoughtful man said that annoyance without pain and greatness without strength are profound sources of the comic,[31] so one can add that deliberate clumsiness and awkwardness produce a highly comic and pleasant effect with their hidden strength.

Enthusiasm for Herr Narciss and Mlle. Landerinette also swelled just as quickly; the shouting, the clapping, the calls of "Bravo" became ever more general; purses opened, and the take was considerable. A stranger who was also at the window regretted that the troupe no longer included a certain child who had performed various stunts with great skill and, especially, the egg dance[32] as beautifully as he had ever seen. Since night was coming on, the performers left the structure and were brought home in triumph by the throng.

On the third day when the number of people had increased extraordinarily through crowds from the neighboring localities, the snowball of applause became ever greater. The leap over the swords, through a tub with a paper bottom, and all that goes with them put the crowd beside itself. To general horror, consternation, and astonishment, the strong man lay down with his head and feet on two well separated chairs, had an anvil put on his unsupported body and a horseshoe prepared on it by three stout blacksmith's apprentices.

The so called Pyramid of Hercules, where a row of men position themselves on the shoulders of others and then others upon them so that finally a living pyramid is formed which a child standing on its head completes like a finial on a weather vane. This had never been seen before in these parts and provided a worthy end to the whole spectacle. Herr Narciss and Mlle. Landerinette allowed themselves to be borne in sedan chairs through the most elegant streets of the city amid loud cries of joy from the people. They threw ribbons, bouquets, and silk handkerchiefs to them and pressed forward to get a good look at them. Everyone seemed happy to see them and to be honored by a glance from them.

"What writer, what actor would not be happy if he made such a general impression? What an exquisite feeling that would have to be if

[31] A reference to J. Möser's "Harlequin or A Defense of the Grotesque-Comic" (1761).

[32] One where the performer moves blindfolded among eggs arranged upon the stage. It is described below in Book 4, Chapter 3.

one could spread good and noble feelings worthy of mankind just as broadly by an electrical charge and thereby arouse such rapture among men as these people did by their visible feats. If one could give the people or the best from among them compassion for everything human and excite and shake them with the vision of happiness and misfortune, of wisdom and folly, of nonsense and foolishness, and set their hesitant feelings in motion! Then perhaps there might occur what the old philosopher promises of the tragedy, that it will purge the emotions." Wilhelm entertained himself with such thoughts as he walked home after having looked about in vain among the whole group for a person with whom he could share these observations.

Chapter 3

When Wilhelm came into the inn, he met Herr Narciss standing in the entrance hall and invited him to come with him to his room. He found him to be a good, cheerful fellow who related his adventures with much levity and was anything but lord of the troupe. When Wilhelm wished him every success he accepted it rather indifferently. "We're accustomed," he said, "to having people laugh at us and admire our skills, but we're in no way helped by extraordinary applause, for the owner pays the same set wage whether receipts are good or not." Wilhelm asked about various things and the other man answered everything factually and finally seemed to have things to do and excused himself.

"Where are you off to so quickly, Monsieur Narciss?" said Wilhelm. The young man laughed and confessed that his figure and talents had gained him approbation which he found more important: he had received tender missives from some young women of the town and had an urgent invitation for this evening and night. He continued to relate his adventures with great candor and would have given names and addresses if Wilhelm, who abhorred such indiscretion, had not declined and allowed him to depart.

In the meantime his young traveling companion had conversed with Mlle. Landerinette, and during supper he let it be known quite clearly with what sort of hopes she had flattered him.

A few more days passed which Wilhelm spent in collecting various debts, and although he did not proceed with asperity and was instead generous and considerate, he was successful and, with what he had received in Hochstädt, had now collected almost fifteen hundred Taler. It gave him great pleasure to report this in his next letter to Werner and to send him the greater part of it. He also commended himself to some tradespeople, who were so pleased by his manner that they placed orders with him, which he carefully noted. Finally he found it advisable to continue his trip, and because his former party had dispersed, he ordered a post chaise, packed his bags, and departed in good time in order to arrive at the next station before night.

Time passed for him amidst all manner of thoughts, night came on, and he noticed, since the coachman took first this road, then that one in the forest which they had entered, that they might have taken the wrong one. He found this was the case when he inquired about it, but the coachman assured him he could not be far from their destination. It was deep in the night when they arrived at a village and inquired about the region. They had come far away from the main route; since they had moved away from it at almost a right angle, the station they were going to lay almost six hours away and, moreover, no direct road led to it. Wilhelm demanded that they remain here for the night and that he bring him there the next morning. The coachman begged urgently that he let him return home again, he was new in his job, and because he had overworked the horses he had much to fear from his master. He was going to say that he had delivered him to the next station and hoped that this lie would suffice. In turn he suggested procuring for him for a modest sum the local preacher's old touring coach and work horses, about which he had already inquired. These could bring him the following morning to the next town in good time, which was a respectable regional center and only three hours away. There he could again obtain post horses and regain his route without difficulty. The innkeeper himself also advised this, and since Wilhelm was good-natured, he acceded.

The following morning, when his new coachman brought him near the city and he saw it lying before him, he heard from the man that a large garrison was in it and that one was sharply questioned at its gates. "It always strikes me odd," Wilhelm said to himself, "whenever I give my name and am supposed to call myself 'Meister.'[33] Truly I'd do better to call myself 'Geselle,' for I'm afraid I'll always be stuck in bachelorhood. I'll do it as a joke, especially since I know no one and have no one to call on. The name doesn't sound nice but it does have a meaning; it would sound better translated, but let's stick to the mother tongue."

---

[33] This passage involves a pun and then a pun on the pun. *Meister* was the title for a master artisan in the guild system. Under him were the *Gesellen*, the apprentices or journeymen. Since they usually were poor and unmarried, the term acquired the meaning of "bachelor."

He came to the town gate where his name was so recorded. It was still early when he arrived before the inn. The innkeeper told him that most of the rooms were taken by a troupe of actors who were staying here, but he could give him a very nice room that faced on the garden. "Must fate always lead me to these people," Wilhelm cried to himself, "with whom I neither should nor want to have anything in common!" He answered the innkeeper that he didn't need a room, that he just wished to descend for a moment and then order post horses in order to travel on immediately.

On the gatepost was posted the playbill from yesterday, and to his great astonishment he found on it the names of Herr and Frau Melina. "I must pay my respects to them," he thought, just as a young creature came bounding down the stairs, attracting his attention. A short vest with slit Spanish sleeves and wide trousers looked quite nice on the child who had long black hair in locks and braids wound about its head. He observed it quite keenly and couldn't decide right away whether he should take it for a boy or a girl, but he soon decided for the latter. He greeted this apparition as she went past with a "Good Morning" and asked whether Herr and Frau Melina were already up. She glowered at him as she ran past him and into the kitchen without answering. He sent the landlord up and entered the room soon after him.

Chapter 4

As he entered Madame was throwing on a white coat to cover her décolleté nightgown, her spouse was pulling up his sagging stockings and removing the nightcap from his head. They tried to free a chair to offer to the newcomer, but the table, the bed, even the stove and the window sill would hold nothing more. They were very pleased to see one another again, and Mme. Melina in particular did not hide her intent to impress Wilhelm. She laid some claim to wit, poesy, and whatever else belongs with these. During her protracted unmarried state she had been the oracle of her small town, and the haughtiness with which she currently displayed herself to Wilhelm indeed did not cause her to appear in so favorable a light as she had formerly in the aura of misfortune. Her efforts left Wilhelm cold, or rather he didn't notice them at all. They presented complaints about their directrix, for it was a woman who held this troupe together. They complained about her as a business woman who put nothing aside in good times; instead she squandered everything with a member of the troupe whom she had chosen for her favorite. When bad weeks then occurred, she was compelled to pawn things, and she still could not pay her actors their promised wages. People even believed she had additional debts, things were not going well for her, and one should be wary.

During their conversation Wilhelm recalled the singular figure whom he had encountered and inquired about her. "We ourselves don't know," said Mme. Melina, "what to make of this child. Approximately four weeks ago a troupe of acrobats was here which presented very artistic acts. Among them was also this child, a girl, who performed everything quite well, she danced the fandango most charmingly and performed various other stunts with great agility and grace, yet she was always quiet, whenever anyone spoke to her or praised her or asked her about something.

"One day shortly before their departure we heard a frightful noise downstairs in the house. The leader of this troupe was cursing the child frightfully, whom he had thrown out of her room and who stood unmoving in the corner of the hall. He heatedly demanded something of her which she, as we had heard, refused to do. He then fetched a whip and beat the child unmercifully, the child didn't move, scarcely made a face, and a feeling of compassion overcame us so that we ran down and became embroiled in the affair. The furious man now swore at us and kept striking until finally, restrained by us, he poured out his indignation in a frightful torrent of words. He screamed, stamped, and foamed at the mouth, and as far as we could understand, the child had refused to dance and had been moved neither by begging nor by force. She was supposed to go onto the rope, she didn't do it. Many hundreds of people had hurried here to see the announced egg dance; they demanded it loudly, but in vain. The manager was furious since the audience was leaving unhappily and consequently refusing to pay. 'I'll beat you to death,' he cried out, 'I'll leave you lying in the street! You can die on a manure heap, for you'll not get another bite from me!'

"Our directrix, who was standing nearby and had long had an eye on the child because the girl who usually played Fiamette in *The Governess*[34] had been lured away and a maid had left. Thus she thought she could use her and with her usual tricks was immediately after the angry man, seeking to convince him the best thing would be to give the child away. She carried out her intention, too, and in his initial fury he turned over the creature on the condition that a certain sum, which was set rather high, was to be paid for her clothing. Mme. de Retti, no dawdler, paid the money on the spot and took the small girl with her to her room. Not an hour had passed when the rope walker

[34] A singspiel by the Viennese actor Franz Anton Nuth (1763).

regretted his decision and wanted to have the child back. Our leader resisted bravely; she threatened that if he insisted for one more minute she would file charges of child abuse against him with the magistrate, who was a very just and strict man, and he would surely not get off with his skin intact. This scared him off, and after a few more exchanges of words the child remained ours.

"But we've already regretted a hundred times that we took on the creature. She's of no use to us at all. She learns her roles very quickly but she performs miserably. We can get nothing out of her. She's very willing to work but doesn't do what's asked of her. We would have liked to spank her a hundred times ourselves. On the first morning after she had slept with us, she appeared in the boy's clothes in which you saw her and no one's since been able to persuade her to take them off. When the directrix, half jokingly, half seriously, asked how she intended to replace the money spent on her, she answered, 'I will serve you!' And from that time on without being asked she has performed for the directrix and the entire troupe all services, even the basest, with a speed, alacrity, and good will which have reconciled us to her stubborn nature and her poor talents for the theater."

Wilhelm wanted to see her more closely and Melina went to fetch her. When the child entered, Frau Melina said, "You didn't thank the gentleman this morning." She remained standing at the door as though she wanted to slip out again immediately. She put her right hand on her breast and the left to her forehead and bowed deeply.

"Step closer, dear child," said Wilhelm. She looked at him uncertainly and approached. "What is your name?" he asked.

"They call me Mignon," she answered.

"How old are you?"

"No one counted."

"Who was your father?"

"The big devil is dead." The explanation for these last words was that a certain acrobat who called himself The Big Devil had been regarded as her father. She produced her answers in a broken German and a manner that puzzled Wilhelm, and with each one she put her hands to her bosom and brow and bowed deeply.

"What are these gestures supposed to mean?" said Frau Melina. "That's something new again; she comes up with something odd every day."

She was silent and Wilhelm delighted in watching her. His eyes and his heart were irresistibly drawn by the mysterious state of this creature. He guessed her to be twelve or thirteen years old. Her body was well built except that the bones and joints promised a marked growth or indicated one that had been stunted. Her features were not regular, but striking; her forehead proclaimed a secret, her nose was extraordinarily beautiful, and her mouth, although somewhat pouting and occasionally twitching, was nonetheless still guileless and charming. Her face was brown with somewhat freckled cheeks and quite marked by makeup which she now would wear only with the greatest reluctance.

Wilhelm kept looking at her and was silent and in his observation forgot the others. Frau Melina awakened him when she gave a sign to the child, who, after bowing as before, departed like a flash.

Wilhelm could not get this figure out of his mind. He would have liked to go on questioning her and hearing about her when Frau Melina found it enough and changed the conversation to her own talents, performing, and destiny.

Chapter 5

It was soon agreed that Wilhelm was to remain the day, to become acquainted with the directrix and the rest of the troupe, and to see the play this evening; he could depart tomorrow in good time. The temptation was too great for him to be able to resist for long, although in the beginning it caused him some difficulties, for he had promised Werner to be in a certain town on a specific day. This deadline was approaching; at his last stop he had already remained longer than he should have; through the coachman's mistake he had again been delayed. He was accustomed to obedience and order as a given, he regarded duty and one's word as sacred because he respected himself only to the extent that he honored them. Yet his inclination outweighed everything, he remained with the firm intention to travel on early the next morning. Mme. Melina invited him to supper, he invited her and her husband to his room, and ordered the meal. When the landlord asked him for his name which he was obliged to submit to the Commandant's staff in the evening, he presented himself as he had at the city gate and begged his friends to also call him so and to be silent about his true name.

At dinner things were very merry. Madame did everything possible to please, her husband made a dry joke from time to time, and Wilhelm, who for the first time in a long while was breathing quite freely, was open and vivacious, conversing with much enthusiasm about his interests. They enjoyed the wine, which was by chance good, and remained long at table.

Mme. Melina did not lack a kind of intelligence, only her mind and wit were not well formed. She sometimes found a good point but often she lapsed from the exaggerated into the common. The period of her principal education had fallen in the time of the *Bremer Beiträge*,[35] and she had joined the party opposing Gottsched. In generally she had progressed no farther except that Lessing's plays, which appeared in the theater from time to time, had given her thinking a new direction. In her unmarried years she had had some success with occasional poems and madrigals, and she had written some prologs for the troupe and presented them to great applause. She recited this one or that one to her host, who praised their good points. She knew no foreign language, nor any foreign literature, and thus her horizon was rather limited. It might have been even more so and Wilhelm in his innocence would still have regarded her as a universal genius, for she was what in a word I might call a good listener. She knew how to flatter someone whose attention she coveted with a special attentiveness, to enter into his ideas to the extent she could, and, as soon as they had exceeded her horizon, to accept ecstatically anything new to her. She understood how to pose questions and to remain silent, and, although she was not malicious of spirit, to observe with keen attention where the opponent's weak side might be. Let it be added that she, although no longer young, was nevertheless well preserved, had friendly eyes and a pretty mouth, if she didn't contort it, and one will understand that our hero thoroughly enjoyed her company.

The time for the play approached without anyone's having spoken to the directrix. Holberg's *Bramarbas*[36] was performed. Mme. Melina complained about the role of Leonore, about the dull and tasteless aspects of the play, which the public had greatly enjoyed. The audience departed and Wilhelm went backstage. He soon found the actors to be as he was accustomed to finding them. Most had performed in extemporized comedy and had become so accustomed to a certain individual pace which pleased them that they regarded this piece simply as a scenario and through interpolations and burlesques gave it an even broader shape than it possessed by nature. Leonore made a charming entrance, searching out her friend with her eyes and applying and using to best advantage not only in her delivery but also in her gestures some of the good precepts which he had discussed at dinner. This pleased him greatly and although she appeared seldom, he as usual forgot the rest and praised her greatly when he was taking

---

[35] The name given to two journals (Bremen and Leipzig, 1744-1757) published by former allies of Gottsched who turned against him in their desire to liberate German literature further from the influence of French literature.

[36] A work by the Danish dramatist Ludvik Holberg (1684-1754), published in German by Gottsched in 1741.

her home; he commented on her performance and assured her that she could go far if she would pay attention to herself and to her art. This conversation was continued in her room to which Wilhelm escorted her; on this occasion, too, no one remembered to visit the directrix as had been intended, and no one noticed that it was late until Herr Melina entered the room.

"Oh," she cried, "how happy I would be if I could enjoy your instruction! How much happier if you could see me perform all my roles! If I could learn to perform them from you!"

Wilhelm expressed his regrets, but they urged him to remain the following day when there was no performance, where there was only an early morning rehearsal at which he could become acquainted with Mme. de Retti. Everyone could spend the remainder of the day most pleasantly in conversation. The married couple grew insistent. She in particular became so cajoling, almost familiar, that in the end she found it impossible that she now could take leave of him, so that it became impossible for him, too, and he promised to stay.

When he came to his room and examined his things, he missed the large leather briefcase in which he carried all the documents and the papers necessary for his business. In the beginning he was frightened, but it soon occurred to him that he had left it at the home of his friend at his last stop. A few things had been left unfinished there and he had asked that they be sent to him when he had announced his arrival in a specific town. Thus he regained his composure and thought that it might all be done at once — his stay wouldn't be all that long.

On the following morning he arose early and found the whole house silent, with only Mignon in the hall. He was cordial to the child and spoke to her, asking about various things. She looked at him sharply but answered no question and displayed not the slightest emotion or inclination toward him. She seemed to be unfeeling. Finally he reached into his pocket and offered her a piece of money; the little creature's features became more cheerful, she seemed doubtful and hesitated to take it. Finally when she saw that he was serious, she moved quickly and with obvious delight examined his gift in her hands. Later he expressed to Frau Melina his surprise at the child's strong inclination to money. "I can explain this," she said. "Soon after the directrix had taken this strange creature from the rope walker, she once said to her, 'Now you are mine, you must always behave nicely.' 'I am yours,' said Mignon, 'I saw that you bought me. What did you pay?' The directrix said as a joke, 'A hundred Dukaten. If you repay me, I'll free you and you may go where you wish.' Since then we've noticed that she's saving money, we sometimes give her a few Pfennige, and she's given me a large box of copper money to keep. We suspect that she's saving for her ransom, especially since she recently asked how many Pfennige make a Dukat."

Chapter 6

At ten o'clock Wilhelm appeared at the theater and the entire troupe assembled about him. He looked about and tried to find a person to whom he felt drawn and believed he found a response here and there. When Mme. de Retti entered, she succeeded in drawing all his attention to herself. Her whole manner was masculine, her carriage and conduct proud without being offensive. The others stood about her like courtiers. She greeted the stranger with friendliness and respect. During the rehearsal she sat down beside the newcomer in order to converse with him about theatrical matters. At the same time she remained singularly attentive to the performance of the actors. One actor she cheered along with a joke, the next was not treated so gently. She guided the neophytes in the art and to the egotists she gave instructive advice without insulting or shaming them. Quietly she expressed regret to Wilhelm that so few actors took their work seriously and especially that one couldn't persuade them to treat the rehearsals as important.

Our friend greatly enjoyed hearing her opinions on this because they were his own. "An actor," he said, "should have nothing more important than memorizing most accurately. Even at the first rehearsal he should know his role completely in order then to study carefully the many nuances which it may assume. In the various rehearsals he should think through his exits and entrances, his sitting and standing, his actions and omissions, and every gesture in order to assure himself of their mechanical aspects so that during the performance, he can entrust himself to his heart, his mood, and to luck. Thereby a diversity would enter into his acting so that with repeated performances, a play would always remain new to the audience. How variously the singer can express a single sustained note, a single passage, without violating the character of the aria if he has method and knows how to employ various mannerisms with taste. It is just the same with roles where a limited actor will see only chains and bonds, but a clever and skillful actor will find an open road."

Mme. de Retti was very pleased to hear from the mouth of a third party the good precepts which she preached to her actors so often, and usually in vain. The conversation picked up and Wilhelm was quite enchanted by her great theatrical insights. They forgot those rehearsing to the not slight annoyance of Mme. Melina, who was among them and saw the attention of her new friend diverted from herself. Wilhelm was now completely in his element and for almost the first time in his whole life in a conversation on his favorite subject with a person who was far more familiar with it than he, who through her experience could confirm, develop, and correct that which he had thought out for himself quite alone. How pleased he was when he met with her, how attentive when he encountered something new, and how careful in his questions and analysis when she was not of the same opinion as he! In her conversation she referred to various works that he should see performed by her and her troupe.

His reluctance was removed more quickly than yesterday and he promised to remain a few more days. He reflected to himself that his itinerary was in any case arbitrary and a week more or less would not worsen the outstanding debts which had already existed for years. He abandoned himself entirely to his inclination, and in the company of the two women, in conversations, reading, declamation, with visits to the theater and conversations about them, first one week and then another had passed before he noticed it.

Before man abandons himself to a passion, he trembles a moment before it as if facing an unknown element; but scarcely has he surrendered to it when he finds himself, like a swimmer pleasantly supported and borne by the water, happy in his new circumstance. He does not concern himself about firm footing until his strength fails or a cramp threatens to pull him beneath the waves.

Mignon's person and manner grew ever more appealing to him. In everything she did she had something singular about her. She did not walk up and down the stairs, rather she leaped or climbed up the banisters of the passages. Before anyone noticed it she was sitting atop the armoire, where she remained quietly for a time. Wilhelm had also observed that she had a special type of greeting for everyone, and for some time she had greeted him with her arms crossed on her bosom. Some days she gave answers to various questions and always oddly, but it was impossible to tell whether this was deliberate or from her inability to express herself, for she spoke a quite broken German interspersed with French and Italian. She was up at daylight and untiring in her service. In the evening she disappeared early and Wilhelm discovered only much later that she slept on the bare floor in an attic chamber and could not be persuaded to accept a bed or a sack of straw. He often found her washing herself and she was always cleanly dressed, although almost everything on her had been patched twice or thrice.

He was also told she went to mass quite early every morning. When after taking a very early walk he passed the church and entered it, he found her in a corner by the church door, kneeling with her rosary and praying very devoutly. She did not notice him. He returned home and had a thousand thoughts about this figure and yet could come to no conclusion in his thinking.

Chapter 7

Since they lived together in one house and had the opportunity to see one another at all times, they became more familiar, and the two women took Wilhelm between them. Each tried to attract him, each found him pleasant, and the circumstance that they sensed he had money and wasn't niggardly spoke greatly in his favor. Without the slightest tenderness having entered into his feelings, he found it quite comfortable between the two women. Mme. de Retti expanded his mind and broadened his knowledge when she spoke of herself, her talents, her endeavors and achievements. Mme. Melina attracted him in her seeking to learn from him and to fashion herself after him. The former imperceptibly gained a power over him through her decisive and imperious character, the latter through her desire to please and her submissiveness. he soon depended solely on the desires of the two, and the company of both was extremely necessary to him. It was not long until they became even better acquainted and more confiding. Wilhelm did not hide from Mme. Melina his passion for Mariane and found the greatest pleasure in the painful recital of his story. He revealed to the directrix the secrets of his literary efforts, recited to her passages from his plays which were received by her with great praise and with flattering comparisons. In exchange they had nothing to reveal to him other than secrets of the business; in discussing these, the former discussed these quite openly, whereas the latter revealed no more of these than she thought advisable.

They had often conversed about the inspired and splendid aspects of the art, but in its performance they unfortunately lagged far behind. Wilhelm, who placed great importance on costuming, was struck most by the deplorable state of the poor and inappropriate costumes. Mme. Melina shrugged her shoulders and confessed to him that her best pieces had been pawned and, indeed, for the petty sum of fifty Taler. In an emergency the Jews occasionally would let her have a piece again on the evening of a performance, for which she had to pay dearly. No sooner had Wilhelm heard this than he took counsel with himself and he soon found occasion and sufficient cause to lend this sum to his friend, especially since he was assured by her promise to repay him as soon as possible. The pawnbroker was summoned, some things of her husband's were included, and there was interest to

satisfy so that it came to over seventy Taler, which he nevertheless gladly paid.

As is natural, this generous act did not remain unknown, and Mme. de Retti also found it convenient to take advantage of his attitude. As we have already heard earlier, her economic situation was indeed very bad. On her entire journey through the world, with all her talent she had gained little and saved nothing. Whatever she had earned in large towns in times of good fortune soon disappeared in merry living. Her restless character did not let her derive great advantage from fortunate circumstances, and her imperious and unyielding nature could not condescend to concession and submission in bad times. As directrix she often went hungry when as a lesser actress in another troupe she could have found an ample income.

The women spoke of various tragedies and other important plays that they would have liked to perform in honor of the new guest. They made him aware that he was not only a connoisseur of the theater, but also a devotee and patron. This was repeated on every occasion and was presented and put in such a way that he finally resolved to come personally to the aid of the oppressed art of the theater, which in prologs he had seen protected so often by Apollo. He said to himself that he also had some right to use the money he had collected, that it was to be regarded as found money, that he intended to economize once he was again on his journey, and that here, too, he was on sure ground in that they had promised to sign the entire wardrobe over to him.

It now became quite easy for him to promise his friend an additional three hundred Taler, and ultimately pay out four hundred. Herr Melina, who at first seemed to advise against this deal, assumed responsibility for its legality and summoned a notary to execute the transfer properly. Thereby the captive heroes and sultans were freed, the elegant costumes liberated, a new life entered the troupe, the variety of their plays attracted audiences, the income was greater than ever. Wilhelm advanced more money in order to renew the old sets, and a new spirit emerged. Since she could pay something to her secret creditors, Mme. de Retti again was given credit, the group ate, drank, lived splendidly and in joy, assuring the world and swearing that at this time of year — Spring was already well advanced — they had never experienced such a fortunate theatrical season.

Chapter 8

Things were most jovial when Wilhelm invited them and treated them at his expense. Then they were merry and of good cheer as though

they had never known privation or ever needed to fear it. One day, as
they were sitting at such a meal, it occurred to them to imitate the
characters of various types and everyone picked out something special for himself. The one presented an inebriate, the second a Pom-
eranian nobleman, one a Lower Saxon boatman, the other a Jew, and
when Wilhelm and Mme. Melina could find nothing for themselves
because they were not very practiced in imitation, Mme. de Retti said
in jest, "You can simply play enamored lovers, for this is surely a universal talent." When she bound a round straw mat about her head instead of her usual hat, she did a Tyrolean woman most charmingly,
which was all the more striking in that her droll manner and her
teasing pranks made a pleasant contrast to her customary grand manner. They pretended to be a group who had happened together in a
post coach, had at present dismounted at an inn, and were soon
about to ride on again. Each strained his imagination to make the
most unusual and comical situations from the common occurrences
such parties customarily encounter and to link them together in acceptably good taste. There were complaints, teasing, accusations,
threats, happy scenes, and everything imaginable was put into play so
that finally Wilhelm, who did not feel comfortable in his role, finally
laughed heartily as a spectator and assured the directrix that no play
had entertained him so well in a long time.

"How sorry I am," she said, "that we've abandoned extemporizing.
I've regretted a hundred times that I myself was partly responsible for
this, not that one should have retained the old indecencies and not
have performed good plays in addition. If we had extemporized only
once a week, the actors would have remained in practice and the
public would have maintained a taste for this style. We would have
derived all sorts of gain from it, for extemporizing is the training
school and the ultimate test of the actor. It wasn't a question of
learning a role by heart and imagining that one could perform it;
rather one's wit, lively imagination, adaptability, knowledge of the
theater, and the presence of mind were revealed most clearly at every
step. Necessity compelled the actor to make himself familiar with all
the resources the theater offers. Subsequently he became quite at
home with them, like a fish in water, and a poet with sufficient gifts to
use these tools would have had a great effect on the public.

"But I unfortunately let myself be persuaded by the critics. Because
I myself was serious and took no pleasure in skits and burlesque and
thought myself fortunate to play a Chimene, Rodogune, Zaire, or Mé-

rope,[37] I regarded myself and my troupe as too respectable to entertain the audience as we had up till then. I banished the Hanswurst and buried the Harlequin, and if they had been permitted by circumstances to build their own theater, then they could have done a splendid parody of me as a queen who dismisses her ministers and generals in the time of crisis and thereby falls into the hands of weak and stupid opponents. And what German writer so far has repaid us for that which we surrendered? If we hadn't had the translations of Molière's plays, we wouldn't have known how to save ourselves, for our best original plays have the misfortune of not being theatrical."

Wilhelm objected to this and that. She turned to the actor who played the Jew and was sitting opposite her: "Isn't it true, old man, if we had had enough intelligence and luck to execute our plan at the right time, we could have given the Germans a splendid present which would have become the basis of a national theater and could have been utilized and refined by the best minds. We often spoke about the advantages of the Italian masks,[38] about the interesting feature that each actor has a definite character, homeland, and dialect, about the convenience of an actor's being able to think his way into an individual character and then if he operates imaginatively within this same character, he is certain to delight his public, rather than bore it.

"We thought of producing something of this sort in a German manner: our Hanswurst was a Salzburger, our country squire we wanted to take from Pomerania, our doctor from Swabia, our old man was to be a Lower Saxon businessman. We wanted to give him a sort of sailor as a servant. Our lovers were to speak High German and to come from Upper Saxony, and our fair Leonore, or whatever we were going to call her, was to have with her a maid from Leipzig as our Columbine.[39] We wanted to situate the action in ports, commercial centers, and at large fairs in order cleverly to bring all these people together. We even wanted to introduce a traveling Harlequin, Pantalone, and Brighella and through the contrasts make our pieces even more varied and exciting. Our thinking was only superficial, but how

[37] Rodogune is the title character from a work by Corneille, Chimene from his *Le Cid*; Zaire and Mérope are title figures from plays by Voltaire.

[38] In the *commedia dell'arte* actors wore masks characterizing their traditional roles.

[39] The beloved of Harlequin in the Italian comedy. Additional figures are Pantalone, a Venetian businessman, and Brighella, a peasant yokel from Bergamo.

much we could have added to it with the aid of time and leisure! Every new actor who would have come to the troupe would perhaps have brought a new idea, a striking imitation of some regional custom, just as we especially hadn't forgotten the Jews. Some people have gimmicks that suit their individual character especially well. Through some sort of flaw, stuttering, limping, or whatever one might want, the figures would have received an even more detailed definition of character, and we believed at least at that time that we would be quite successful at it.

"But unfortunately the experiments that we presented to the public in defiance of the purists, with whom we had split, misfired. They prejudiced the best people against us, and the first attempts, which some years before certainly would have been well received, failed completely. They also didn't accomplish what we had in mind: the actors were out of training, we lacked people to make the characters diverse, and we simply had to retire, give up our plans, and follow the current in which we are still drifting. I'm now convinced that no one could bring back this epoch without a miracle. We are like people who have happened on an uncomfortable or poor path and who nevertheless are too far advanced to be able to turn back and take a new one from the beginning."

She was going to add various things when they heard a great tumult outside. Shortly thereafter Mignon plunged through the door and a strange man followed her with threatening gestures.

"If this creature belongs to you," the stranger said, "then I want to see you punish her for her ill breeding. She struck my face so that my ears are still ringing and my cheek is burning."

"What caused you to do that, Mignon?" asked Wilhelm.

Mignon, who had calmly taken refuge behind Wilhelm's chair, answered, "I have hands, I have fingernails, I have teeth; he's not going to kiss me."

"What, sir?" cried Wilhelm. "Then you're surely the wrongdoer! What right do you have to demand something improper of the child?"

"In truth," answered the stranger, "I'm not going to make a great fuss about such a creature. I wanted to kiss her, and she behaved impertinently. I demand satisfaction."

"Sir," responded Wilhelm, whose anger was aroused by the stranger's insolence, "you would do best to beg the child's pardon and thank her for the lesson. In that way we'll still be able to think well of you."

To this the stranger responded haughtily and menacingly, "If you deny me what I'm due, I'll use the whip to teach manners to this ill-bred thing, wherever I find her."

"Sir," Wilhelm cried out, as he leaped up, his eyes glinting from anger, "I swear I'll break the neck and legs of anyone who touches a hair on her head." He wanted to say even more but anger prevented him. To give it vent, he probably would have thrown the stranger out the door, which would have been the first act of violence in his life, had not Mme. Melina discreetly grabbed him by the coattail and pulled him back.

The stranger hesitated at this confrontation, and when the rest of the group noticed this, their courage also came to life, and all of them, especially the directrix, fell upon him with hostile words so that he regarded it as most advisable to withdraw and leave the group while muttering threats. When he was gone, they talked about him, jokes were made especially about his flushed left cheek. Mignon was praised, Wilhelm ordered a couple bottles of wine, they grew cheerful, jovial, and familiar.

That evening Wilhelm was sitting in his room and writing; there was a knock at his door, and Mignon stepped in with a small box under her arm. "What are you bringing me?" Wilhelm called to her. Mignon had laid her right hand over her heart and, by bringing her right foot behind her left and almost touching the ground with her knee, offered him in all seriousness a kind of Spanish curtsy. A similar bow followed in the middle of the room, and finally, when she came up to Wilhelm, she knelt down completely on her right knee, placed the box on the floor, seized Wilhelm's feet and kissed them with great zeal, yet without any apparent stirring of the heart, without any expression of emotion or tenderness. Wilhelm, who did not know what to make of this, wanted to lift her up, but Mignon resisted and told him solemnly, "Lord, I am your slave. Buy me from my mistress so that I will belong to you alone."

She then took the box from the floor and explained to him as well as she could that this was what she had saved in order to buy her freedom. She begged him to accept it and, because he was rich, to add what was missing to make up a hundred Dukaten. She would pay him back fully and not leave him until his death. She stated all that with great solemnity, seriousness, and respect so that Wilhelm was stirred to the depths of his soul and could not answer her. She then unpacked her cash holdings, the sight of which wrung a kindly smile from Wilhelm. All the varieties were separate and divided into rolls and paper wraps. For silver and copper coins she had made special sorters and had carved alternating signs on the different sides to indicate the various species. At the lower end of its frame she had especially marked unfamiliar and stray coins and with the help of this sorter she presented her wealth to her master and protector. Wilhelm saw clearly that the incident this noon had made a deep impression on her. He sought to calm her by promising to keep her money and to look out for her, and he struggled in vain to make her understand that he could not keep her nor take her along with him. She left by backing to the door with the same bows with which she had entered, and from this time on, whenever she met him or came to him, she greeted him in just this manner while keeping herself at some distance.

Chapter 9

Gradually Mme. de Retti had performed for her theatrical guest and friend all the plays that showed off her talents, and in several passages she had surprised and astonished the young connoisseur. The remaining members of the troupe had done their utmost, especially since the applause of the public increased and an improved circulation of money completely restored the flow of their sluggish humor.

Now Wilhelm at last began to think seriously of his departure, of which a kindly admonishing spirit occasionally reminded him.

Most of the translated tragedies which Mme. de Retti had performed were, as everyone knows, forged in poor alexandrines. She complained often about this and, as a favor to her, Wilhelm translated some moving passages for her into good verse that pleased her so much that she often recited them with great satisfaction. On quiet evenings he sometimes read things from his works, which were well received. He carried them at the bottom of his bag more carefully than his business papers. But he had not yet fallen into the mood to read from his tragedy *Belshazzar*. He had kept postponing it and now wished to present it at a farewell dinner. He brought it out, looked it over, corrected a clumsy verse here and there, and though he didn't approve of it as a whole, it still pleased him for the most part when he read through it again.

While he was busy with this, Mignon stepped in. The child now regularly served him as her master, though she didn't neglect the others. She stepped up to him and said: "Your vest is blue, you love blue, I want to wear your color."

"Gladly," replied Wilhelm, "that will just make seeing you all the nicer," and he gave her a blue and white silk neckerchief. "You dear child," he thought to himself, "what's to become of you, how can I care for you other than by commending you to your mistress most compellingly? If you were a boy, you should surely travel with me, and I would take care of you and raise you as well as I could." He walked up and down in his room, thinking about the child's fate, simultaneously feeling that he had to abandon her and that he could not abandon her.

He took his manuscript and went over to Mme. de Retti's room, for which he had ordered a bowl of punch and where he found the better actors assembled. "I don't know," he said, "if you're in the mood to hear a play that is perhaps here and there too intellectual?"

They all assured him they would be very attentive although it might not have been completely true since some would have rather played cards, some would have preferred conversation. He began to read and, for the sake of what followed, it will be necessary that we mention some of the plot.

The King, his character, life, and manner are known to us from the previous Book. At his court was staying a princess by the name of Kandate, whose father had been deposed from his empire by Nebuchadnezzar. She nurtured a secret, implacable hate of the conqueror's son and was thinking about an opportunity to avenge herself and her father's spirit, and indeed, if possible, to exchange her present state for the throne.

Eron, her friend, a gentleman from the old court, who finds it insufferable to be ignored by the young king and is prepared to gamble everything to regain his former influence, has initiated a plot with the Princess. They have entered into negotiations with the Median king Darius and the latter has promised to help her if it should fail. Darius himself has designs on Babylon. He comes to the court in disguise and appears before Belshazzar as a Median general. He reveals to the plotters that he is aware of their secret, yet even they do not recognize him to be the King. On the night that precedes Belshazzar's birthday which has been selected for carrying out their plan, the plotters assemble one by one in a hall of the palace, and the plot gradually develops.

Eron's intention is to put the Princess upon the throne and to marry her to the king of the Medians. Disguised as an ambassador, Darius gives them hope of this, but no firm promise. Without suspecting his high position, the Princess feels drawn to the disguised hero and wishes to share the throne in Babylon with him. But the breast of the Prince nourishes quite different desires, and quite different concerns. As much as he wants to tear the empire away from an unworthy king, he is equally repelled by the treason which would aid him. And — oh strange fate! — love also enters here. The spouse of Belshazzar, Nitokris, has stirred his heart, he burns for her with the strongest passion and fears that she would never grant her hand and heart to the murderer of her husband. He seeks to persuade the plotters through all manner of arguments to postpone their enterprise for

a brief while longer, and they break up indecisively, much to the annoyance of Eron.

Wilhelm, who knew the piece almost by heart, read it very well
and with nicely nuanced delivery. Each listener in his thoughts was already seeking out a character whom he hoped to play, each praised
the young author and toasted him with a glass of punch. The directrix
was quite taken by the role of the princess as if it had been written for
her; she requested the manuscript for a moment and immediately read
a few proud, troubled, imperious passages.

Wilhelm felt as great a pleasure as perhaps a master ship builder
may when he launches his first large ship and sees it floating before
his eyes for the first time. He intensified his mood through the fiery
drink and began the Second Act, the opening soliloquy of which we
saw in the preceding Book.

The young King, firmly resolved to begin his birthday with the
adoration of the gods and reflections on himself, is about to send for
Daniel to have a talk with him. A courtier, who intervenes, diverts him
and he yields to the flow of the festivities prepared for him. He
scarcely wishes to hear the felicitations of his wife, whose presence
bothers him because he feels he has not been treating her, the most
delicate, most lovable queen, as he should. A monologue, which
Darius interrupts, presents her quiet suffering. This last scene did not
receive the applause it deserved, for it was too elegantly conceived for
this audience. The young hero reveals his passion while trying to hide
it, and the feelings of the queen for him remain hidden although she
speaks with an open, good heart. Again, when the Second Act was
finished, there was general praise at which an older writer, one better
acquainted with the public, would have been less flattered.

The first bowl of punch was finished, a second was ordered, and
the innkeeper, who had prepared for this, brought it immediately. The
Third Act was begun with even more enthusiasm. In a conversation
with Daniel, the Queen reveals her heart completely to the wise man.
Her quiet acceptance of her fate and the inner certainty of her good
nature make her person most lovable. One sees Darius alongside her
husband, and the appearance of the young hero makes a favorable
impression on her, the sense of his worth casting a gentle glow over
the gloomy twilight of her circumstances. She feels nothing wrong in
this pleasant sensation, and Daniel is wise enough not to disturb her.
One of the queen's ladies-in-waiting enters and relates the events of
the festivities up to the moment. The King steps in, surrounded by the
great of his realm, who offer him congratulations; the Queen and
Daniel add their own. They rise to go to the banquet, and Nitokris

asks that she be excused from joining in. This is granted and thus closes the Third Act.

The question whether one should have brought one of the four great Prophets to the stage was debated at length, and these critical considerations diminished somewhat the good impression of this act.

At the opening of the Fourth Act, Eron appears with one of the plotters, greatly annoyed that they are going to miss a precious opportunity to carry out their plan. He begins to mistrust the Median ambassador and perhaps suspects that the latter has secret intentions of putting his king on the throne without their assistance and thus of completely excluding the Princess. When out of annoyance at the insane debauchery at the table she leaves it and approaches Eron, he reveals his suspicions to her. They decide to execute their attack without informing him, to keep a watchful eye on him, and in any case to hold him prisoner until the deed is done. Just then Darius joins them with a vivid description of the wild depravity of the table, which he had left without being noticed. He tells them that the gold and silver vessels which were consecrated to the god of the Jews had been brought in and they were worshipping the king as a god. Eron leaves them with a gesture to the Princess to find out the foreigner's thinking. Their conversation continues very coolly. Eron returns and tells them the frightful story of the miraculous phenomenon and urges the completion of the deed since the gods themselves have given a sign. Darius seeks excuses in vain.

At the beginning of the Fifth Act the downcast King enters, who is shaken by the interpretation of the mysterious words. His muddled mind sees apparitions everywhere, and only his wife stands by him in this tragic state. After a moving scene he takes leave of her and is murdered at that moment by the plotters. The Princess appears, claims the empire, and places the Queen under guard. She gives orders to free the stranger, who has been held prisoner until now. Darius, who has overpowered his guards, arrives leading Median soldiers who have entered the city by a secret way. He reveals his identity, demonstrates he is in power, and the plotters submit. He grants the Princess a royal share of the estates and riches and then consoles the sorrowing Queen in so kind a manner that the audience has good hope of his future happiness, although here the curtain falls.

Now there arose a babbling, a screaming, everyone talked only of himself, and no one could hear himself for the others. They all agreed loudly, the play had to be performed.

Wilhelm, who saw them all excited, was highly pleased to have inflamed so many people through the fire of his poetic skills. He thought he saw spread among them the fire which burned within him.

He felt them, like and with himself, lifted above the ordinary. He spoke words full of spirit, full of nobility and love.

The attentive innkeeper in the meanwhile had never let their punch bowl run dry, and its contents tasted better and better to the guests. They shouted their approval, and their joy grew ever less restrained. They toasted Wilhelm quite loudly and screamed so that it sounded horrible to him. His spirits which had been elated by many a glass of punch and the recitation of his play were brought down forcibly and unpleasantly. The tumult grew worse and worse, they repeated their toasts to the poet and to the art of the drama. They swore that after such a celebration no one was worthy of drinking from these glasses and bowls and hurled the stemmed wine glasses at the ceiling. The directrix protested in vain. They broke the punch bowl and the dregs flowed everywhere. The glasses that refused to break were hurled violently against the walls and, ricocheting, flew with the shattering window panes down to the street. Here and there a person lay passed out in the corner, others staggered, all were ranting, some sang, some howled. Wilhelm, after he had summoned the innkeeper, slipped away to his room with confused, highly unpleasant emotions.

Chapter 10

Wilhelm had slept through most of the Sunday morning following this dissolute evening, and upon awakening he found himself out of sorts. His intention of still packing last evening after the reading had ended, of finally writing to Werner, of ordering post horses and leaving early this morning remained unfulfilled. He dressed and reflected on what he should do. Mignon came in, bringing water as usual, and asked what were his wishes. The sight of the child cheered him, for she had put on his white and blue neckerchief, had begged together various scraps of blue taffeta from the actresses and attached them cleverly to her vest as facings and the collar, so that it looked quite attractive. She brought the compliments of the directrix, who requested yesterday's play for just this morning. He sent it with the assurance that he would soon follow.

When he came to her room, he found Mme. Melina and Mme. de Retti both busy reading the play aloud to themselves, especially the scenes with the Princess and the Queen. "We must perform it," the directrix called to him. "You must leave it with us!" Mme. Melina cast her most telling glance at him and begged in the warmest manner. It was the first time the two women were completely of one mind. The directrix already saw herself in the role of the Princess, Mme. Melina yearned to play the Queen. For Belshazzar they proposed a handsome young man who was showing great promise. A skilled old actor was to do Eron, Daniel was assigned to Herr Melina, an actress was found for the lady-in-waiting. The remaining roles were unimportant save for that of Darius, for which quite at the end Mme. de Retti, with some embarrassment, proposed her darling, Herr Bendel.

This person we would simply call Herr Bengel,[40] were it not improper and a pun offensive to good taste, and thereby characterize in a word his character and nature. He was a clumsy, stocky type without the slightest decency, without feeling. Not only did he lack all the qualities of an actor, but he also had all the flaws which render an actor dispensable. To mention only one, he noodled with language by which we mean to characterize a whining tone poorly articulated by an unhelpful tongue. Small eyes, thick lips, short arms, a broad chest and back — enough, he had found favor in the eyes of his mistress. Up to now we have avoided mentioning this unfortunate figure save in passing and do it here against our will, especially since he emerges to the great annoyance of our hero.

The surprised author made various objections to this person, but only mildly because he knew the situation, but he was contradicted, and unfortunately contradicted by impossibility, for there was no one in the troupe who would have performed the role better than he. They mentioned that he had played Lord Essex[41] to applause; unfortunately this Lord Essex, in which role Wilhelm had seen him, lay like a heavy stone upon the young author's heart.

They talked so long and so much that Wilhelm, the eternal optimist, thought it might be just possible that the actor could improve himself through practice and effort, and he was already idealizing him in his mind. Finally he yielded, and it was agreed to go to work as soon as possible.

On this occasion they had gone through the whole troupe and spoken of Mignon and of the child's inability to perform at all. Wilhelm had seen her in some plays where she acted her small roles so dryly and stiffly that one might say she didn't act at all. She said her lines and saw to it that she exited. He took her under his wing and had her recite, but even then he was not at all satisfied with her. If he asked her to get a grip on herself, her expression remained strained in both routine and important passages. She recited everything with a fantastic exaltation, and if he demanded natural behavior from her and

[40] *Bengel*, "rascal, boor, hooligan."

[41] The hero of *Le Comte d'Essex* (1678) by Thomas Corneille, brother of the more famed Pierre. It was translated into German in 1747.

asked her to imitate him, she never understood what he wanted or how he wanted it.

On the other hand, he chanced to hear her picking away at a zither which was among the theater properties. He had it properly strung, and Mignon began to improvise and play all sorts of things on it in stolen moments, and always, as usual, in wondrous poses. Now she might be sitting on the top rung of a ladder with her feet crossed under her, like a Turk on his carpet, now she was walking along the eaves above the inn's courtyard, and the lamenting tone of her strings as well as a pleasant although somewhat hoarse voice made everyone listen to her in surprise and wonder. Some compared her to a monkey, others to other unusual beasts, and they were agreed that the child possessed something strange, exotic, and fantastic. They could not understand what she was singing; they were always the same or similar melodies which she seemed to vary according to her mood, thoughts, situation, and whim. In the evening she would sit on Wilhelm's threshold or on the limb of a tree that stood beneath his window and sing most charmingly. If she caught sight of him behind the window panes or he moved in the room, she was gone. She had made herself so necessary to him that he could not stir in the morning until he had seen her, and in the evening he usually called for a glass of water in order to wish her a good night. If he had pursued his inclination, he would have treated her as his daughter and assumed complete responsibility for her.

Chapter 11

The parts were written out and memorized. Everyone more or less accepted Wilhelm's good advice, read the scenes with him or in his presence, and even the directrix listened to his suggestions. They strove for a genuine, impassioned, forceful delivery. In a short time this unity brought such a harmony into the play that even the rehearsals went pleasantly to both eye and ear. Mme. Melina took the greatest pains, and Wilhelm did not fail to support her in her enthusiasm. She knew her role by heart in a few days. Wilhelm had to read each passage to her, perform them scene by scene with her, and she came rather close to the proper expression. But, to be sure, the quiet purity, the gentle tone, the inner tenderness of the Queen was not in her character. There was a certain quality, a certain calm emotion that she could not express, yet she had achieved a great deal, and Wilhelm daily grew more satisfied.

The coarseness, ill manners, and foolishness of Herr Bendel made the worst possible contrast to the actors' harmony with one another and with the play. He was by nature vain and had a high opinion of his acting. This time, however, he was doubly or triply ill-mannered because he felt a fierce and uncontrollable jealousy of Wilhelm, for whom the directrix expressed so much respect. This manifested itself sometimes in his rudeness, especially when learning and rehearsing the play. Since this tedious person drank every day and was scarcely sober by morning, his poor and dissolute appearance became more and more insufferable. In his aggravation he poured even more wine into himself and with his overly sanguine constitution suffered from dizziness a few times in the theater, so that he had to be taken home and there be bled. Thus during studying and rehearsals he disturbed the peace, the order, and the congeniality of the hard-working troupe, which for a long time had not felt so agreeable and unified and which displayed double and treble zeal at the prospect of the rich earnings this play was to provide.

Wilhelm in the meantime made a new acquaintance. In the theater he had occasionally sat next to an officer and found he judged the plays and the actors soundly. Out of boredom Wilhelm had occasionally joined the promenade in the theater foyer, where this man usually approached him and talked with good taste about theatrical matters. With great admiration and interest he finally asked Wilhelm whether it were true that a play of his would soon be presented. Wilhelm admitted it, and the former evinced friendly interest.

The officer was one of those good souls who are destined by nature to take a genuine interest in what occurs to others and what others accomplish. His caste, which damned him to a hard, refractory existence, had made him even gentler within while covering him with a rough exterior. He was in an exacting service, where for years everything followed a predetermined path, where everything was measured off, and iron necessity was the sole goddess to whom one made sacrifices, where justice became harshness and cruelty, and the concept of the human being and humanity disappeared completely. Here his good soul, which in a free and open society would have shown its beauty and would have found its true existence, was completely suppressed, his feelings deadened and almost destroyed. The one innocent pleasure remaining for him was the recent budding of German literature. He was familiar with it down to the smallest detail; he knew what we had and did not have; he hoped; he wished; and although he knew some foreign languages and read their best authors, in his heart he nevertheless gave precedence to the narrow concerns of his fatherland over those riches, because he felt closer to them.

He was partisan in the good sense and expected from the next generation everything he could not yet find. One could call him a true patriot, one of those who, without wishing it or knowing it, have contributed so much to the reception and encouragement of learning.

They sometimes went to play billiards, sometimes for a walk and became quite important to one another. Wilhelm, who was not well informed except in the area of drama, was guided by him into the broader field of belles lettres, and not a day passed without profit and joy from a new intellectual friendship.

When Herr von C** read through the tragedy of his young friend, he was delighted and astonished. He found it superior to all the known works written in German verse and begged him to continue on this path, and wished for him only more knowledge of the world and men in order to impart true worth and the proper character to his works. "This piece," he said, "much as I like it, is written only from the inside out: it concerns a single person who feels and acts. One sees that the author knows his own heart, but he doesn't know people."

Wilhelm conceded this and even more, throwing out the baby with the bath water, but also gladly let himself be refuted when, with understanding and intelligence, the officer demonstrated the play's true worth.

Chapter 12

Now Mme. Melina did not let go of our young writer. She was clever enough to see the many advantages she could obtain from him. Up to now she had been received indifferently in tragic roles; she hoped to be more fortunate this time. He rehearsed with her almost daily and she was delighted by the way he played Darius.

Mignon usually sat down in a corner whenever they were reciting and was sure to be present when Wilhelm was reading or declaiming. She did not take her eyes off of him and seemed to forget herself. She sometimes demanded of Wilhelm a passage to memorize which he then usually gave to her from his own works. She also learned quickly, but her delivery did not seem to improve.

One day when Wilhelm and Mme. Melina had ended and were talking about various lines, the child asked if she might say her part. She was given permission to do so and began to recite with great emotion the following passage from *The Royal Hermit*, which he had written down for her the day before. He paced up and down in the room without paying special attention to her, since he was thinking of something else.

Bid me speak or not one word dare,
My secret is a sacred vow.
For you my soul I'd gladly bare,
But that's a thing Fate won't allow.

Its hour has come, the sun comes forth to scare
Away the gloomy night, and splendor brings.
The stony cliff unlocks its heart to share
With all the earth its deeply hidden springs.

Within a friend's embrace we each find calm,
For there the flood of sorrows can pour free;
An oath has sealed my lips, I'll find no balm
Until some god can fashion me their key.

Wilhelm did not look up as she delivered the first verses, but when she came to the last ones, she spoke them with an emphasis imparted by fervor and truth so that he was awakened from his dream and it sounded to him as though another person were talking. In his pacing back and forth he had just turned away from her, he turned about quickly, looked at the child, who, when she was ended, bowed as usual.

The plan with which Wilhelm put his mind to rest was now drawn. He had decided to wait for the performance of his play, then to depart immediately and to ask Werner's pardon for his prolonged stay.

Work progressed and they considered what sort of costumes and sets would be necessary to do justice to the play. Our officer helped out with books and travel guides from which one could best choose the Near Eastern dress. There were few sets worthy of a tragedy available, and although the scene was to be changed only a few times, that also had to be provided for, and, as though obvious, here too the burden fell on the good author. He had to pay for cloth and taffeta, canvas and paint, tailors and painters. He placated himself with their promise that, although he had not received much up till now, they would repay him immediately from the expected income. In the meantime the necessities to be acquired along with the rest were to be signed over to him as security. Everything was coming together. It had even been felt that the usual musicians were unworthy for so festive an affair, and the principal players from among the regiment's oboists received permission to assume this duty — in return for good compensation.

All these lovely prospects were disturbed by the single and unfortunate figure of the loutish Darius at every rehearsal. Wilhelm did everything possible to draw the wool over his own eyes, which otherwise rarely failed him. Now he hoped the creature would look better in a handsome costume and that the harmony with which the others were acting would be strong enough to carry him through. He even consoled himself with the expectation of a miracle that perhaps could break the hard crust of this nature on the evening of the performance and bring to light a pleasant person. Finally he abandoned himself to the lighting and makeup, finding solace and aid in all natural and unnatural possibilities. But in vain! As soon as this person opened his mouth, all illusion was destroyed, and if Wilhelm on the one hand looked forward with great yearning to that day, it was a great shock to him whenever in his thoughts he saw that discordant figure appear.

Chapter 13

The public now began to show some interest in our author. They pointed him out to one another as the person whose play was soon to be performed and he became the talk of the town. He made the acquaintance of many officers. Herr von C** introduced him into a house where a lady and her two sisters were the heart of a pleasant circle. They knew their Gellert[42] by heart, made rather clever use of Rabener's witticisms, sang Zachariä's songs, and played the piano quite nicely.

Wilhelm was received well everywhere because he was very modest and yet upon closer acquaintance proved quite open and vivacious. He also felt at ease in this new world, except that here he fared like other young people. Out of good nature and adaptability he abandoned himself to the prevailing mood of every gathering: in the one he was gentle, reserved and undistinguished, in the next he would rave enthusiastically; with officers he was loud and also occasionally drank to excess. This switching of life styles put him into some confusion with himself.

The title and plot of his play had now become known, several people had heard passages from it, some followers had slipped into the rehearsals, people talked and were already judging it from all aspects. The clergy became attentive when they heard that Daniel, the fourth among the great prophets, was to be performed by an itinerant actor. They brought the matter to their superiors and, in the absence of the Chief Magistrate, an order was issued to Mme. de Retti prohibiting a performance of the play.

---

[42] C. F. Gellert (1715-1769), G. W. Rabener (1714-1771), and F. W. Zachariä (1726-1777), perhaps the most popular German authors at the middle of the eighteenth century.

What an unexpected event! What aggravation! What problems! Herr von C** soon learned of it, it annoyed him, and the concern he always showed for his friends here came to the help of the author and the actors. He made calls, he explained, he persuaded. Fortunately Racine's *Athalie*[43] had been performed in French at the local palace; he showed that this play was much more insidious since, even though the story was in the Bible, the characters were out and out heathens save for the one exception of Daniel, who did express splendid moral precepts. His efforts and arguments, but even more the influence he had on some intelligent women and his friends had on some less so soon had this matter back on track, and the prohibition was lifted.

The day was now set, and the final rehearsal was to be on the evening preceding. People wanted to see the sets and the costumes by artificial light. Wilhelm ran and raced about the entire day. He had not only equipped the theater as well as possible, but had also had the proscenium and even the boxes, heretofore covered with poor rags, draped with canvas and, wherever necessary, decorated with architectural motifs. In order to double the illumination, he had acquired more lamps and sconces. This activity was highly pleasing to him since in good part he could employ everywhere all his accumulated knowledge and put into practice the ideas he had simply been bearing within him. He cleaned the house up as if it had been a Christmas creche and felt so good in it that he didn't even go home at noon, but had his meal brought to him. He acted, recited to himself, made plans for new works, and his heart beat for joy and expectation whenever he envisioned row upon row of faces instead of its empty benches and walls.

In the evening Herr and Mme. Melina came first and brought the bad news that Monsieur Bendel had had a new occurrence of his illness. He had been attacked by the ague, the blood had rushed to his brain, and it often seemed as if he were about to choke. A doctor was sent for immediately; he assured them it was fleeting as was the first and of no significance. It was the result of overindulgence, and if he spent the night quietly and took the prescribed medicine, he would certainly be able to perform on the morrow.

"You'll be kind enough," said Mme. Melina, "to take his role this evening; you know the play so well that you could prompt from memory. It's a great advantage to all of us that you're directing the main rehearsal yourself so that the directrix won't be saying first this, then that, so that in the end she's no longer sure herself."

---

[43] A tragedy of 1691.

The others came later and made similar remarks. Also the music had been ordered. They were looking for appropriate, serious, and splendid pieces from various symphonies to play between the acts. They began to rehearse and Wilhelm, who in order to light a fire under the others also caught fire himself, outdoing himself in delivery and acting. Everyone did his part so that in the end all were greatly pleased with themselves and the others.

"Alas! How different it will be tomorrow," said Mme. Melina, "when our heavy hero enters so that the boards will groan until the stage is about to sag! Would to Heaven, my friend, that you were destined for this art and didn't mischievously have to hide and bury that beautiful talent which Nature has given you!"

"You see, my dear lady," he said, "that path is blocked for me."

"It only seems so," said Mme. Melina. "I was in the same situation, but it's only a paper door you can push through with your elbow."

The tailors, who arrived with the costumes, interrupted them. The people withdrew and tried on their costumes. These were found to be handsome although they were not yet fine enough; more taffeta would have to be added and a few more spangles sewn on. Finally they went home, where the first question concerned how the patient was feeling. They heard he was sleeping, and it was the first time that his being asleep or awake had interested anyone save the directrix.

Chapter 14

The following morning appeared and awakened Wilhelm in due time. He heard Bendel had passed a quiet night and was still sleeping. He took hope from this and hurried to the theater where various craftsmen were still busy. Towards midday everything was finished. The set changes, although they occurred between the acts, had been carefully rehearsed, and when he was on his way home, he met various post coaches filled with strangers whom the publicity had attracted. For the first time he enjoyed the pleasure of seeing the public being stirred by him. The not yet dry playbills circulated from house to house, and the name Belshazzar confronted him at every corner.

When he arrived home, he found assorted servants and people who were clutching money in their hands. It was the first time the directrix did not know what to do, for all the boxes had been taken and all the tickets sold. Someone had started to print some more, but Wilhelm stopped this since the people would not all find room and either be miserably crowded or simply turned away.

Bendel meantime had arisen, stretched out in an arm chair and was consuming a considerable breakfast. He was the only one who still didn't know his part by heart. What was worst of all, from the very beginning he had read some verses wrong and in his ignorance become used to substituting their words with others, whereby various important passages became nonsensical. From many corrections he was aware of this, but before anyone could stop him, the accustomed error slipped out of his clumsy brain. He began to stutter, and instead of correcting the mistake, his artless tongue became doubly or triply confused. He had his part lying next to him and when he recited it, he simply seemed to have forgotten it at just this moment. Wilhelm, who had stepped into the room, could not bear it; he raced away indignantly and the directrix was greatly embarrassed.

How many times has it been observed that the most beautiful wish of man, when it is finally fulfilled, is usually spoiled by some earthly additive through which the most pleasant enjoyment of it becomes martyrdom. Our friend now saw at hand the day for which he as a boy had wished so often.

We see how children are first attracted by the surface appearance of the work their fathers pursue or by one they are otherwise tempted to take up. They take sticks and make mustaches to appear like soldiers, tie string onto sticks to be coachmen, or fashion clerical tabs of paper. Things had been no different for our young author: as a boy he had composed theater handbills on which in large letters were announced works by himself that were not yet written nor ever would be. When he subsequently created the names of the characters of a play and wrote the first scenes for it, he thought to himself, how beautiful it would have to be one day to see it printed in a format as nice as that of the first edition of Lessing's works.[44] Whenever he sat in the parterre and the opening music was arousing the spirits of the audience, he thought, "If only you could be so fortunate as to be sitting before that curtain, listening to the overture, and awaiting your own play!" The good child thought at that time, his own works would then appear as extraordinary and he himself as praiseworthy as did at that time the sublime writers and their works. And who among us does not feel that way when he see others above him resplendent in wealth, rank, titles, offices, and honors?

The day had finally come! Yet how far short it fell of that rapture with which he as a child had for the first time attended the marionette show in his home! Tired from the rehearsals, the play itself seemed almost trivial to him. Nervous about the responsibility to his family

---

[44] The first edition of the works of G. E. Lessing (1729-1781) appeared 1753-1755.

because of his long stay and held captive by the money that he had loaned foolishly and in recent days had even converted into a structure of boards, he was less than healthy throughout; but his passion would have outweighed everything if only the confounded Darius had not ruined his composure completely. He felt like a dancer who is quite confident in all respects save that his big toe begins to hurt miserably as soon as he steps onto the stage.

Soon he hastened back to the theater, finding satisfaction in the calm and order which prevailed. The carpet man was there, spreading a large rug of green baize on the stage, another order that strongly attacked Wilhelm's purse although he was convinced that with it he gave his play the final polish. The hours ran past, and already at about four the idlest spectators were seeking the best seats; about five the house was rather full except for the subscribed loges. The musicians had arrived and their unbearable tuning and plunking gave the audience genuine hope the arena would soon open. In full costume the actors appeared one after the other, the front lamps were lit, and only the two princesses and the Median hero were lacking; otherwise everything was ready to begin. Every actor presented himself in his costume to our friend, who was straightening this and that for them when some servants from the city hurried in and inquired whether the play was going to be performed? Rumor had it an actor had fallen ill and the play could not be given. Wilhelm assured them it was an error, he had improved and one would begin at the appointed hour, which was drawing near. Among them was also a servant of his military friend, whom he sent off with these same message.

Scarcely had this happened when Mme. de Retti sent word he should come to the inn hastily, and the messenger did not keep from him the news that Monsieur Bendel was suffering another attack. Quite shocked Wilhelm ran and found the two women in royal garb concerned with the half-naked creature, who was lying in the arm chair, senseless, with a doctor at his side while the surgeon opened one of his veins. Mme. de Retti was beside herself, Mme. Melina was about to become hysterical, the doctor was complaining about this person who ignored moderation, who had eaten his usual meal and had not denied himself a bottle of wine, because of which the illness lurking in him had been given new life. He assured them they should not excite themselves, should change their costumes, and give a different play. When the blood began to flow, the doctor ordered the theater tailor standing nearby to undress him quickly and help him get to bed.

Wilhelm stood immobile, a burden lay on him like a person held by a nightmare: he could not move a limb, his blood seemed to freeze, and his heart stood still. He went with the two ladies to a different room. "What will we do!" he cried. The coaches, alerted by the news he had given the servants, commenced their rattling. He began to grow fearful like a person who cannot hold back a load that begins to roll downhill, like a person who wants to coast and then begins to skid.

"What can we do?" cried Mme. de Retti and looked the crestfallen Mme. Melina in the eyes.

"Oh," the latter cried with emotion, "there's only one way! Good sir! My friend!"

"Yes, our friend," cried the directrix while she, like the other woman, took him by his hand, "you must save us!"

He stood between the two women whose whole souls had been shaken by the shock, the fear, the predicament, the worry that seized them in this moment. He didn't understand them at first, but then immediately thereafter he did, and suddenly he returned completely to life. With the thought that someone could demand it of him, that it was possible, the burden that had weighed on his bosom was suddenly lifted, the oppressive silence was gone. But he felt himself exposed to a flurry of doubts, wishes, courage, and fear, to which he almost succumbed. "What are you saying?" he called out. "No, it won't do."

"But understand our difficulty," said Mme. de Retti. "and feel your own. We are lost if we don't satisfy the public, our fate depends on your desire, and all this confusion can be removed by one word from you, removed most wonderfully, for no one can perform this role like yourself."

"How lovely our rehearsal was yesterday," cried Mme. Melina. "When I think of today's performance like that, I lose myself in rapture, and all my anxieties are transformed into ecstasy."

They took turns, each saying something more urgent and more beautiful. Their excited souls stirred him more than their words; their handsome costumes and their noble composure made what they said even more compelling. "You can't fail us," the Princess said, "our whole future depends on this very day. You also owe it to me since this is the only way for me to cease to be your debtor. I've often been unfortunate, but if we assemble an audience and disappoint it, I'll be worse off than ever." Tears ran down her cheeks, a tear was gleaming in Mme. Melina's eye, his own eyes grew moist, and he no longer knew how he should turn them down.

"Do you want to see me at your feet?" cried the proud Princess as she threw herself upon her knees before him.

"Can we beg you any more urgently?" cried the charming Queen and fell down before him on the other side.

He could not bear it and he compelled them to rise. He couldn't say "Yes" and he didn't have the strength to produce a decisive "No."

Mme. de Retti stood up and went to the window to dry her tears.

"Make up your mind," said Mme. Melina in a low voice "No one knows your real name save my husband and I. You're a total stranger here, your current stay is a secret to your relatives. I swear to you that in no way will it ever cross our lips."

"If only," cried Mme. de Retti, who had turned her back to him, "the smallest fraction of what you said back then about the theater would soften your hard heart."

It struck six.

Even before they expressed their wish, it had proved effective. What the two women thought possible in the torment of their souls, he could finally also find possible. How moved he was when he sensed it fully in this happiest moment! Wasn't his own wish fulfilled? A kindly spirit had paralyzed the miserable sinner who was destroying the total harmony of his beautiful creation. It had fallen to him to determine success or failure; he had been compelled to decide the fate of his own play and that of his friends. The congruence of all circumstances down to this present day seemed to demand this sacrifice that strongly resembled the greatest triumph a human being could achieve. He became pensive, he hesitated, the women ceased talking, they took him by the hand and looked at him movingly. If only a friend had been present whom he could have asked for advice!

Someone charged noisily up the stairs and cried, "You ought to come, you oughtn't wait any longer, the whole house is full, the audience is growing restless and has been clapping for a quarter of an hour.'

"A single 'Yes'," said the women, "would put an end to this unimaginable misfortune."

"It's impossible," said Wilhelm. "How in these straits am I supposed to recall entirely my role? Where am I supposed to get a costume that would be acceptable and fit in with the others, which are all new?"

Once he posed objections, he was lost. Mme. Melina answered the first one immediately; for the second, the directrix summoned the troupe's tailor. "Can you quickly fit Herr Bendel's costume to this gentleman?" she said.

"It won't do," cried Wilhelm, "he's much taller and heavier than I am."

"That's of no importance," replied the tailor, "you can take things in much more quickly than let them out, better too big than too small. I'll be finished in a quarter of an hour. This sort of thing happens all the time." The directrix gestured to him, he went over and picked up the clothes.

"What are you doing," said Wilhelm, "I haven't made up my mind."

"We have no other choice," she replied.

A second messenger stormed in. "What are you waiting for?" he cried urgently. "The audience is getting out of control, the parterre demands the play and is raging, the crowded gallery is filled with disturbances, some people are demanding their money back, the loges are threatening to send for their coaches, the musicians are playing as well as they can to quiet the storm a little." The two messengers stood next to one another and waited for an answer. The tailor returned with the costumes on his arm.

"I'll send down to ask the audience to have patience," called the directrix. She went to the door with the two messengers, Wilhelm didn't say either "Yes" or "No" while he was being dressed. Outside she ordered the old man who was playing Eron to step before the curtain and with his usual skill to address the public, to explain the cause, to ask for but a quarter hour's postponement, and to promise the best with all humility and modesty.

The skillful hands of the tailor and of a seamstress who had been called in quickly transformed our friend into a hero before he had time to reflect on it. Mme. Melina herself combed his hair into flowing locks that were destined to support an exquisitely decorated helmet with large plumes. The cuirass and skirt, the tunic and belt shone as if they were real and fit as though made for him. Fortunately, a new pair of laced boots were found, which fit the hero perfectly. He was armed in almost less time than Homer's heroes when they were preparing hastily for battle.

He examined himself in the mirror, and the old spirit of the drama came over him. He straightened out the pieces which adorned him, to the left and the right the ladies worked away and didn't let him escape the spell. Before he could recover, he sat in the chariot and stood on the green carpet to the total astonishment and great pleasure of the other actors.

With trembling he peered through the opening in the curtain at the crowded audience. The overture to the play began, and his spirit which had been cast from one passion to the other, gathered itself and summoned from his memory the first verses of his role. Several times with rapid, heroic paces he measured the green carpet, discussed this and that at the last moment, warned the prompter and the grips who had been hired for the scene changes, and in less than a minute seemed as familiar with his situation as if he had been in it for years.

Like a person who laboriously hurries over the frozen, humped earth and uncertainly steps with his leather soles onto the flat ice, once he has on his skates is quite soon carried away by them and in smooth flight abandons the shore, forgetting his former pace and situation as soon as he is on the smooth element, floating with re-spectable grace past the casually assembled curious along the dikes — or like Mercury, as soon as he has tied on the golden wings, moves easily across the ocean and the earth according to the will of the gods — just so did our hero in his half boots pace across the stage in exaltation and without care until the presto of the overture compelled him to hide behind the flats. The curtain rustled up, and I hope that I may be permitted to let it fall here.

Book 4

Chapter 1

D'you know that land where the lemons grow,
Midst foliage green the golden oranges glow,
A gentle breeze beneath the azure sky,
The laurel smiles, the myrtle rests nearby,
D'you know it then?
      That's where! That's where
With you, oh Master, I would like to go.

D'you know that house, its roof on columns rides,
Its hall gleams forth, its chambers glow besides,
And marble statues stand and gaze at me:
Oh, what, poor child, has someone done to thee?
D'you know it then?
      That's where! That's where
With you, oh Master, I would like to go.

D'you know that hill, its trail through clouds inclined,
In fog the mule his footing has to find.
In caves resides the dragon's ancient brood,
The scarp drops down as o'er it hurls a flood:
D'you know it then?
      That's where! That's where
Our road must lead; oh Master, let us go!

Among the songs that Mignon sang, Wilhelm had noticed one whose melody and expressiveness pleased him particularly although he could not understand all the words. He asked her for it, she explained it to him, he memorized it and translated it into German, or, rather, imitated it as we have shared with our readers. To be sure, the childish innocence of expression was lost amidst her broken speech, yet the charm of the melody was incomparable. She began each verse with solemnity, with a dignity as though she wished to draw attention to something remarkable, to tell something important. By the third or fourth line her singing grew more subdued and darker. "D'you know it then?" she phrased mysteriously and gravely. In the "That's where! That's where" lay an irresistible yearning. And as often as she sang it, she knew how to vary the "oh Master, let us go!" so that it was variously pleading, urging, compelling, hurried, and promising.

Once, when she had repeated it, she paused for a moment at the end of the song, looked intently at her master, and asked: "D'you know that land?"

"It must refer to Italy," replied Wilhelm. "Where did you learn the song?"

"Italy," replied Mignon. "If you go to Italy, take me along. I'm freezing here."

"Have you been in Italy, dear child?" said Wilhelm.

The child was quiet and would say nothing more.

But I don't know why we concern ourselves with that small creature at a time when we have left our hero in a critical situation.

There will scarcely be one among our readers who would not like to learn how things went for Wilhelm at the theater and surely none who couldn't imagine it better than we can describe it. We find him in his room, sitting reflectively once again, his costume removed.

He was staring ahead of himself, deep in thought, and had he not noticed his half-boots, which someone had forgotten to unfasten for him, he would have regarded the whole adventure as a dream. The loud applause still echoed, the deafening approbation of the audience rang in his ears, he still felt the movement spreading from loge to loge during the more beautiful and powerful passages, and he sensed from this first, odd attempt what he formerly had imagined as the happiness produced by mastery. He enjoyed completely the exquisite impression of being the focal point to which a mass of assembled human beings directed their attention and, if we may speak metaphorically, of feeling himself to be the keystone of a great vault against which a thousand stones press without disturbing it and which holds them together without work and force simply from its position, for otherwise they quickly would hurtle down in a jumble of rubble. His imagination did not let the audience disperse when the piece was ended; at least in his spirit he held them together and was convinced that each of them at home with and within his own family would relive the good, noble deeds and vivid impressions of the play. He had not ordered supper, for the first time Mignon was sent away without her nightly salutation, and he didn't consider going to bed until his burned-down candle compelled him to do so.

The next morning, after he had recovered through a long sleep, he rose up as if awakening from a period of intoxication. The traces of makeup on his cheeks and his hair falling down in wondrous locks recalled vividly his condition of the evening before and in his sober state made a strange impression on him.

It was not long before Herr Melina stepped in, to whose visits Wilhelm was not accustomed and especially so early. "My wife sends her greetings," he said, "and if I could be jealous, then I'd have to be so now, for she's babbling like a fool about you and your performance yesterday."

"My thanks to her," said Wilhelm, "if she chooses to be satisfied with me. I can assure you of this: I don't know how I performed and I'm sure you believe me. It seems to me most of all that everyone performed his task quite well, and I remain quite indebted to them for that."

"Well, all right, more or less," said Herr Melina. They spoke further about the play, the performance, and the effect of various scenes. Finally Melina said, "Permit me as a friend to remind you of something, for I'm afraid you're forgetting a very important matter. The applause of the public is all very well, but I only hope that you'll use it as you deserve. Yesterday's receipts were very respectable and the directrix must have a nice piece of change in her cashbox. Don't waste this opportunity to regain what is yours, for I've figured up what in part you've loaned to her, in part spent on the performance of the play. In the last two days you still had acquired or done much in haste, and the bills for that will come to you. As far as I know, you also haven't yet paid the innkeeper, who will draw up a considerable bill for you, and I wouldn't want to see you embarrassed."

It was highly disagreeable for our friend, while strolling the pleasant path of intellectual pleasure, to see suddenly this abyss of domestic concerns opened before him. "I'll count out my money," he said. "pay the bills when they arrive, and speak to the directrix in good time."

"My friend," Herr Melina called, "consider what you're doing and take advantage of this moment! You must do it this very moment when Madame de Retti hasn't yet paid out the money or found excuses for not doing so. I wouldn't bet you have until noon to act."

"She's not the kind of person," replied Wilhelm, "who would keep back what she owes me. Just yesterday when things were critical, she promised to pay me back most conscientiously. We're surely doing her an injustice. Perhaps she's right now counting up the sum she owes me in order to free herself from her obligation to me."

"You must not know her," said Herr Melina, "and must have paid poor attention to her conduct up till now. If she had been serious, she could have done her duty long ago and paid you back gradually. If you keep on like this, you'll accomplish nothing with her, and I must insist that you become serious. Do you know what you've laid out already and have you calculated what's owing to you?"

"I think," said Wilhelm, "that six hundred Taler will take care of it or let's make it seven hundred with the seventy I loaned you. I figure fifty Taler for the innkeeper's bill, and enough's left over for me that in no way can I be embarrassed."

"It seems to me you don't keep your books properly," replied the other. "I'll bet you've spent eight hundred Taler since you've been here. Just check, I beg you, and forgive me for being so insistent."

With some reluctance Wilhelm went to his bag and was greatly astonished when he found his friend's calculations correct and his holdings much further reduced than he thought. "You're right," he said, "although I'm not worried at all."

"It's not appropriate for me," replied the former, "to ask how much remains for you at present, but I must say to you, be prepared for tradesmen's bills of a hundred Taler and an accounting from the innkeeper of at least two hundred Taler.

"That's impossible," cried Wilhelm.

"Excuse my curiosity," replied the other, "it's well intentioned. Yesterday I asked to see the innkeeper's books and I found it amounted to that much. Your hospitality and generosity couldn't come for less." The estimate was soon completed and scarcely a hundred Taler remained for Wilhelm from his cash. He was dismayed, and Melina pressed him harder. "You see it's not a laughing matter," he said. "We have the directrix in our hand, for everything she has and owns is pledged to you as a security, and we can take possession of it immediately. Before she ruins herself and allows herself to be driven out of town, she'll surely do her utmost and you'll get what's yours. Insist that you receive your first payment immediately and that the remainder be sent to you gradually from her earnings, that she likewise assume the outstanding tradesmen's bills, and then you'll save whatever's possible, for you're not going to get away completely unplucked. I beg you, get dressed and go over to see her. If I didn't fear ruining things with her and appearing too aggressive, I'd gladly spare you this fateful step."

A young prince, who is about to ride out to the hunt, booted and spurred, cannot grant an audience to a protesting minister of finance more reluctantly than Wilhelm did in following the wish of his friend. How differently had he thought to spend this morning! He had hoped to refresh himself with his friends, to savor again and enjoy with them last evening's adventure, the delight, the applause.

Chapter 2

At the moment when Wilhelm was dressed and about to go over to
the directrix, he received a note from his friend Herr von C**, who
with ebullient enthusiasm praised him for the surprise of yesterday's
play and his unsuspected acting skills. At the same time he invited
him for the evening; he wanted to introduce him to a couple of
splendid young ladies who had come to the city from their estates in
order to see the play and who desired greatly to meet him in person.
He gave word that he would attend and then went to the room of
Mme. de Retti.

At her door he heard her engaged in a heated dispute and he soon
recognized the voice of Herr Bendel, who was expressing himself to
her most ungraciously. She did not hear him knock, and when he
opened the door he could understand the words of the coarse creature, who shouted, "Enough, you didn't have to be in such a hurry.
You could have put on a different play, and by tomorrow I could
have acted myself."

The arrival of the third party interrupted his vehemence. Wilhelm
greeted him and expressed pleasure at finding him recovered. For his
part, the boor responded by mumbling a few incomprehensible
words, picked up a small chest that was standing on the table, went
out, and slammed the door behind him.

"I wish you had taken over this role right away and Herr Bendel
hadn't learned it. Now he's angry that you played it before he did."

"He'll have time enough to play it after me," replied Wilhelm. "I've
stayed around too long already; my business compels me to move on.
I've come to tell you this and to ask you repay me that which is mine,
with which I've gladly helped you out up till now. I ask you especially since the yesterday's receipts will almost suffice for that."

"I don't know how much we took in; I just gave Herr Bendel the
cashbox in order to sort and count the money. This evening I'll be
able to give you an accounting of it."

"Madame," replied Wilhelm, "I wish you'd have the cashbox
brought back. I'm offering to take on that task myself. Everything will
be finished in an hour."

"You're not going to press me at the moment," replied the directrix. "I owe the innkeeper a considerable sum, and if I hope for some
credit from him, I must pay it right away."

"Madame," said Wilhelm, "consider that my debt is no less urgent,
for I can't stay here another day."

"Nor do I expect you to," said Madame. "Leave me your address and I promise to send it to you by the first post."

"I cannot yield on this point," he interrupted. "Remember that the entire wardrobe, the sets and everything have been pledged to me as security. It would be regrettable if you compelled me to exercise my right."

"Would you be capable," Mme. de Retti cried out sharply, throwing onto the table a roll of paper she had held in her hand as she paced up and down the room, "would you be capable of being so hard and unjust toward me?"

"I see nothing wrong," replied Wilhelm, "in my seeking to obtain that which is mine."

"No," she cried out as she clapped her hand to her forehead, "no, I never thought I'd experience anything of the sort! How greatly I've been mistaken about you till now! How very wrong about you! I will never forgive you as long as I live!" In heated anger she continued to complain about his conduct and to make him feel how greatly offended she was by his demand.

Wilhelm stood quite astonished, for to his way of thinking *he* was actually the offended party; *he* was the one to complain, *he* the one to seek forgiveness! And it struck him as quite strange when he sought to quiet Madame and assured her that he had not intended to infuriate her and cause her annoyance.

"In order that you see I'm serious," she said, "I'll immediately make a start and give you a partial payment of twenty-five Taler from yesterday's receipts and that same amount from each of the following performances until the capital and interest have been discharged. Do not believe," she replied in a proud tone, "I willingly remain in debt to anyone."

Our good friend was stunned and ashamed. He had never learned to think of his own interests, so he forgot the good advice of Herr Melina, and the emptiness of his own cashbox, and acquiesced in her proposal without accepting or rejecting it. And Mme. de Retti was clever enough to send the promised partial payment after him when he went to his room.

Herr Melina, to whom Wilhelm, however unwillingly, gave a report of the outcome of this matter, was highly displeased at his complaisance and his courteousness and especially at the fact that he was willing to accept a partial payment, had not agreed on a larger sum, nor referred the outstanding tradesmen's bills to her. At the discontent of her husband, Mme. Melina lost her composure completely and could scarcely express to her theatrical friend a hundredth of all the pleasant things she had prepared herself to say, and her most beautiful thoughts had to yield to financial considerations. Herr Melina considered back and forth how he might give the matter a different turn, but Wilhelm could not resolve to take things up once again with the distraught directrix.

After the meal, as had been anticipated, some artisans came who wished to be paid. On Herr Melina's advice they were sent to the directrix, who, however, protested and bade them return, assuring them she had ordered nothing; they should address the gentleman who had arranged everything. Following this interpretation, they returned and Wilhelm asked only that they wait until the following morning when he would straighten everything out.

That evening he went to his friend, who introduced him into very pleasant company. Everyone and especially a few young ladies of fine qualities concerned themselves with him and could not say enough about how happy he had made them yesterday and for a long time to come. They spoke at length about the play, went through it in detail, and demonstrated their satisfaction with the harmony of the sets and the costumes. Indeed, even the green carpet was not forgotten so that Wilhelm could have been completely satisfied if all the praised objects had not reminded him of the predicament in which he found himself today on their account and which would be worsened tomorrow. Thus the entire, delightful pleasure which had been prepared for him was snatched away from his lips by the evil spirit of worry.

Chapter 3

Meanwhile the public with great expectations was awaiting the following day when the troupe promised to repeat the tragedy. And on this day, too, their house should have been much larger if it were to hold the throng of those waiting. There was no doubt in the city that the new actor would again appear in the role of Darius, although in Wilhelm's heart it had been agreed that he would never again enter the theater and Monsieur B. had had the costume let out and fitted to his body, as it originally had been. The directrix was clever enough to ignore custom and not have the performing actors listed on the playbill, which heightened curiosity all the more and strengthened everyone in his assumptions.

For Wilhelm it was an annoying day. He had to let Mme. Melina bemoan how poor the play would go today and to hear worried reproaches from her husband for not having followed his good advice and not having dealt more firmly with the directrix in the matter of repayment. He grew so irritated that he wished he had never seen this place. He reproached himself for not having tried to get the money all at once this morning from the directrix, since then he could have followed his heart and traveled on this evening. He could not resolve to go to the theater, for he could already feel his stomach churn when that unfortunate creature would stumble over his lines and destroy the mood of the audience through fumbled lines and inappropriate gestures. Thus, when everyone was getting dressed and departing, he remained quietly in his room in order to settle his account with the innkeeper and to pay him.

Scarcely had it become quiet in the building when Mignon entered bearing a lit candle, which caused Wilhelm to wonder, for it was still daylight. He did not have time to inquire as to the cause for the child closed the shutters, making the room quite dark, and quickly went out again. After a short time the door reopened and the young girl stepped in. Over her arm she was carrying a rug, which she spread on the floor. Wilhelm did not interfere. She set four candles on it, one at each corner. A small basket of eggs, which she fetched, made her intention clearer to Wilhelm. With deliberate paces she now measured the rug and placed the eggs at specific distances from one another; then she called in a person who was with the troupe and played the violin. He stepped into a corner with his instrument, she put on a blindfold, gave a sign, and immediately began to move with the music like a mechanical toy while she accompanied the beat and melody with the click of her castanets. Nimbly, lightly, quickly, precisely she performed the dance. She stepped so firmly and surely among the eggs and alongside them that one thought at any moment she would have to break one or skid it aside with her quick movements. Not at all! She did not touch even one though she wove her way through their ranks with all kinds of steps, both short and long, even with leaps, and finally half- kneeling.

Inexorable as a clockwork she ran her course, and at each repetition the exotic music gave a new impulse to the continually restarting and explosive dance. Wilhelm was quite taken by this strange show; he forgot his worries and followed each movement of the dear creature. He was surprised how fully her character was revealed in this dance, which was strict, severe, dry, emotional, and more solemn than pleasant in its gentler poses. In this moment he sensed all at once everything he felt for Mignon. He yearned to wrap this abandoned being in his heart as a child, to take her in his arms, and with the love of a father awaken in her the joy of living.

The dance came to an end. With her foot she gently rolled the eggs into a pile, forgetting none, damaging none, and stood beside them as she removed her blindfold and ended her piece with a bow.

Wilhelm thanked her for having performed so nicely and unexpectedly the dance which he had wanted to see for so long. He patted her head and regretted that she had worked so hard. He promised her a new dress, to which she answered intently, "Your color!" And when he promised her that, she collected her eggs, then her rug, and asked if he desired anything more, adding that she was going to the theater. He learned from the musician that for some time she had taken great pains to do the dance for him until he was able to play it. Also she had offered him some money for his efforts, but he had refused to accept it.

Chapter 4

The innkeeper, whom our friend had summoned for this hour, stepped in shortly thereafter and tendered the desired accounting. Had Wilhelm not been prepared by Herr Melina, he would have been very shocked by the sum, for he found that indeed he did owe over two hundred Taler. There was nothing to object to in the individual entries, which he found to be correct in scanning them, and the innkeeper assured him he had kept them to a minimum. Save for a small discount he paid the bill, whereby his cash was greatly reduced.

The gratitude of the innkeeper was all the more effusive and he was just taking his leave when Mignon burst through the door and cried, "Come, sir, come! They're killing each other!" The child took him by the hand and pulled him after her. He asked what it was all about, but she was so out of breath and seemed to have run so fast that she could not say another word. She pulled him to the window in the entrance hall and called, "There! There!" as she pointed toward the street that led to the theater.

It seemed to him there was movement in the lane but he could not make it out clearly since dusk had come on. Shortly thereafter a whole troop approached, running toward the inn in full course and with great shouting. Wilhelm soon realized that a number of wanton and ill-bred youths were running after a man who seemed to be fleeing from them in a ridiculous costume and hastening toward the road to the great gate. At a glance he recognized that the quarry was Monsieur Bendel himself.

How astonished and shocked our friend was! But he had little time to recover; the former scrambled up the stairs and ran toward him breathlessly. "For God's sake, what's happening?" cried Wilhelm quite seriously and in consternation, forgetting to laugh at the odd figure standing before him. This tall and broad monster, who through his inappropriate, heroic garb had grown even broader and more unshapely, had thrown a short, black coat about himself that the Crispin[45] usually wore and that he had grabbed in desperation in order to cloak somewhat his gleaming figure. The helmet, whose straps had become entangled, had fallen backwards in his running and was bouncing about his shoulders. Further down one saw the beautiful boots and the skirt shimmering forth, and his stupid, broad face was twisted in foolish contortions through anger, fear, and ignorance, and smeared with blood and filth. "For God's sake, what's happening?" cried Wilhelm.

"You're going to pay for this!" the other stammered. His face was burning, his eyes protruded from his head, his breathing was heavy, and it seemed as though he were about to burst. The youths had followed him up the stairs, were pushing in, screaming, calling him Santa Claus and Rübezahl[46] before they were forcibly ejected by the innkeeper.

The shocking condition in which Wilhelm found the dissolute creature aroused his compassion completely. He attempted to calm him, but the former ran about the hall as if crazed, wrapped the coat more closely about himself, and roared so that any other observer would have broken out in loud laughter. Amid convulsive gestures he gradually came to himself and progressed to a violent and furious vehemence, cursing at Wilhelm and threatening him. When the latter displayed all possible moderation and reasonableness, it seemed as though the frantic man might even attack him.

Wilhelm was not idle; he leaped into a corner and seized a cudgel he chanced to see there, and, by swinging it several times quickly through the air, he kept the barbarian at a distance. The latter in single-minded rage reached for the sword which hung at his side and whose blade fortunately was made only of silvered wood. It very quickly broke into pieces on the club that our hero held before him, and the blows which Wilhelm executed were so quick and earnest that the madman was compelled to draw back. When he caught his foot on a loose plank in the flooring, he fell full length on the floor at the moment when the innkeeper leaped in to separate them and above all to assist his young, friendly, and generous guest.

At the same moment a corporal with several guardsmen occupied the stairs, and Wilhelm, who heard the uproar in the street continue to increase, leaped to the window and saw to his surprise the coach gate

---

[45] A clever, unprincipled servant developed in seventeenth century French comedy.

[46] A playful, bearded spirit in the mythology of the Riesengebirge region.

similarly occupied and the royal family, whose clothes glittered in the twilight, arrive amidst an escort of a number of soldiers who cleared their way. He ran toward them, but at the bottom of the stairs Mme. Melina fainted into his arms. She was brought upstairs, and who can describe the tumult, the figures, the state of things, the gestures, the shouts, and above all else, who could describe the horror and confusion of our friend, for whom this event was an incomprehensible riddle? He sought its solution in vain, for every shout, every fragmentary word only made him more curious and more uncertain.

Chapter 5

"If the Commandant doesn't defend us, they'll tear the theater down and we'll be completely ruined!" cried the directrix. "My dear Bendel, my love! What haven't I endured for you!"

Melina came and discreetly demanded the key to Wilhelm's room, who up till now had been concerned with the good Queen, who was gradually recovering. Her husband soon returned and gave the key back to Wilhelm, who earnestly implored him for a proper account, an explanation of this confusion. Melina took him to the window and responded, "The house seemed even fuller than the first time. There was a general curiosity and desire to see the play or see it again. Everyone anticipated you would act. When the substitute Darius appeared, a general murmuring and whispering arose. Fortunately in the First Act he didn't have much to say and few difficult passages. Everyone was doing his best. Mme. de Retti performed splendidly and was rewarded with general approval and applause.

"In the final scene of the Second Act, which had made so great an impression the preceding time, things went all the worse. The whole success of this scene depends on him, on the insistent though restrained affection of the hero. Even I grew fearful for him. His delivery was completely without emotion. In the parterre they began to stomp their feet, he lost his place, he got stuck in the middle of an important passage, and when the prompter helped him out, he hurriedly delivered some lines he'd just recalled, without any sense and reason. The contrast with the earlier performance was too striking; the manner in which you treated the act was still the impression in their minds. The stomping grew louder, and it was fortunate the act came to an end and the curtain fell. Enraged, Bendel ran from the theater and swore never again to tread the accursed boards. Mme. de Retti did everything to calm him and meanwhile ordered that the Third Act begin. My wife, seized by fear, made her entrance and, without knowing it, delivered the first scene better than ever. Her timidity made her even more appealing to the public, and with several passages she received loud applause.

"The Third Act, in which the ill-bred creature doesn't appear, began, the scene where everyone wishes the King the best went off well, and the public seemed mollified. Meanwhile Monsieur Bendel had also calmed down. The plotters and the princess at the beginning of the Fourth Act did everything possible, but regrettably during this time no change had come over the Darius. The audience had scarcely caught sight of him when their whim again began to stir. He was supposed to deliver an emotional description of the depraved orgy of the banquet. Unfortunately even in the rehearsals some verses in this passage struck us as extremely amusing on his clumsy tongue and from his transposing the letters L and R. As if smitten by his evil genius, he always paused at such passages and, while trying to avoid mistakes, then flung them in the face of his audience as if on purpose.

"Loud laughter arose, he raised his voice even more, soon was stuttering, soon became trapped in transpositions. The stomping, whistling, hissing, clapping, and calls of 'Bravo!' became general. The venom and gall that were boiling in him soon erupted; he forgot where and who he was, stepped down front center to the lamps, called out and cursed at such conduct, and offered to fight anyone who demonstrated such impertinence to him. Scarcely had he finished speaking when an orange came flying and struck him with such force in the breast that he retreated a few steps; immediately thereafter another one, and when he stooped to pick it up, an apple that broke his nose so that a stream of blood ran down his face. Beside himself in rage, he hurled the apple he had picked up back into the audience.

"He must have hit someone squarely, for immediately thereafter a general uproar developed. A boy who was selling rolls and pastries was completely plundered in a trice and the hated target covered with them. Even an old snuff box came flying that shattered on his helmet and filled his eyes and mouth with a cloud of tobacco. He stomped, foamed at the mouth, sneezed, sputtered. All the other actors had fled backstage. By his defiant presence he alone excited the anger and the laughter of the mob, and almost too late he recognized the danger that threatened him. A great number of the audience, armed with staves, broke through the orchestra in order to ascend the stage. The directrix had the curtain dropped, whereby some were struck, others shut out for the moment. Meanwhile she shoved her lover out the back door, who had thrown a black coat about himself.

"Shocked by the tumult, a large part of the audience had taken flight themselves, and because the exits were blocked, the majority of them surged from the parterre onto the stage. They tore pieces out of the curtain, cut the ropes so that the flats fell down, trampled and broke everything that came under their feet amid such screaming and tumult that the pleading of the directrix was drowned out and our shock increased, but none of us was assaulted. Rational people deplored the situation and protected us in the midst of the bedlam. The rowdies searched through the entire theater for the object of their revenge, and soon complete ruin threatened us and our house. Outside a mob had assembled and now forced their way in, that portion of the populace that participates least in the theater, regards it as a school of the Devil because it costs money, and believes that arson, hard times, and plagues are magnetically attracted by such a group. In holy zeal, heightened by a lust for looting, they quite soon broke through some boards of the walls. Before one noticed it others had climbed to the roof and were beginning to remove it.

"We saw our demise before us, for we didn't dare go into the street, and the house was becoming less safe by the moment. We had long since called for the guard, but, being few in number, they soon were trapped in the throng and could scarcely defend themselves. Finally we were saved by a detachment that the Commandant had march out as soon as he heard the noise. The officer took us under his protection, and you saw us arrive."

Chapter 6

During his narration, Herr Melina, somewhat upset, occasionally glanced aside in the direction of the room of the directrix, to which she had withdrawn with her lover as soon as the first storm was past. Scarcely had it ended when she tore open the door and cried out with a violent gesture, "We are lost! We are ruined! During the tumult someone robbed me and took the cashbox from my room! Have any strangers been up here?" She asked for the ticket collector, where he was, so that he could give her what had been taken in at the door.

"Don't be alarmed, Madame!" said Herr Melina quite calmly. "The cashbox is not far; right at the outset I secured it in our friend's room where it's safely locked. Also this evening's receipts are resting peacefully in it; I took them from the old man when we met in the confusion."

"A very unnecessary precaution!" cried the directrix. "And I warn you earnestly to return it to me immediately."

"My friend has his key back," said Melina as he pointed to Wilhelm, who was standing alongside, "and I think he'll regard it as more advisable to keep this treasure at least until tomorrow."

The argument grew more heated, Melina remained calm, the directrix turned on Wilhelm, who was compelled by a glance from his
friend to refuse her the key although he himself would have been
inclined to give it to her. Mme. de Retti began to throw about abusive
epithets, beginning with "scoundrel," and it was quite timely when up
the stairs came the officer of the detachment that had quelled the dis-
turbance. "Can't the rabble keep order even among themselves?
What's happening? Must I make peace here, too?"

Wilhelm was highly offended at this term and was of a mind to
return an equally coarse compliment, but Herr Melina, who was concerned about other matters, answered him calmly and amiably. "Do
not have a worse opinion of us on this account and come protect us
from the violence and malice of our directrix."

"I'll straighten out her thinking," the former cried. "What do you
think you're doing, Madame?"

Melina did not let her speak and said, "In the confusion I put the
cashbox in this gentleman's room to protect perhaps all of us from
misfortune. The directrix is screaming and acting as though it were her
own money, as though she had been robbed, yet basically she owes
us and this gentleman more than it all amounts to. She has nothing in
the least to complain about: we plan to straighten out the matter tomorrow morning." Since Mme. de Retti responded with violence and
abusive language, she was immediately deemed wrong in the eyes of
the officer. He ordered her to keep quiet. Melina continued, "In order
that you see, sir, that our intentions are quite honorable, we ask you
to place a guard before this door and likewise before that of the room
in which our wardrobe is kept. If you also wish to have the key, it is
at your service; or if you wish to seal things, that's completely agreeable to us. Whatever serves security and convinces you we're not doing anything wrong."

The directrix was near to exploding in wrath, but that did not help
her: The officer took the key, posted his guards, and departed to give
the Commandant an account of his expedition. On the stairs he met
another officer whom he immediately recognized as the General's
Adjutant. He requested to speak alone with the directrix, who showed
him into her room. Everyone waited, curious to know what that
meant, and they noted a visible embarrassment of the directrix when
he again left her. He was cordial toward the others, spoke with them,
but they could not learn what his message had been.

Everyone departed to his own room and this time Wilhelm found
his night's lodgings with Melina. After they had discussed many
things, he lay down with an aching head and very oppressed heart on
a bed that had been hastily prepared in a corner.

Chapter 7

In great confusion and perplexity he tossed his head back and forth on his pillow; sleep was not so kind as to ease his condition. The loss of his money, concern about his family, his old desires, and his present associations stirred within his soul. The officer's insulting language rang in his ears, and he found it unbearable to be put into such company even though he could not find himself offended thereby. The illusions of his youth were scattering like a beautiful cloud bank drifting around a bald mountain. He felt sorry for himself, for the theater, and for poetry. "Alas," he cried out, "if only my example might teach the many foolish youths who chase after this phantom, who let themselves be lured from their appointed path in life by this siren!"

He had been lying for some hours in such varying, aggravating thoughts and was comparable to a soldier who by chance has been surrounded along with his troops by an enemy. First he climbs a hill, then reconnoiters the valley, then he hopes to escape by a river, and after he finds the circle completely closed, with varying thoughts of fighting his way out or of surrendering, begins his explorations and deliberations all over again.

He heard some noises in the house that seemed to him as though strangers were arriving or departing. He heard a wagon move, trunks being hauled; whether upstairs or downstairs he could not tell exactly. In the morning Melina, who had been up earlier and had inquired about the guards, stood before him and called, "Get up, my friend, and view the empty nest with me! Our birds have flown and it's fortunate we took precautions."

Wilhelm was surprised and could not quite grasp what he was saying. Enough, the directrix had made off in the still of the night with Monsieur Bendel. It was now learned the Commandant had her informed that without further ado she should get rid of the depraved creature who was so displeasing to the public; otherwise he offered her no guarantees, and she had to realize that the mob would attack him on the street and create a riot. When the house had grown quiet, she summoned the innkeeper and revealed this injunction to him and asked him to order post horses and a wagon since she wanted to accompany Herr Bendel to the next station and then return. In the beginning he had not wanted to believe her, but at her bidding he went quickly to the Adjutant, who assured him it was true. In order to show she was serious, she had given him a partial payment of Herr Bendel's bill, pointed out the guarded cashbox and wardrobe, and said naturally she would not abandon those, and that she was taking little clothing with her.

"My good friend," said Melina, "this time your wits have abandoned you, for you'll never see her again. The wardrobe and the cashbox and whatever may be there as security or for petty cash belongs to this gentleman." He pointed to Wilhelm. "But be calm; we shall see how we emerge from this and help one another survive our losses." There was another large trunk in her room. Melina maintained it should be opened and would be found to be filled with straw and stones. Others had different opinions and it was left standing.

The news spread with the dawning day. All the actors, who lived partly within the house, partly without, hastily assembled. There were questions, counsel was taken, plans were rejected, proposed, and abandoned again; everyone cried out that he had found the best solution, and each had to become silent in the face of his neighbors' loud opinions. When some saw the inn occupied by soldiers, they had visited the theater and found it in the most frightful disorder. Mme. de Retti still owed most of them their pay. Everyone asked about the cashbox, about the money, and Melina was confident that at least a part had been saved. He bade the others to remain calm and to wait and see how things turned out.

He then summoned a notary who had recorded that pledged security for Wilhelm. They shut themselves in, deliberated, went to the town clerk, and Wilhelm was as irritated, as put out of any good humor by the complaints and boredom of this business as our readers probably would be if we continued to relate the precise details of this bankruptcy.

Chapter 8

The considerations and plans people were making were interrupted suddenly by the unexpected return of Mme. de Retti, who protested most solemnly against all that had happened. Melina, who here saw a new obstacle, was furious. When she expressed her astonishment that anyone could have proceeded so swiftly without any regard for her, he replied, "Madame, you cannot demand of us that we anticipate the bold moves which occur to your extraordinary mind. In the present case probably no one save you would have been capable of daring such a trip that necessarily had to arouse the suspicion that you wouldn't return at all."

"I forgive you," she said, "for not being able to see into my heart; it's not something just anyone can do."

"And I," replied Melina, "certainly can't judge what one is obliged to do or capable of doing for so worthy an object."

Wilhelm stepped in when this argument started to become heated. Since the entire matter was highly irritating to him, he asked Herr Melina if, without becoming angry and bringing up personalities, he might seek to save whatever was possible of the money and to not increase the difficulty in which they found themselves. "I turn the whole matter over to you," he continued, "for I'm no longer in a condition to think or say a word about it, nor to consider my interests in the slightest. I beg you, Madame," he said, "also consider what I am losing, be content and reasonable, and do not increase our difficulties." Mme. de Retti began to address him with glib words, but Melina saw to it that he soon withdrew.

In order to divert himself, Wilhelm went to the promenade in order to look up his friend Herr von C**, whom he, however, did not find. The other officers, whom he more or less knew, stared at him, gathered around him, and left him standing so that he sensed something unusual in their behavior yet could not define it. He asked for Herr von C** and was told in an odd manner that he was ill. Wilhelm decided to visit him but was turned away when he arrived at his door. He was told that the gentleman was sleeping, but that his illness was not of special significance.

He went walking for a while, but this did not satisfy him. He wanted to find a sympathetic soul with whom he could converse. There was nothing left for him other than to go to Frau von S**, who along with one of her sisters had been especially kind to him, but he also did not find her at home and returned to his quarters reluctantly. There he found a very pleased Herr Melina, who told him of the start he had made. He hoped through concessions to bring about an agreement in order that the matter not come before the court and they might save the majority of what was left. Wilhelm was impatient and assured him that he didn't want to hear anything more about this business. He then turned to Mme. Melina and said, "I'd like to know what's wrong with my friend C**. I hear that he's ill. I hope it's of no significance."

"I was just going to ask," she replied, "whether you had visited him. We hear he was in a duel, and that it was on your account."

"What!" cried Wilhelm. "How is that possible?"

"For a long time now," she replied, "some people are said to have been jealous of the favor he enjoys in Frau von S**'s home. They've sought out all sorts of things to hurt him and to annoy him. Recently they specifically criticized his keeping company with an actor, deeming it inappropriate that he had introduced you into the lady's com-

pany. He grew furious at this and in a duel which followed this exchange, he wounded his opponent severely, but did not himself
emerge unscathed."

The cold words of Mme. Melina were a thousand stab wounds in
his heart. He concealed his emotions as well as he could and hurried
to his room, where he gave free rein to his anger, pain, and regrets.

Chapter 9

This news and the state into which he was put were as surprising to
him as Mariane's faithlessness, as insufferable as that letter from his
unworthy rival. For the second time he had felt compelled to follow
an innate passion, had seen himself drawn imperceptibly by it, and
because of it was now thrown into such confusion, into so painful
and fearful a condition, he was so pressed from all sides that he was
not able to bear it. "Why from my youth on," he called out, "did I
have to be gently charmed, tempted, and driven in order to end up in
this trap that is closing about me so ruinously?"

He seized his pen and in a note to his friend von C** gave vent to
his most impassioned annoyance. He asked the good man for his forgiveness for having put him in such a dilemma, scolded himself, and
could not find words sufficient to blame himself and to show his suffering. The letter was dispatched immediately, and the reflection and
the meditation began anew.

He had never experienced suffering of this sort, for even the first
quick despair and the quietly lingering sadness at a misfortune in love
have something fascinating, something appealing. We submit to it
gladly, where usually our soul casts off, the sooner, the better, every
annoyance that comes from without. Also in this period a more manly
trait had come into his soul, albeit unnoticed, although otherwise he
was still completely a youth. He felt anger rather than pain, and
whenever his own mistakes became apparent to him, it was simply
this which oppressed him most.

To create breathing space for himself through a voluntary confession, he sat down to write Werner the whole story in vivid detail, to
confess his follies and ask for forgiveness. He closed his letter with
the assurance that he now intended to continue his journey and to
take better care of the business he had undertaken. He did not hide
from him how much money had been spent, but he believed that ultimately it had been well used because he had gained valuable experience that would be useful his whole life.

He felt quite well when he had this burden off his chest, he felt as
if reborn, and although his annoyance at the disgraceful behavior of

the public, so it seemed to him, often returned, nonetheless he quite soon straightened himself out. He excused himself and forgave himself everything. Then it attacked him anew, he stamped his foot, gnashed his teeth, and tears came to his eyes; soon he felt shame and then regained his composure.

"Is it possible," he said to himself, "that one can despise a whole class of people who are welcome everywhere, whose talents are praised and encouraged, whose skill everyone rushes with money in hand to see, to hear, to admire? What a contradiction! What nonsense!" Thus agitated he walked up and down and probably would have torn himself out of this state if a friend or fate had been able to offer a helping hand. While sealing the letter he found to his great annoyance that he had taken a sheet of paper whose back side was already half written on. This and the much too casual penmanship of the letter caused him to leave it where it was, in order to copy it carefully the following day.

Soon hereafter his business agent Melina stepped in. The cheerful face of his friend proclaimed something good. "I've spoken with the rest of the troupe and we've agreed on a plan that, if you approve it, can give our situation a new turn."

"What are you proposing?" asked Wilhelm.

"They think I can guide the administration of the theater skillfully and honestly," replied the former. "The directrix agrees she'll have to leave and follow her lover. I'll take over the wardrobe at a fair appraisal and thus become your debtor. As we've now learned, the house can be restored quickly, the public will come back to us, we hope for good earnings and for nothing more earnestly than to satisfy our noble creditor soon and in full."

When Wilhelm inquired about the ready cash that had been found, he unfortunately had to learn that most of it would have to be paid out to the actors, workmen, and the innkeeper. The new director also could not start without any money, and Wilhelm soon saw that at least at this time he would not receive anything for the money he had advanced. He also had not relied especially on this; rather he simply sought and hoped to continue his journey with what little was left for him, and to reach a place where he would not lack for money and credit.

When Wilhelm on the following day reread yesterday's letter in relative calm and composure, it seemed to him exaggerated, too emotional. "What will Werner think of you," he said, "when you posture so foolishly, and why do you find it necessary to babble about your own misfortune and a relationship that could hurt you in its consequences?" The letter was not copied; rather it was torn to pieces, and he intended to inform Werner in a cleverer fashion only of that which he needed to know. A generous, moderate, and understanding response from Herr von C** confirmed this thought even more and calmed him for the moment, for soon his soul began its examination anew and to investigate his pain and annoyance and, if possible, to gain control over them.

Mignon up till now had been entirely neglected by him, however much the child, now as before, strained to serve him attentively. When she noticed Wilhelm was preparing to travel, she was happy and unusually busy. "Your trunk isn't large," she said. "A mule can carry it quite easily."

"What is it, my child?" said Wilhelm.

"When we cross over the mountain," replied the little girl. She had gradually approached him from a subservient distance. When she rolled up his hair in the evening or took it down in the morning, she did not do it expertly, to be sure, and took longer than he cared to comb out his hair and brush it, and she brushed him off carefully whenever she caught sight of a crumb or a bit of dust. When he was writing or reading, she sometimes stood before him or sat down quietly on the floor by his chair. Whenever he looked at her, he thought he caught sight of a gleaming ember smoldering beneath the ashes. At the present she was cheerful and busy, her spirits were stirring, she seemed to be anticipating a pleasant change. Wilhelm felt without doubt that she hoped to travel with him; this was a new torment for him and a weight upon his heart.

Chapter 10

The directrix had departed without any discussion of who was to keep Mignon or assume responsibility for her. The troupe was very busy with the new arrangements and would have finished up in a short time, had not the events of the outside world consumed this small town. News of the outbreak of war arrived quite unexpectedly. The regiment was to prepare to march, all was confusion, and the quieter muses did not survive the pandemonium. The beautifully conceived plan of our new director suddenly came to naught, for one could easily see that under such circumstances there would be little to earn in a provincial city. Thus it was necessary to think of something else and to reach a decision quickly if the danger of suffering privation was to be avoided. The worst thing was that one could easily predict the war would spread throughout the greater part of Germany and everywhere the theater would be exposed to privation and danger. They knew of few troupes to whom they could have turned even under more favorable circumstances. Finally they decided that going to H** might be the best thing. The geographical situation of the town let them anticipate peace there and its conditions favored a good reception of the theatrical art. The troupe in residence there had a good reputation and Wilhelm knew the director; moreover, his business compelled him to go there. Thus he could accompany and recommend his friends and so garner a double pleasure.

Since this thought had occurred first to Melina and his wife, it was deemed advisable to keep it from the remaining actors in order not to be burdened with too many people and to enjoy the advantages alone. Wilhelm also especially favored this because he had no desire to travel with an entire large company.

When they were busy making arrangements for this, Mlle. Philine came to his room, a cheerful young actress, whom we so far have not mentioned, or only in passing. Our friend often suffered reproaches from Mme. Melina for allegedly having treated this small, wanton figure more nicely and for having a greater inclination to her than her conduct merited. And indeed he did regard her with attentiveness and a kind of favor, even though he could never respect or love her. From an early age she had led a life of unbelievable frivolity and heedlessly dedicated every day and every night, just as if it were the first and the last, to her own pleasure. She confessed she had never felt an affection towards any particular man and was accustomed to saying in jest that they were a monotonous gender, that one could hardly tell one from the other. She could scarcely cast her eye at someone who didn't then seek to win her favor, and there were not many at whom she did not cast her eye.

She was the kindest-hearted person in the world, had a sweet tooth, liked to dress up, and could not live without going for a ride or finding some other diversion. She was most charming, though, when she had a glass of wine in her head. Whoever could provide her this pleasure was pleasing to her, and whenever she had some money left over, which was quite seldom, she spent it with some wandering knight who pleased her sufficiently and whose strength was not in his purse. In times of plenty nothing seemed good enough for her, and soon thereafter she would tolerate anything. She would honor a generous lover by bathing in milk, wine, and scented waters; soon the village well served the same purposes. To the poor she was very generous and extremely sympathetic, but not to the laments of a lover whom she had dismissed. Whenever she discarded dresses, ribbons, bonnets, and hats, she usually threw them out the window. Her whole manner possessed something childish and innocent that gave her new charm in the eyes of everyone. All the women were hostile toward her, and rightly so. She associated with none of them and for her own servants always found some old adventurer or a young beginner.

The reader will recognize her sufficiently from these traits; for this reason we won't add any more and simply come to the surprise which our friend displayed at her visit, since she rarely came to his room and never alone. She did not leave him in doubt for long, for it became apparent she had learned of the impending journey. She insisted upon going along and conducted herself so nicely, so flatteringly, so eagerly, that Wilhelm could not turn her down, at least at that moment.

When Wilhelm, albeit somewhat bashfully, told this to Mme. Melina, it caused some discussion; however, the project soon became even more broadly known and more people stepped forward, each in the conviction that the troupe would be better received if he were included. And when they gave their consent to some and decided to take a second coach, then quite soon a third was necessary. Others wanted to make the trip on horseback, and finally even the coach boxes were occupied. Herr Melina and his friend were regarded as the leaders of this caravan, and the troupe set forth.

Chapter 11

Many of our readers who were satisfied when we changed the scene at the end of the preceding chapter will perhaps lose patience if we return once again to mention various things that transpired at the departure.

The first conversation with Herr von C** after that event, which Wilhelm had so dreaded, went easily, passed without incident, and now was their last one, to the regret of both friends. There was no mention of that incident. "My good friend," Herr von C** called out when he caught sight of him, "you see me also about to hasten to a theater where more serious plays are performed, where each acts his part only once, and where no one who has ended his fifth act can ever return."

"How wrong you are, sir," replied Wilhelm, "to compare the broad arena of those free, manly deeds with the narrow confines of our childish games! How fortunate you are that your fate leads you to places where the entire man can apply his best strengths, where everything that he's become in his life, for which he's trained himself, can achieve its effect in one moment and must reveal itself in its highest glory. How greatly do I hope to exult in my own circle when Fame cites your name to me and simultaneously assures me that Fortune has fought on the side of the deserving!"

"I expect, my friend," replied Herr von C**, "my fate will take a much quieter and more insignificant end, and I'm quite content with that. You may well be right if you don't wish to allow anyone to compare what we find, what we undertake to a play, since it is truly more serious by a good bit and only the smallest part of what happens can be seen. The good, idle observers view from afar the dangerous tumult in which, as in the rest of the world, the noblest deeds transpire in secret, obscured by night or by smoke and clouds, while only a few, favored by undeserved fortune, gather unto themselves the glory which belongs to many and carry it off. It is a game of chance; and you know well, my friend, how little difference this makes between noble and ignoble men, between the wise and the foolish, between the brave and the cowardly."

"What!" cried Wilhelm. "Doesn't your whole soul burn to distinguish itself? Aren't you motivated by a fierce desire to leave behind your name and your deeds as a model for posterity?"

"By no means, my friend," replied the other. "I'm accustomed to doing my duty in my trade and in the place where I am. I shall do my duty and calmly await what comes. If I thereby provide my officers and the soldiers of my company with an example so that they act more decisively, more courageously, and more surely in doing what they're supposed to do, and if I die as a good man and only they know it or at best my regiment is aware of it, then I've done more than many a person whose name is spread about in newspapers through an accident that provides no advantage to his people.

"Believe me, Fame is an impotent god; it resembles the wind in its fickleness and is strongly dependent on chance. One gives it a hundred tongues, and if these were increased to millions, then it still wouldn't be able to proclaim the millionth part of the good that occurs quietly every day among all classes. And if it were to proclaim this, who would pay attention? Only the crudest granting of favor by fortune and the worst attacks of evil can attract the attention of its distracted eyes.

"And what does the hero need before all else to be the most famous of the famous? Nothing, save that the lowest member of the mob can see and understand that he routed his enemy and marched over him. Perhaps another, perhaps even this very man, at another time has had far more dangerous enemies to overcome, has applied greater magnitude of spirit, more strength of soul, more heroism, and who noticed it or who was capable of noticing it?"

"You've known the world longer and better than I," replied Wilhelm, "and I myself have no cause to expect the best from it, yet what you're saying to me is so contrary to all our childhood conceptions and to all our wishes that I can't make up my mind to say you're completely right; rather I'm inclined to grant to a depressive trait of your character a greater role in your attitudes than it may deserve."

Herr von C** smiled and replied, "I wouldn't want to infect you, and our time is too short for us to discuss this matter thoroughly. But as a dramatist, remember one thing and repeat it over and over again, no matter how much and how long we have agreed on it: Learn from this that one must offer the people only quite visible, strong, obvious, striking traits; those which are relatively fine, heartfelt, and sincere have less effect than one thinks, especially when one wants to make an impression on the masses, who ultimately are the ones who always pay the admission."

They had to part at this moment, saw each other a few days later only for a few words, and then disappeared from one another's view without their ever really having said good-bye.

Chapter 12

Wilhelm sat in a carriage with Mignon, Frau Melina, and her husband. The latter, who did not like to be driven, soon had to climb out and ask for another's horse. The clever Philine noticed this change immediately and requested the empty seat, which could not very well be denied her. Scarcely had she taken her place when in her usual manner she turned her attention to Wilhelm, the only man in the company, and soon knew how to draw his attention to herself. She sang some songs pleasantly and they discussed all sorts of subjects that could be treated dramatically.

This favorite topic put the young writer into his best humor and from the wealth of his vivid imagination he composed for them an entire play with its acts, scenes, all entrances, characters, and complications, and even the sets were not forgotten. It was decided to work in some arias and songs; these were composed and Philine, who entered into everything, immediately set them to familiar melodies and sang them off the top of her head. Wilhelm, in the happiest and most cheerful mood, went on now cheerful, now serious, and in devoting himself to the frivolous creature almost forgot his more serious lady friend and his beloved child. Philine was simply having a fine day, a very fine one, and knew how to approach him with all sorts of teasing. He felt better than he had in a long time.

After a journey of some days they finally had to come to a halt in a small village because the area was not secure and marauding troops were swarming about in the vicinity. Against their desire they had to crowd into an inn; they made out as well as they could with several in each room, except for Philine, who had set her cap for our hero and preferred a small chamber on the upper hallway in order to be alone and undisturbed.

At the urging of Mme. Melina, Wilhelm had taken occupancy of a nice room immediately by the stairs. Since that frightful discovery had torn him out of Mariane's arms, he had taken an oath to guard himself from this closing trap, to avoid the faithless sex, to contain within himself his suffering, his yearning, his sweet desires. The diligence with which he observed his oath gave his entire inner being a secret nourishment, and when his heart could not remain completely without involvement, a loving sharing became a painful necessity for his entire being. He again walked about as if wrapped in the first cloud of youth, his eyes perceived each charming object with joy, and never had his judgment concerning a lovable object been more tolerant. One can easily understand how dangerous in such a situation the young woman became to him, and we probably need say no more in order to excuse to a certain degree the kind of affection he felt for her without knowing it himself since our readers, as we are convinced, have long since absolved him.

Scarcely had they arrived and gained some rest when during a walk Mme. Melina quite seriously confronted him with these emotions which he had not yet noticed on his own. He swore to high heaven, and he could so swear, that nothing was further from his mind than to turn to this girl whose conduct was entirely known to him. He excused himself as well as he could for his friendly and polite manner toward her and in no way satisfied Mme. Melina.

Upon their return they also found her husband in the foulest mood. He had inquired high and low whether it might be possible to continue the journey. Everyone had advised against it for the best of reasons: The armies were not so far apart; one could anticipate a battle in the area through which they had to pass. There remained nothing for them other than to stay put, a necessity which was almost as dangerous as the danger itself.

Herr Melina administered the communal cash box, which actually consisted of the remains of what Wilhelm had been able to save, to meet the travel expenses and the lodging for a part of the troupe. It was gradually becoming emptier. Others who still had something left and had decided to provide for themselves lived foolishly, soon experienced shortages, and went wherever they suspected there might be money, borrowed it, or attempted to do so. "We'll soon have to beg from door to door!" cried Melina.

"Don't be so dispirited!" replied Wilhelm. "Something will turn up soon."

"If only we were alone and hadn't taken on the burden of so many people," said the former.

"My last Groschen is at your service," replied Wilhelm. "As long as we're together, everything I have I'll share."

"We'll only be hungry a few days later, and who'll get us out of this hole?"

The other man had no answer to this.

At table Melina also unleashed his foul humor towards the others, for they ate together, and he was interrupted only by the inquiry of the innkeeper, who announced a harp player, saying ,"You'll certainly be pleased by his music and his songs. No one who hears him can keep from admiring him and giving him a little something."

"Keep him away!" replied Melina. "I'm in anything but the mood to hear some organ-grinder, and anyway, we have our own singers who would like to earn something." He accompanied these words with a malicious side glance cast at Philine.

She understood him well and was secretly angered, but to not let her annoyance show, she turned to Wilhelm. "Oughtn't we hear the man?" she said. "We're going to die of boredom! For my part I'll gladly contribute something."

Melina started to answer her and the argument would have become heated, had not Wilhelm at that moment greeted the entering man and bade him approach.

The figure of this strange guest surprised the whole group, and he had already taken a chair before anyone had the heart to ask him a question or bring up anything else. A bald pate surrounded by a few gray hairs, large, blue eyes which peered out from under long white eyebrows, a well proportioned nose, and a white beard of medium length had to present an unusual picture to the party. A long robe of dark color covered a slender body from his neck to his feet. He took up his harp and began to strum it. The pleasant sounds he brought forth from the instrument, the cheerful, gentle melodies that resounded from its strings soon put the group into its best mood.

"You usually also sing, old man!" said Philine.

"Give us something that will delight our spirits!" said Wilhelm. "Since I'm no connoisseur, these melodies, runs, and arpeggios are to my ear not much more than brightly-colored snips of paper and to my eyes would appear as dappled feathers that the wind blows about in the air. Song, on the other hand, lifts itself into the sky like a butterfly or a beautiful bird and incites both heart and soul to accompany it."

The old man looked at Wilhelm, then up to heaven, strummed a few chords on his harp, and began his song. It contained a praise of song, it lauded the fortune of minstrels and admonished men to honor them. He presented it with such great vitality and realism that it seemed as if he had created it at this moment and for this occasion, and Wilhelm could scarcely keep from hugging him. Only shyness in the presence of the group drew him back to his chair. He was afraid of loud laughter if he rapturously embraced a stranger, about whom they were still arguing whether he was a monk or a Jew. They asked enthusiastically for the composer of the song, to which he gave no specific answer but simply assured them he had a great number of them and hoped they might please the gathering.

They had become cheerful and ebullient, chattering and joking with one another, and he began to sing most imaginatively the merits of a life spent among friends. He praised its harmony and kindness in ingratiating tones. His singing was dry, coarse, and confused when he lamented hateful exclusivity, short-sighted hostility, and dangerous discord, and every heart gladly cast off these burdensome trappings when he, borne aloft on the wings of a surging melody, sang the praise of the peacemakers and the good fortune of souls who are re-united.

Wilhelm felt as if he were born again. Without his having noticed, his unfortunate situation had glued up his feathers one after the other until, without knowing or understanding it, he felt himself captive. Now the spirit of the old man had breathed fire into his soul again. It was as if a gale had torn away all the clouds. Just as the first glimpse of the sun after a long cloudy period suddenly restores an entire region to its fair weather rights, so it was in his heart, which again felt itself blessed by an unconditional freedom. He no longer perceived who or where he was; every object about him was ennobled, and, seized by his former, happy folly, he called out, "Whoever you are, who comes as a helpful protecting spirit to us with a voice both blessing and stirring, accept my homage and gratitude. Know that we all admire you, and rely on us should you need anything."

The old man was silent, let his fingers slide across the strings, then addressed them more firmly, and sang:

"What do I hear outside the gates?
What echoes from the trestle?
Unto my ear there penetrates
A voice, a rapturous vessel."
The king had spoke, the page off hied,
The boy returned, the king then cried:
"Go let the old man enter!"

"My greetings to the noblemen,
Fair ladies, salutations!

With star on star, so rich a hea'n!
Who knows your many stations?
In this hall with splendor filled,
Now close, my eyes, you must not yield
And stand in rapturous wonder."

The minstrel closed his eyes anon,
And played away right loudly;
The ladies gazed demurely down,
The knights stared forth quite proudly.
It pleased the prince in every way,
And as reward for his sweet play
He bade a chain be brought him.

"Don't give me any chain of gold;
Your knights are more deserving,
Those men whose countenances bold
Produce your foes' unnerving.
Or join it to your chancellor's fate
And let him add this golden weight
 To all his other burdens.

"I sing just like the bird must sing
That in the tree is dwelling,
The song that from my throat does ring
Rewards beyond the telling;
But if I might, one wish there'll be:
Your finest wine poured out for me
Into a golden goblet!"

He raised it up and drank it all,
Oh drink of sweet refreshment!
He cried: "Oh, fortunate the hall
Where that's a petty present!
When all goes well, remember me,
And thank your God most ardently
As I do for this potion."

Chapter 13

When after finishing his song the singer picked up a glass of wine poured for him and, turning to his benefactors, emptied it with a friendly smile, a general delight arose among the group. They applauded and cried out, "May this glass of wine suffice for your health, for strengthening your aged limbs!" He then sang a few romances and aroused more and more cheerfulness in the company.

"Old man, do you know the song 'The Shepherd Dresses for the Dance'?" Philine called.

"I used to be able to play it," he said, "but now I'm not sure. Do you want to perform the shepherdess?"

"With all my heart," she cried out. "I've hoped for a long time to find someone with whom I could sing it once again. Just don't get confused in the comic rolling syllables of the refrain!" She playfully sat down beside him on the floor.

Since the song is anything but respectable, we cannot share it with our readers, and since it actually has to be sung by a dancing, gesticulating couple, it lost some of its impact at this performance. It was, however, received with great applause, and the droll whistles, the skillful turns and clever gestures with which Philine made clear the ambiguities while she seemed to be trying to hide them were approved by all and even in Wilhelm's eyes.

The party was quite delighted, but since the unfortunate consequences of their merriment were long since known to our friend, he sought to break things off and pressed into the old man's hand a generous recompense for his efforts. The others also gave something; they asked him to go rest and promised themselves a second enjoyment of his skills for the following evening.

When he was gone, Wilhelm said to Philine, "I can't, to be sure, exactly praise the morality of your favorite song, but if you had performed something pleasant and appropriate at the theater with this same naiveté, then well-earned admiration would have raised you to the level of the first actresses.

"Truly, this man puts us all to shame! Did you notice how correct the dramatic expression was in his romances? Certainly there was more characterization in his singing than there is in our actors on the stage. We would do better to regard the performance of some plays as a story and thus bestow a physical presence on their poetic accounts."

"He shamed us on another point," cried Melina when the others had grown quiet, "and, indeed, on a major point. The strength of his talents is revealed in the gain he derives from them. He moves us, who perhaps in a week won't know where our next meal is coming from, to share our meal with him. With a ditty he knows how to lure from our pockets the money so necessary for reaching our destination. I myself with mixed feelings of inclination and reluctance consigned a few Groschen to him. But truly, I'm also firmly determined, and you won't be opposed, to regain this tuition with interest."

"With all our hearts!" some called. "We're with you if an opportunity appears."

"It can occur anywhere," said Melina. "We simply mustn't be too particular. I looked at a large antechamber at the town hall today. If we hung the fire buckets elsewhere and removed some old scaffolding and partitions, there'd be room enough for stage and audience. I checked the hooks and beams from which an acrobatic troupe hung their ropes and curtains a year ago."

"But you're not going to try to compete with such riffraff for a few Pfennige from the local public?" cried Wilhelm.

"I certainly shall, with your permission," Melina replied vehemently, "for we ought not always play the big-hearted fool and, like young fops, use up our capital along with the interest!"

Our young friend choked on these words, for he felt this ungrateful reproach attacked himself and the generosity through which he had been drawn to feed this whole tribe for an entire half year. With contemptuous eyes he looked at the base-minded director and called to him as he reached for the door, "Do what you wish; as soon as possible I shall continue my journey and abandon you to your cleverness."

Having said that, he hastened downstairs to sit down on a stone bench in front of the door. Oppressed by annoying thoughts, he had scarcely taken a seat when Philine sauntered singing from the front door and sat down next to him — one might almost say on him. She leaned against his shoulder, played with his locks, caressed him, and told him ever so sweetly that he ought to remain and not leave her prematurely. Finally, when he sought to push her away, she wrapped her arm about his neck and kissed him with the most ardent expression of desire.

"Are you crazy, Philine," said Wilhelm, while he tried to free himself, "to make the public street witness to such caresses, which I in no way deserve? Let me go! I cannot and will not remain here!"

"And I shall hold on to you," she said, "and I'll kiss you here on the open street until you promise me. I'm about to laugh myself to death," she said. "After this familiarity the people will surely regard me as your wife and the husbands who either see such a charming scene or hear about it will praise me to their wives as a model of truly ingenuous affection." She caressed him most compellingly just as some people were passing, and he, in order to avoid any scandal, was forced to play the role of the patient husband.

When the people had gone past for some distance, she broke out in unbearable laughter, then, full of high spirits, she pursued all sorts of uninhibited naughtiness. Finally he had to promise he would stay on today and tomorrow and the day following.

"You're truly a dunce," she said as she gave him a poke and pulled away from him. "Truly I've never wasted so much kindness on even the oldest and hardest of men." She arose with some reluctance and returned laughing. "That's why I think I'm crazy about you," she called. "I'm just going to go and fetch my knitting so that I have something to do."

This time she wasn't fair to him, for no matter how much he attempted to keep away from her, at this moment if a bower had surrounded them with privacy, he probably would not have left her caresses unanswered.

"Do you remember if I brought my knitting to the table?" she said.

"I saw nothing," he replied.

"Then it must be lying in my room." She went into the house after casting a glance at him. He had no inclination to follow her; rather he felt a reluctance and annoyance at her behavior, yet he stood up without truly knowing why, in order to follow her.

He was just about to step into the door when a boy stopped him who had come up the lane and was carrying a bindlestiff on his back. Judging by his clothing which was dusted with powder, one would have to take him to be a journeyman wig maker. With an open, impudent, spirited forwardness he asked Wilhelm, "Can you tell me if a group of actors is staying here?"

"There are some players here," he replied.

The innkeeper had just stepped up and the young chap continued, "There must be a young miss among them named Philine. Is she in?"

"Yes, indeed," said the innkeeper. "Her room is upstairs on the second floor at the end of the hall. I just saw her go up."

The stranger heard this with great blue eyes shining with joy, and, without tarrying, he was up the stairs in a few leaps.

A secret annoyance stirred in Wilhelm's bosom: he was undecided whether he should follow or remain. A cavalryman, who reined up before the inn, attracted his attention through his fine appearance and his almost defiant countenance. He held back at the threshold, especially when the innkeeper extended his hand with the pleasure of familiarity, bade him welcome, and said, "Ah, Herr Equerry, how do we chance to see you again?"

"I only want to feed my horse," the stranger replied. "I have to hurry over to the estate to arrange all sorts of things in a hurry. The Count is following tomorrow with his lady. They'll be residing here for a good while in order to play host to the Prince of ***, who'll probably set up his headquarters in this region."

"It's too bad you can't stay with us," replied the innkeeper; "we have nice company."

A groom, who came running up, took the horse from the Equerry. He spoke in a low voice with the innkeeper, glanced at Wilhelm, and the latter, when he noticed that he was being talked about, removed himself and ascended the stairs in great irritation.

Upstairs Mme. Melina received him, talked to him, and tried to show him her husband was not all that wrong. He was annoyed, did not wish to hear any reasons, and was pleased to find a cause for acting irritated. Mme. Melina, who was not accustomed to his being in a bad mood, found this quite strange. "I see I've lost your friendship," she cried out and took to her room. He did not follow her as usually happened whenever a small difference developed between them and he was inclined to atone for his mistake.

In his room he found Mignon busy at writing. For some time now the child had made a great effort to write down completely everything she knew and had asked her fatherly friend to correct what she had written and to give her instruction in proper penmanship. She was untiring and truly had come quite far in a few weeks. She was a delight to Wilhelm whenever he was in a quiet mood; this time he paid little attention to what the child showed him, who was saddened by this since she believed she had performed her task quite well and was expecting praise.

After Wilhelm had tarried a while in the hallway trying to discover something about Philine and her young adventurer, the uneasy state in which he found himself drove him to seek out the old man through whose harp he hoped to dispel his evil spirits. When he inquired about the man, he was directed to a mean tavern in a distant corner of the town and, once there, up the stairs to the attic, where the sweet sound of the harp came toward him from a chamber. He heard heart-rending, lamenting sounds accompanied by a sad, fearful song. He crept up to the door and, since it was a kind of fantasy in which the old man almost always repeated the same words to his accompaniment, the eavesdropper after listening briefly could understand more or less the following:

> Who never ate with tears his bread,
> Who never spent tormented hours
> While seated crying on his bed,
> He doesn't know you, heavenly powers!
>
> You lead us out onto life's plain
> You let poor man grow obligated,

> And then you leave him to his pain,
> For on this earth no debt's negated.

The mournful lament pierced deeply into the soul of the listener. It seemed to him as though the old man were sometimes prevented from continuing by tears; then the strings alone sounded until softly in broken tones the voice again joined in. Wilhelm stood at the doorpost, his soul deeply moved; the sorrow of this stranger opened up his heart. He did not fight compassion nor restrain the tears that the old man's heartfelt lament drew from his eyes. All the pains that oppressed his own soul immediately melted; he surrendered to his feelings, pushed open the chamber door, and stood before the old man, who had been compelled to take as his seat a poor bed, the only piece of furniture in this shabby dwelling.

"What feelings you have stirred within me, good old man!" he cried. "Whatever was stuck in my heart you have freed. Don't let me disturb you, just continue to make a friend happy while you ease your own sorrows."

The old man wanted to stand up and say something; Wilhelm did not permit either, for at midday he had noticed the man did not like to speak. He chose to sit down next to him on the straw mattress.

The old man dried his eyes and began to smile amiably. "How did you get here? I was going to call on you again this evening."

"It's quieter here for us," replied Wilhelm. "Sing me something, whatever you wish, that agrees with the state of your soul, and behave as though I weren't here; it seems to me as though you could not go wrong today. I find you very fortunate in being able to occupy and entertain yourself so pleasantly when alone. Since you are everywhere a stranger, you find the most pleasant company in your heart."

The old man looked at his strings, and after he had gently strummed, raised his voice and sang:

> Whoever seeks out solitude,
> Soon learns that he's alone.
> The world continues on its route
> And leaves him there to moan.
> Yes, leave me to my pain!
> Oh, when I once again
> Am by myself,
> Then I won't be alone.
>
> A lover softly creeps to ascertain
> If his sweet friend's alone:
> Thus day and night comes creeping pain
> To strike me when I'm prone,

Renewing all my pain.
Oh, when I once attain
The quiet of my grave,
Oh then I'll be alone!

We would become too diffuse and still not be able to express the charm of the unusual conversation our friend conducted with the romantic stranger. To everything the young man said, the old man answered in purest agreement through chords which aroused all related emotions and opened a broad field for thought.

Whoever has attended an assembly of Amish or other pious people who are edifying themselves in their fashion will be able to have an idea of this scene. He will recall how the reader is able to weave into his sermon a part of a hymn that lifts the soul to where he wishes, so that it might take flight; how he soon thereafter adds a verse from another song and then joins a third to this that also brings along related ideas from the passage from which it is taken. Through the new association it is renewed and seemingly individual as if it had been invented at that moment, so that from an entire cluster of ideas, from songs and sayings that have much in common, this particular group is provided what it needs and is thereby enlivened, strengthened, and refreshed.

Thus did the old man edify his guest while he brought to life immediate and distant, wakeful and slumbering, pleasant and painful emotions, whereby our friend was put into a state that truly separated him from his former oppressed and impoverished life. A consciousness of the nobility of his being, of the loftiness of his calling to arouse among his fellow men a feeling for what is good and great was reawakened in him. He praised the old man while simultaneously envying him for having been able to produce this mood in his soul; he wished for nothing more than to join him in the common cause of bettering and converting the world. His old ideas of hope and confidence, which he had presented to the theater, were again aroused; with unbelievable rapidity he also added the idea of the ultimate, so that any rational person who had examined his brain at that moment would necessarily have had to think him crazy. He left the mean chamber with the greatest reluctance when night forced him to depart, and he had never been more undecided about what he would, could, and should do than when he was walking back to his quarters.

Scarcely had he reached home when the innkeeper revealed to him in confidence that Mlle. Philine had made a conquest with the Count's Equerry: after he had completed his assignment at the estate, he had returned in greatest haste, ordered supper, was at this moment upstairs with her, and it seemed as though he were making plans to spend the night.

In order to hide his irritation, Wilhelm went to his room, when all at once a horrible screaming arose in the house. He heard a youthful voice crying uncontrollably and howling angry threats. Then he heard the person from whom it came running from above, past his room, and down to the inn's courtyard. When curiosity drew him downstairs, he found the young fellow who had asked so eagerly today for Mlle. Philine. The boy was crying, gnashing his teeth, stamping his foot, threatening with clenched fists, and from anger and frustration was beside himself.

Mignon stood opposite him and was looking at him in astonishment, and the innkeeper gave a partial explanation of this scene. The boy had been happy and cheerful at his reception by Philine, had been singing and jumping about up to the time the Equerry had returned, at which point he began to display his annoyance by slamming the door and running up and down. Philine had ordered him to wait on them at supper, at which he immediately expressed his displeasure. Instead of placing a bowl of stew on the table, he had thrown it between Mademoiselle and her guest, who were sitting rather close together, at which the Equerry had boxed his ear sharply a couple of times and had thrown him out the door. He, the innkeeper, had helped the two people clean up. He could not find the words to describe how awful they looked. When the boy heard that, he began to laugh loudly while the tears were still running down his cheeks. He seemed to enjoy it greatly until the insult, which the stronger man had dealt him, reoccurred to him, at which he again began to cry and make threats. Wilhelm, to whom all this was doubly and triply annoying, hastened to his room and from boredom and ill humor went to bed early.

His restless sleep was disturbed by a sound that almost frightened him since he was already somewhat excited. In the large hallway he heard a shuffling of feet that was accompanied by a quite unnatural moaning and alternated with a mysterious rattling and a muffled thumping. He could not compare the noises to anything he knew. Curiosity urged him to get up, while a frisson held him in his bed. His jealous imagination, which hovered about Philine's door, pursued the phantom that far, and he thought he clearly heard it stop in the corner not far from that beauty's room. All at once a loud, piercing scream startled him and mechanically lifted him from his bed. Immediately thereafter he heard a mighty bumping like that of a person falling down a steep stairway, and shortly after that an even louder one as though another person had tumbled after him, and both came to rest before his door. He tore it open and in the glow from a glass lamp hanging opposite he saw the strangest group that might better have been called a clump. Wrapped in a large white sheet, two men lay across and around each other on the floor, wrestling and scuffling most earnestly; one had just gained an advantage over the other and was heartily pounding him with his fists. Wilhelm had scarcely cast his eyes on the figures when Philine appeared at the top of the stairs in the extreme disarray of a nocturnal apparition, carrying a candle that burned smokily from its untrimmed wick. When she caught sight of the two warriors and Wilhelm with them, she screamed loudly, set her light on the floor, and ran toward her room.

The victorious phantom, meanwhile, was still flailing away with furious ardor until Wilhelm finally stepped in and separated them. How astonished he was when he recognized in the victor, whom he pulled away, the blond newcomer from this noon and in the vanquished, the Count's Equerry, who sprang up quickly. Neither presented the prettiest picture when the sheet fell off. The battle seemed about to begin anew with fury, so Wilhelm quickly shoved the boy into his room and requested the other, who stood before him with fearsome threats and curses, to calm himself at least until tomorrow morning and then to demand or provide satisfaction as the circumstances warranted or permitted.

These gentle arguments would have helped little had the furious man not begun to feel the pains the fall had caused him. Aided by the innkeeper, who had come running up at the noise, he limped to one side, and Wilhelm took possession of the candle from the head of the stairs in order to light the way for his new guest and to enlighten this wondrous event for himself.

Chapter 14

When Wilhelm stepped into the room, the boy was jumping about like a senseless bacchant; he kicked out his legs, threw his head back, waved his arms, and shouted in unbridled merriment. He exulted in the triumph he had carried off, in the revenge he had executed, in the bliss he had interrupted, and until this paroxysm had passed, Wilhelm had to postpone the questions he wanted to ask him.

To be sure, one could easily guess the relationship of this young person, and he did not relate anything surprising when he confided to Wilhelm his story which was roughly the following. As a trainee he had had to do Philine's hair in the absence of an apprentice; she had attracted him, and he had become a kind of servant to her until, out of jealousy, he broke up with her and had run away. His passion, however, gave him no peace so that he had to keep seeking her out. Already he had moved three times to follow her, and even if he had declared and sworn he was leaving her, he nonetheless had had neither rest nor peace whenever she was away; she must have infected him. But now he didn't want to hear another word about her. In telling his story he lost his courage, began to cry uncontrollably, threw himself on the floor, and displayed an unrelieved suffering.

Wilhelm believed the whole story, just as he had told it, although it was subsequently apparent that he had not stuck strictly to the truth. But he was such a good story teller, was so sincere, and knew how to bestow such an aura upon what he truly felt and what had really happened to him that the gaps were thereby hidden and the probable became certainty. In all this our friend felt like the readers of those stories in which, by plan or by chance, truth and lies have become so thoroughly intermixed that even the relatively clever person must struggle to determine whether he should accept the one with the other or reject them both.

Toward dawn the thought occurred to the young adventurer that the Equerry would scarcely let things stand as they were and that in any case he would come out the loser. For this reason he collected his things in the stillness, bade farewell to Wilhelm, and hastened on his way.

The morning passed in anticipation of the visit by the noble party, which was supposed to alight at the inn for only a moment, to be sure, yet nonetheless occupied the attention and the curiosity of all the guests, as customarily happens. It was known that the Count was a man of great knowledge and much sophistication. He had traveled widely, and it was said of him that in all matters he had a decided taste. The few idiosyncrasies one knew of him did not come into consideration; rather there was no end to talk about the kindness of his spouse. Meanwhile everyone had gotten himself as well dressed as possible and figured out the place from which he would see them go past.

When they drove up in a heavily packed English coach, from which two servants leaped down, in her typical manner Philine was the first person at hand and positioned herself before the door. "Who is she?" the Countess asked upon entering.

"An actress, your Excellence," came the answer, while the imp bowed with a pious and demure expression and kissed the lady's hem. When her husband heard the same thing from the people standing about him, he inquired as to where they had last stayed, their number, and their director. "If they were French," he said to the

Countess, "we could prepare an unexpected pleasure for the Prince at finding his favorite entertainment at our place."

"It all depends," said the lady. "If these people aren't unskilled, it would still be something, and our Secretary would certainly support them."

They went to their room, and at the top of the stairs the attentive Melina introduced himself as the director. "Call your people together," said the Count, "and introduce them to me so I can see what they're made of, and bring me a list of the plays you could perform."

With a bow Melina hastened off and in a short while his people were standing before the Count in the room. Amidst jockeying for position, some presented themselves poorly from an excessive desire to please and the others fared no better because they presented themselves in a frivolous manner. The women all attested to their respect for the Countess, who was extraordinarily gracious and kind. The Count meanwhile mustered the troupe. He let each one say what roles he usually played, had him recite something, and expressed his opinion to Melina, which was received with the greatest humility in each instance. He told each to what he should pay special attention, what should be improved in his posture and gestures, showed them clearly what Germans were always lacking, and displayed such extraordinary knowledge that they all stood in greatest humility before such an illustrious and enlightened connoisseur and patron. No one dared take a breath.

"Who's that creature there in the corner?" asked the Count as he glanced toward the door and caught sight of a person who had not introduced himself. A gaunt figure in a torn coat and a poor wig, who had managed to hide until now, had to approach like the others. This person, otherwise of no importance, customarily played the pedant, schoolmaster, and poet and usually had to assume the roles where someone was supposed to be whipped or drenched. He had acquired a certain groveling, ridiculous, and obsequious bow, and his stammer, which suited his roles, usually made the people laugh so that he was not a complete outcast. He approached the Count in just this manner, bowed before him, and answered his questions in the style to which he was accustomed from his roles on the stage.

With courteous attentiveness the Count looked at him for a while as if weighing things and called out as he turned to the Countess, "My dear, observe this man closely. I'll swear he's a great actor or can become one." The person made a whole-hearted, foolish, and bashful bow, so that the Count had to laugh out loud. "Begone with you! Begone with you!" the gentleman cried. "You do your job excellently.

I'll bet this person can play whatever he wants to. It's a shame that he's not been used for something better."

This extraordinary preference was a thunderclap for all the others, save for Melina, who replied with a respectful attitude, "Yes indeed, for him as for several of us, there's been missing only such a connoisseur and such encouragement as we've had the good fortune to find in Your Excellence."

The Count stepped to his wife at the window and seemed to ask her about something. One could see she agreed with him most heartily and seemed to be asking him eagerly for something. Thereupon he turned to the troupe and said, "I cannot remain here at the moment; I shall send my Secretary to you, and if you pose reasonable conditions and want to exert yourselves, I'm not disinclined to invite you to my place for a while."

Everyone expressed great delight at this, and especially Philine, who kissed the Countess's hand excitedly. "Look, dear!" said the lady, as she patted the wanton girl's cheeks. "Look, child, you must come back to me. I'll keep my promise, but you must dress better."

Philine excused herself for having so little to spend on her wardrobe, at which the Countess ordered her chambermaids to bring out an English hat and a silk neckerchief that were easy to unpack. They came and she herself dressed up Philine, who continued to conduct and comport herself gracefully with a hypocritical, innocent face.

When the Count was gone, they brought the news to Wilhelm with a great cry of joy and jubilation. He wished them luck and had them relate all that had happened, which he heard with some surprise. Philine produced her presents, and when he cast an annoyed look at her, she left the room singing. Melina requested that he quickly discuss with him what sort of plays they could propose to the Count as though they had already performed them.

"You surely didn't say anything about me?" Wilhelm interrupted.

"I didn't feel authorized to do so," said Melina.

"But you'll go there with us in any case," said Madame quite quickly.

"I'm not of a mind to," replied Wilhelm.

The excitement of again having favorable prospects for some weeks seized the entire troupe, and everyone returned to life, made suggestions, spoke of roles he would play, and the cleverest went into the kitchen and ordered a better midday meal than they had been accustomed to up till now.

Chapter 15

The Secretary arrived. He was a small, lean, active person, one of those who at that time were called friends of the arts and who actually should have been called lovers of the useless and the mediocre, for as they left the sphere of necessary and useful knowledge, they believed they were devoting themselves exclusively to the beautiful and the pleasant. But in this they deceived themselves greatly, for each also felt the urge to produce something and yet loved only that which is beautiful to the extent it lay in his field of vision. His taste quite gladly seized upon the ordinary and mediocre as something good and splendid. Then with this justification he could judge his own productions to be of equal rank. Thus a great number of young and old congratulated one another in mutual adoration.

They were all afraid of the Secretary, and Melina was particularly fearful lest he, as a knowledgeable person, might soon discover the weak side of the troupe, observe quite easily that it was not well established since in almost all of the proposed plays principal roles were vacant. He soon removed their concerns by greeting them with great enthusiasm, regarding himself as fortunate in having encountered a German troupe so unexpectedly, in having made contact with it, and in introducing national muses into his master's castle. Soon after his greeting he produced from his pocket a manuscript and asked them to listen to a comedy that he had written. They eagerly formed a circle about him, happy at being able to assure themselves of this indispensable man at so slight a cost, although from the thickness of the text each of them was afraid it might take an inordinate amount of time.

And thus it proved to be. It was a play in five acts, of the type which never wants to end, and of which the Germans are said to have quite a few, even though those are the unfounded accusations of fickle, foreign-minded spirits. During the reading all had sufficient freedom to think of themselves and to rise up slowly out of the humility in which they felt themselves only an hour ago into a happy self-complacency, and from there to survey the sweet prospects which had unexpectedly opened up before them. The delighted author lost nothing through these secret lapses in attentiveness, for his audience displayed its approval all the more often, and whenever someone characterized a passage as splendid, the others joined in the chorus.

Their business was soon concluded. He promised to pay their bill at the inn, to provide room and board at the castle, and finally to add a bonus to their travel money when they departed. He assured the women gifts of clothing and trinkets would not be lacking, so that it was as if by some magic word they were all transformed into different beings. Only this morning they were still sneaking about in subservient humility, quite modestly requesting a glass of beer from the innkeeper, were polite and considerate to everyone and quietly cooperative even with one another. In the house there now arose cries, shouts, commands, and curses; everyone demanded something better than what his neighbor had and to have it quicker, so that the innkeeper's head was swimming and he had to think the number of his guests had increased by two or threefold.

Frau Melina sought to persuade Wilhelm that he should go with them, a decision he had not been able to reach. "Surely I should go my own way at last," he said to her in a low voice, yet one that Mignon could hear, who was standing not far away and secretly listening to the conversation.

Chapter 16

When Wilhelm was by himself, going over and evaluating what he had seen and heard this day, he exclaimed, "How uncertain is man's judgment, even that of the most understanding! This noble gentleman, this experienced man of the world, a great connoisseur, probably through some capricious mistake of the moment, directs his approbation to the most miserable and tasteless member of the troupe, and an intelligent, clever, splendid lady bestows her favor upon a loose creature who seems trying deliberately to draw upon herself the contempt of every right-thinking person. And they regard their Secretary as a connoisseur, and even as a good author. It can't last long until they'll have to open their eyes, the sham is too tangible. Meanwhile so many others are treated unjustly, and the influence of the nobler and more respected, which ought to be purposeful and helpful, is harmful."

These thoughts were interrupted by a return to his own problems, for he still vacillated between doubt and necessity. He could see already that he would have to go along to the Count's castle, and he had a thousand reasons not to do so. When a person finds himself in circumstances that bear no relationship to the space his mind should occupy, when he is constrained, bound, and tied and has struggled against this for a long time, he finally becomes accustomed to a somber, tolerant patience and passively follows the gloomy path of his destiny. When then sometimes a bolt of lightning from a higher sphere illuminates him, he looks up joyfully, his soul rises up, he again senses himself. Soon, however, the gravity of his condition draws him down again, with slight grumbling he relinquishes his rediscovered happiness and submits with little resistance to the force that drives the strong and weak alike. And yet one can call such a creature happy in comparison with others who find themselves in circumstances like those of our friend.

Ever since the surprise that had drawn him to the stage, he had not had time to come to himself. The hidden effects of that decision still marched on in his heart without his being aware of it. As if dreaming he remembered that happy evening when he had rapturously surrendered to his dearest, inmost passion. In silent memories the sweet satisfaction of applause still revived him, nurturing a strong desire to experience that pleasure once more.

The attachment of the child, this mysterious creature, gave a certain consistency to his being, more strength and weight, something which always happens when two good souls unite or simply approach one another. The fleeting attraction to Philine aroused his spirits to a sweet yearning. With his harp playing and songs the old man had raised him to the highest feelings, and at moments he enjoyed a truer and worthier bliss than he could recall from all his life.

On the other hand, all the tiresome earthly burdens placed themselves in the opposite pan of the balance: the troupe in which he found himself and which could almost be called bad, their incompetence as actors and their vanity at their talents, Philine's insufferable pretensions, Melina's limited thinking, his wife's demands, the necessity sooner or later of leaving the dear child to her fate, the lack of money and of any appropriate means of alleviating it.

Thus did the balance sway back and forth or, much more the case, the fabric was woven of such contrastingly dyed threads that, like a vilely shimmering taffeta, it struck the eye simultaneously with pleasing and repulsive colors from one single fold, and, if I may be permitted to pile up images, this yarn was twisted from silk and coarse hemp, woven, and tied in addition, so that it was impossible to separate one from the other, and our hero had no other choice than either to submit to these bonds or to cut through all of them.

Such are the conditions in which a good, even resolute person drags along for years, unable to stir either hand or foot, remaining in a state of suffering if direst necessity does not compel him to choose and to act. But even then he is not helped. It is seldom that after a series of sufferings and a chain of events a person is capable of making, or that fortune lets him make, a clean break with himself and with others. A man chooses bankruptcy as gladly as death and seeks to hold out for as long as possible through borrowing, repaying, and reassuring, through pretense and improvisation.

The mind is busy, always working on how it can attain a free, whole, clean condition, but the moment always compels him to half-way measures, even to wrong ones, to substitute one evil for another, and, if he is lucky, to hover between the frying pan and the fire. As often repeated, this is what assumes mastery over the best head, what sends active, passionate persons into a kind of madness that subsequently must become completely incurable.

How keenly did Wilhelm feel the oppression of this condition and how vainly did he work to free himself of it! His former, middle-class world was already separated from him by an abyss, and he had been accepted and initiated into a new estate while he still thought he was tarrying in its entryway as a stranger. His mind grew tired of weighing pros and cons. Finally he walked mindlessly up and down, his tormented heart strove for relief, and a fearful melancholy took possession of him. He threw himself into a chair and was very restless. Mignon stepped in and asked if she might roll up his hair. For some time the child had grown quieter and ever quieter. Without noticing it, Wilhelm had neglected her and she felt it all the more deeply.

Nothing is more moving than when at the right time a love that has been silently nourished or a loyalty that has strengthened itself in secret finally emerges and becomes obvious to the person who until now has not been worthy of it. The bud which had been firmly closed for a long time was now ready, and Wilhelm's heart could not be more receptive. She stood before him and saw his distress. "Master," she called, "if you're unhappy, what's to become of Mignon?"

"Dear child," he said as he took her hands, "you're included among my sufferings." She looked into his eyes, which glistened from repressed tears, and knelt before him emotionally. He held her hands, she lay her head upon his knee, and didn't stir. He played with her hair and was affable. She remained quiet for a long time. Finally he felt a kind of quiver through all her limbs that began quite gently and spread with increasing strength. "What's wrong, Mignon?" he cried. "What's wrong with you?" She raised her head and looked at him and suddenly reached for her heart with an expression as if fighting back pain. He picked her up and she fell into his lap; he pressed her to him and kissed her. She answered neither with a squeeze of the hand nor any movement. She clutched her heart and suddenly gave a scream that was accompanied by convulsions of her body. She jumped up and immediately fell down before him as though all her joints were broken. It was a fearful sight.

"My child!" he called as he lifted her up and embraced her tightly. "My child, what's wrong with you?" The convulsions continued, traveling from the heart to the twitching limbs; she simply hung in his arms.

He pressed her to his heart and sprinkled her with his tears. All at once she again grew tense and tenser, like someone enduring the greatest physical pain. Soon and with a new intensity all her limbs again came to life and she threw her arms about his neck with the finality of a lock snapping shut, while deep within her something like a mighty rent occurred and at that moment a flood of tears poured from her closed eyes onto his bosom. He held her fast. She wept and wept and no tongue can express the force of these tears. Her long hair had come loose and hung about the weeping girl, and her whole being seemed to be melting irresistibly into a stream of tears. Her rigid limbs relaxed, her inmost self poured out, and in the aberration of the moment Wilhelm feared she would melt in his arms and that he would retain nothing of her. He simply held her ever more firmly. "My child!" he called, "My child! You are indeed mine, if that thought can comfort you! You're mine! I will keep you! I won't leave you!"

Her tears were still flowing. Finally she pulled herself up. A faint cheerfulness glowed from her face. "My father!" she cried. "You won't leave me! You'll be my father! I am your child!"

Gently the harp began to sound before the door. The old man was presenting his most moving songs as a vesper gift to his friend, who, holding the child ever more firmly in his arms, experienced the purest, most indescribable happiness.

Book 5

Chapter 1

With how much higher spirits, with how much lighter a heart do I begin this Book than I did the last one, where I saw my friend facing only hindrances, worries, and displeasure! How I wish happiness for my readers and myself at his approaching a path that he will set out upon with joy and honor!

Toward the end of the preceding Book we could already guess that he will let himself be persuaded to go to the Count's castle with the rest of the troupe and draw nearer to the great world with its rich and respectable inhabitants. What an advantage for him that he possessed all the qualities necessary to develop in this new climate! The pressure, the anxiety, shortsightedness, and want which up till now had been his masters must be lifted from his head and from his bosom if a good genius is to guide him out of the confines of his station when his horizon broadens and becomes acquainted with the goals a noble soul must yearn for and to which it must adhere and devote itself in order to satisfy its destiny and to feel happy. In the upper classes there will be no lack of men who show him the way. They will make it clear to him that man's nature cannot be more badly misdirected than when he abandons himself to an accidental passion for base goals, when he surrenders to an obscure attachment to a society whose members do not accord with his own being. He thus becomes the slave of a state in which loyalty, the most beautiful and most human quality, holds him fast only for his own pain and ruination.

Thrice blessed are those whose birth immediately lifts them above the lower ranks of humanity, who don't need to endure circumstances in which many good people must torment themselves throughout their whole lives, nor do they even need to spend any time in them! Their outlook on the higher viewpoint must become general and correct, as early as every other step in their lives. From their birth forward they are as if set in a ship in order to take advantage of every favorable wind or wait out an ill one during the voyage that we must all make, while others work themselves away swimming before them, enjoy little advantage from a favorable wind, and soon perish in the storm, their strength quickly exhausted. What comfort, what facility

congenital capability confers! And how surely a business flourishes
that is solidly capitalized so that not every failed venture results in its
becoming idle! Who can better know the value or lack thereof in
earthly things than he who has been in a position to enjoy them from
childhood on? Who can direct his mind to the useful, the necessary,
and the true earlier than he who must convince himself through so
many errors to begin a new life at an age when he still has all his
powers? Thus hail to the great of this earth! Hail to all those who
come near them, who can draw from this well, who can share in such
advantage! And once again hail to our friend's guiding spirit, who is
making preparations to lead him to this happy step!

Chapter 2

The Count's secretary often came over to arrange things with the
troupe. Melina produced a respectable list of what they allegedly had
previously performed. Only unfortunately with the one play it was
noted that an indispensable actor had left in the meantime, with a
second that the wardrobe was not adequate, a third was dropped
from the list for some other reason. This was accompanied by complaints that the actors who had been long since engaged and to whom
travel money had been sent had not appeared and were probably delayed by disturbances from the war. The Secretary, who was quite
credulous, let none of this deter him; rather he hoped to perform
miracles with his small army. They selected some plays, he himself
included some of his epilogs, and so the two parties reached an
agreement and satisfaction increased daily. With what delighted familiarity they often sat together as the Secretary related to them in
detail about the hospitality of his lord, the order which prevailed in
his house, the care for even the least of his guests, and let them have
a taste of happy days to come.

Moreover, each person in the troupe was highly satisfied with himself and the director in that he was assigned roles to which he otherwise could scarcely have laid claim. Philine was given the dainty and
sensitive lovers, the principal roles for a young woman, although she
was poor at learning lines and was accustomed only to playing the
chattering chambermaid. Madame Melina, who was in advanced pregnancy, had to assume the serious maternal roles, and her husband,
who was born more for any trade other than actor, had to be content
with the fathers, uncles, and figures of that sort. A handsome young
man who had been treated as a boy before the troupe broke up had
grown quickly; having trained himself through conversation with Wilhelm and from his example, he took over the parts of the leading

lover. Some girls and young women with acceptable faces and clumsy figures, in company with their completely insignificant husbands and friends, divided up the lesser parts. Only Mignon, to whom they wished to assign the role of the chambermaid, rejected it outright and swore she was not going to act.

The parts were copied and diligently learned. The people were full of hope; they ate and drank at the Count's expense and enjoyed in advance many a good thing that one should first earn.

Meanwhile, Wilhelm had also become acquainted with the Secretary. The latter was delighted at our friend's great knowledge. He begged him most earnestly to come to the castle with the troupe. "Our master and mistress have a great love for literature, especially for German literature, they pay it all due respect, and you will certainly be received quite well." Once when he returned he invited him most forcefully in the name of their excellencies and could not find sufficient words to describe the honor and good fortune that he would enjoy. This enticement was irresistible for our friend, although he did not like the familiar and casual tone with which the young man spoke of his master and mistress and treated them in his stories, not as though he was their equal, but that they were his. But since our Wilhelm had proposed to stay connected to the troupe no longer, he requested permission to follow him there on his own and to stay at an inn in the neighboring village, which request was willingly granted.

Daily he became all the angrier at the frivolity and ignorance with which the actors were approaching so exalted a public. They were scarcely able to read their parts correctly, not to mention their not holding proper rehearsals and not making the effort they were obliged to. They now believed that would all take care of itself. He did not neglect to address their consciences, to make them fearful they could be dismissed again quite soon. Finally they submitted to a certain extent, yet they were still more concerned with presumptions of approval than efforts to earn it.

Wilhelm led them through good example. He took them through their plays, improved the language of translations, drew scenes together, assigned roles more according to the actor's skills, prepared new translations of some short French epilogs, and was generally busy with this from early in the morning till late at night. His zeal did not remain hidden from the Secretary, and for the latter the skill with which Wilhelm straightened everything out that he addressed was something entirely new. He was full of admiration for the energy and accuracy of sensibility with which our young poet knew how to distinguish between the effective and the affective, between narration and edification, and to give entire scenes and plays a different shape

through a slight change, and with good humor was careful not to offend decency and propriety. From this the Secretary, who had an extraordinarily good image of himself, was moved to regard the former
as worthy in every way of his friendship. He importuned him more
from day to day and confided to him his inspirations and criticisms, at
which our friend usually noticed with an unpleasant feeling that the
good man was just using big words; his ideas and themes, however,
were quite insignificant.

Finally the time was at hand when people were to prepare for the
move and await the coaches and wagons that had been ordered to
transport the entire troupe to the Count's castle. Even before the start
great quarrels took place as to who was to sit with whom and where
they were to sit; finally with great effort this was settled and agreed,
though unfortunately to no purpose. At the appointed hour fewer
wagons came than were expected and different arrangements had to
be made. The Secretary, who followed shortly thereafter, gave as a
reason the great commotion at the castle because not only was the
Prince arriving some days earlier than had been believed, but also unexpected visitors had already arrived. Room was growing very short;
for this reason they would not reside as well as had been planned
earlier, for which he was extremely sorry.

They distributed themselves in the vehicles as well as they could,
and since it was decent weather and the way was only a few hours,
the heartiest among them chose to set out on foot rather than wait for
the return of the coaches. The caravan pulled out with cries of joy, for
the first time without concern as to how the innkeeper was to be paid.
The Count's castle stood like a fairy palace in their souls; they were
the luckiest and happiest people in the world, and underway each of
them according to his manner of thinking linked with this day a suc-
cession of good fortune, respect, and prosperity.

A heavy rain, which began to fall en route, could not tear them
from these pleasant thoughts, but since it persisted and grew ever
stronger, many of them experienced considerable discomfort. Night
drew near and nothing was more welcome to their eyes than the
Count's palace with all stories illuminated, which shone towards them
from a hill. They could even count the windows. As they came nearer,
they also found all the windows of the adjacent buildings lit up. Each
person secretly determined for himself which room might be his, and
most were content with a chamber in the attic or in the wings.

As they drove through the village and past the inn, Wilhelm had
them stop in order to get off there. But the innkeeper assured him he
couldn't assign him even the worst room. Because unanticipated
guests had arrived, the Count immediately claimed the whole inn; the

rooms had all been numbered yesterday by his chamberlain, a list of them made and assignments of who should occupy them. Thus with great reluctance our friend had to drive on to the castle courtyard with the rest of the troupe.

The kitchen fire in one of the outbuildings and the activity of the cooks was the first thing that revived and delighted them. Servants came running down the stairs with lighted candles, and the soul of the good wanderers rose at these prospects. How astonished they then were when this reception dissolved into frightful abuse. The servants reviled the coachmen for having driven in here. They were to turn around and drive out again, to the rear toward the old castle; there was no room for these guests here. To this unfriendly and unexpected piece of news they added all sorts of derisive comments and there was much joking with one another about having been sent out into the rain through this mistake.

It was still raining, not a star was in the sky, and now the troupe was carried on a bumpy road between two walls into the old inner castle, which had been standing empty ever since the Count's father had built the forward one. The coaches came to a stop, partly in the courtyard, partly beneath an arched gateway, and the drivers, who were stablemen from the village, unharnessed and rode their way. Since no one appeared to greet the troupe, they climbed out, called and searched, but in vain! Everything remained dark and quiet. The wind blew through the tunnel of the gateway, and the old towers and courtyards, which they could barely make out in the gloom, were frightening. They were freezing and shivering, the women grew afraid, the children began to cry, their impatience increased with every moment, and so sudden a change of fortune, for which none of the troupe was prepared, completely upset all of them.

Chapter 3

Since they expected someone would come and open up for them at any moment, since now rain, now the wind disappointed them and they thought the heard the steps of the longed-for castellan, they remained ill-humored and inactive for a good while. It occurred to no one to go into the new castle and there call on compassionate souls for help. They couldn't imagine what had happened to their friend, the Secretary. Their situation was truly quite difficult. Finally some people indeed came and they recognized from their voices that they were the walkers who had followed on the road after those riding in the coaches. They reported that the Secretary had fallen with his horse and had injured his foot severely and that when they had inquired in the castle, the people had fiercely directed them here.

The whole troupe was in the greatest consternation; they discussed what they should do and could reach no decision. Finally in the distance they saw a lantern coming and they acquired second wind. But the hope for a rapid solution soon disappeared again when the figure drew closer and was recognized. It was the Count's Equerry whose way was lighted by a groom and who inquired very urgently about Mlle. Philine. She had scarcely stepped forward from the remaining crowd when he urgently offered to lead her to the new castle where a place with the chambermaids of the countess had been assigned to her. She did not reflect long before gratefully accepting the offer. She took him by the arm and after consigning her trunk to the others, she started to hasten off with him. But people stepped in their way, asked, begged, and implored the Equerry so that simply to get away with his beauty, he promised them everything and assured them that in a short time the castle would be opened and they would be quartered most comfortably. Soon after they saw the glow of his lantern disappear and hoped for a long time in vain for the new light that appeared at last after much waiting, cursing, and complaining and stirred them with some consolation and hope. An old porter opened the door, which they pressed through forcefully. Everyone worried only about his own things, to unpack them and get them inside. Most of these were as soaked through as were the persons themselves. With only one light, things went very slowly. Inside the building they bumped into things, stumbled, and fell. They asked for more lights, they asked for heating. Under duress the monosyllabic porter left his lantern there, departed, and did not return.

Now they began to investigate the building. The doors to all the rooms were open, large stoves, embroidered tapestries, and parquet floors attested to its former splendor, but there was nothing to be found of other household equipment, not a table, not a chair, not a mirror, only a few large, empty bedsteads, but every ornament and everything necessary for comfort had been removed. The wet bags and haversacks were used as seats. Some of the weary wanderers made do on the floor. Wilhelm had seated himself on a couple of steps, Mignon lay upon his knees. She was restless. To his question as to what was the matter with her, she answered, "I'm hungry!" He had nothing with him to satisfy the child's desire, the rest of the troupe had also eaten up everything, and he had to leave the poor creature without refreshment.

He had remained passive throughout the entire incident, quietly withdrawn in himself, for he was angry and furious that he had not insisted upon his intention and dismounted at the inn, even if he should have found his bed in the topmost attic. The others conducted themselves each in his own fashion. Some had brought a large pile of old wood into a huge fireplace of the hall and lighted it with great rejoicing at being able at least to dry themselves. Unfortunately this fireplace was only an ornament and had been bricked up from above. The smoke quickly returned and all at once filled the rooms, the dry wood broke out in crackling flames, but the flame too was forced outward; the draft which came through the broken windowpanes made its direction uncertain, they were afraid of setting fire to the castle, and they had to pull the fire apart, trample it, pour water on it. The smoke increased, the circumstances grew more unbearable, they were approaching desperation.

Wilhelm had retreated before the smoke into a distant room, whither he was soon followed by Mignon, who led in a well-dressed servant carrying a tall, brightly burning, two-candle lantern. The latter turned to Wilhelm and said as he offered him sweets and fruits on a beautiful porcelain plate, "The young woman from over there sends this to you with the request that you come over to provide her company. She wants me to report," the servant added, "things are going quite well for her and she wishes to share her contentment with her friend."

Wilhelm had expected anything but this offer because for some time he had met Philine with decided contempt and had scarcely paid attention to her in rehearsing her roles. He had also resolved so firmly to have nothing to do with her that he was about to send her sweet gift back; only an imploring look from Mignon was capable of making him accept it and having Philine thanked for it in the name of the child. He rejected the invitation absolutely. He asked the servant to have some concern for the newly arrived troupe and he inquired about the Secretary. The latter had taken to his bed but, to the servant's best knowledge, he had already given another person the task of seeing to the miserably housed people.

The servant departed and left Wilhelm one of the candles, which for want of a holder he had to stick on a window sill, yet now at least he could see the four walls of the room illuminated during his ruminations. For it still took a long time before the arrangements intended to bring our guests to rest became apparent. Gradually candles came, however without chimneys, then some chairs, an hour later feather beds, then pillows, all well dampened, and it was well past midnight when finally sacks of straw and mattresses were brought in, which would have been most welcome had they had them first.

In the meantime some food and drink arrived that was enjoyed without much criticism although it resembled a heap of table scraps and gave no special evidence of the respect one had for the guests.

Chapter 4

Because of the bad manners and excessive spirits of some thoughtless young men, the disorder and misfortune of the night increased in that they teased and woke one another and exchanged all sorts of pranks. The next morning began amid loud complaints against their friend, the Secretary, for having so deceived them and given them a completely different picture of the order and comfort they were entering. Yet to their great astonishment and comfort, they had scarcely gotten themselves assembled when the Count himself appeared with some servants and inquired about their circumstances. He was very offended when he heard how badly it had gone for them, and the Secretary, who came limping up with help, accused the majordomo of acting against his orders in this matter and hoped he had gotten him into hot water. The Count immediately ordered that in his presence everything be done to arrange for the maximum comfort of the guests.

Some unfamiliar officers arrived, who immediately reconnoitered the actresses, and in their presence the Count had the entire troupe present itself. He addressed each person by his name and mixed some jokes into his conversation, so that all were completely delighted at such a gracious lord. Finally it was also Wilhelm's turn, to whom Mignon was clinging. Wilhelm excused himself as well as he could for the liberty he had taken, the Count, on the other hand, seemed to accept it as nothing unusual.

A gentleman standing beside the Count and presumably an officer although he was not in uniform particularly engaged our friend in conversation and distinguished himself from all the rest. Large, bright blue eyes shone forth from beneath a high forehead, his brownish hair was casually brushed to the sides, and an average stature indicated a very forthright, firm, and decided character. His questions revealed great interest, and he seemed to be knowledgeable in all the areas about which he asked.

Afterwards Wilhelm inquired about this man from the Secretary. The latter did not have much good to say of him. He held the rank of major, was a protégé of the Prince, saw to the latter's most private affairs, and was regarded as his right arm; indeed, one had reason to believe he was his natural son. He had been on missions in France, England, and Italy; he was highly regarded everywhere, which made him vain and insufferable. He presumed to know German literature thoroughly and permitted himself all sorts of stale jokes about it. He, the Secretary, avoided all conversation with him and Wilhelm would do well to follow him in this. The stranger was called Jarno, but no one knew what to make of the name.

Wilhelm didn't know what to say to this, for he felt a certain inclination to the stranger although there was something cold and repugnant about him.

The troupe was settled in the castle, and Melina gave strict orders that from now on they were to behave properly, everyone was to learn his roles completely, the women were to live separately. On all the doors he posted rules and regulations which consisted of many points and also included the fines every violator had to contribute to a common fund. These orders were scarcely heeded. There arrived one swarm of young officers after another who joked with the actresses in less than the finest manner, played tricks on the actors, and doomed the rules of conduct before they had even taken root. People chased through the rooms, disguised and hid themselves, and quite soon there were attempts to disappear two by two into the corners. Melina, who had attempted to be serious in the beginning, was driven to an extreme by the wantonness, and when the Count soon summoned him to show him the place where the theater was to be erected, the disorder grew worse and worse. The young gentlemen thought up all sorts of stupid jokes, with the help of some of the actors they became still worse, and it seemed as though the entire old castle were occupied by a raging army. Nor did it end until dinner was announced.

The Count had led Melina into a large hall that belonged to the old castle, abutted the new one, and was splendidly suited as a small theater. He himself showed how he wanted it to be arranged. Melina acceded to the Count in everything, partly out of respect, partly because he knew absolutely nothing about the matter. However, he did come to Wilhelm to ask for advice and to beg him to assist him in this matter. Now everything was undertaken in great haste to erect and decorate the theater scaffolding with the properties they had in their baggage and could use; the other tasks were performed with the help of some of the Count's skilled workers. Wilhelm himself pitched in, helped to determine the perspective and define the limits of the flats. He was as extremely concerned that it should not turn out wrong as though it were entirely his own affair.

The Count, who visited frequently, was very satisfied with it. He showed them what they should do, which they carefully followed, and in so doing displayed an unusual knowledge of all the arts. Now the rehearsals began in earnest and there would have been ample space and time for them if only they had not been disturbed by the

many strangers present. Daily new guests arrived and each of them
wanted to have a look at the troupe. For several days the Secretary
had offered Wilhelm the hope that after having been introduced accidentally along with the troupe, he was to have a special introduction
to the Countess. "I have told this splendid lady so much about you,"
he said, "and about your intelligent and sensitive works that she can't
wait to meet you and hear you read one or another of them. Be prepared to come over at the first summons, for on the first quiet morning you will certainly be sent for." Then he named him some of his
own epilogs to be read first through which he would most surely
commend himself. He added, the lady regretted greatly that he had
arrived in such an unsettled period and had to manage so poorly in
the old castle with the other members of the troupe.

With great care Wilhelm then took up the play with which he was
to make his entrance into the great world. "Up till now," he said, "you
have labored away for yourself in private and earned much applause
from a real audience for one of your pieces, yet you still must doubt
whether your talent for the theater is as great as your liking for it.
Before the ears of such practiced connoisseurs, in their chambers with
no illusion present, the situation is much riskier than elsewhere, yet I
would not willingly refrain from adding this pleasure to my earlier
joys and from broadening my hopes for the future." Thus he worked
through some pieces, read them with great attention, making a cor-
rection here and there, and recited them aloud in order to be fluent in
language and expression. Those he had practiced most and which
promised to do him the greatest honor he put into his pocket on a
morning when he was summoned to see the Countess.

The Secretary had assured him she would be alone with a good
friend. When he stepped into the room, the Baroness von C** greeted
him with great cordiality, was pleased to make his acquaintance, and
presented him to the Countess, who was just having her hair done. To
his great surprise he saw Philine kneeling next to her chair and playing the fool. "This darling child," the Baroness said, "has been singing
us all sorts of things. Do finish the song you started so that we don't
miss any of it."

Wilhelm listened to the ditty patiently, all the while hoping the
barber would depart before he began his reading. He was given a cup
of chocolate while the Baroness herself offered the zwieback. He
scarcely tasted it because his thoughts were filled by the play he
wanted to read and he yearned to impart to the two ladies the feelings
within his heart. Also in his way was Philine, who had often been uncomfortable to him as a listener. With agony he followed the hands of

the barber and hoped that at any moment the fashioning of her hair would be finished.

Meanwhile the Count had entered and was speaking of the guests to be expected today, how the day was to be spent, and of other domestic matters. As he left some officers requested permission to pay their respects since they had to ride off before lunch. The valet meanwhile had finished and she had the gentlemen admitted. The Baroness in the meantime took pains to entertain our friend and showed him great regard, which he received respectfully though somewhat absentmindedly. He occasionally felt for the manuscript in his pocket, awaiting the opportunity at each moment, and his patience almost reached its limit when a dealer in fancy goods was admitted, who unmercifully opened his papers, cartons, and boxes one after the other and demonstrated each variety of his wares with an aggressiveness peculiar to his race. The group grew larger. The Baroness looked at Wilhelm and whispered to the Countess. He noticed it without understanding what it meant until, after having spent a torturous hour, he left; it finally became clear to him at home when he found a beautiful English purse in his coat pocket, into which the Baroness had managed to slip it secretly. A little later the Countess's small Negro servant appeared and delivered a nicely embroidered vest to him without saying clearly where it had come from.

Chapter 5

A mixture of annoyance and gratitude ruined the remainder of the day until, toward evening, Melina revealed to him the Count had spoken of a prolog which could also be performed for the first time when the Prince arrived. In it the qualities of this great hero and humanitarian were to be personified. These virtues were to appear together, proclaim his praise, and finally drape his bust with flowers and laurel wreaths, during which his painted name and the princely hat were to gleam forth from a banner. The Count had assigned him to see to the versification and other arrangements for this piece and he hoped Wilhelm, for whom such was an easy matter, would assist him .

"What!" the latter cried with some anger. "Are we here going to honor a prince as we did back in the oil cloth factory where we used portraits, painted names, and allegorical figures? In my opinion he deserves a quite different form of praise. How can it flatter a sensible man to see himself presented in effigy and his name shimmering from oil-soaked paper! Particularly with regard to our wardrobe I'm greatly afraid the allegories could provide an occasion for several ambiguities and jokes. If you want to have it done, I can do nothing to stop you, but I beg you to spare me from it."

Melina begged pardon, that was only the rough commission of the Count, who moreover left it entirely up to them how they wished to arrange the work. "I'll gladly contribute something for the pleasure of these excellent rulers," replied Wilhelm, "and my muse has never had as pleasant an occupation as hearing itself giving even stammered praise to a prince who deserves so much respect. I will consider the matter; perhaps I'll succeed in using our small troupe so that at least we can produce a theatrical effect."

From this moment on Wilhelm thought eagerly about the assignment. Before he fell asleep, he had more or less arranged things, and early on the following morning the plan was ready, the scenes outlined, indeed some of the most significant passages and songs had been put into verse and onto paper.

Wilhelm hastened to speak to the Secretary about certain matters and presented his plan to him. The latter liked it very much, yet he expressed surprise since last evening the Count had spoken of a totally different work which he had ordered and which, so he believed, would be put into verse. "It doesn't seem probable to me," replied Wilhelm, "it was the Count's intention to have the play prepared as he had described it to Melina. If I'm not mistaken, he simply wished to give an indication of the direction we were to take. The amateur and connoisseur indicates to the artist what he wants and then consigns to him the problem of producing the work."

"Not at all," replied the Secretary. "The Count relies on having the piece performed just as he described it and not in any other way. Your work is indeed remotely related to that, and if we want to push it through and bring him away from his original idea, we must do it through the ladies. The Baroness is a master at doing this, and the question will be whether the plan pleases her so that she joins the cause, and then it will be certain."

"We will need the help of the ladies in any case," Wilhelm said, "for our personnel and our wardrobe may not suffice for the performance. I've counted on some pretty children who run here and there in the house and belong to the chamberlain and the major domo." Then he asked the Secretary to acquaint the ladies with his plan. The latter returned soon and brought the news that they wished to speak to him in person. This evening, when the gentlemen withdrew to their gaming which was going to be more serious than usual due to the arrival of a certain general, they would retreat to their room under the pretense of an indisposition. He was to be led in through the secret stairway and then could present his case as well as possible. This kind of secret was giving the affair a double delight, and the Baroness in particular was taking a childish pleasure in this rendezvous and the fact that something was being undertaken secretly and cleverly against the will of the Count.

Towards evening at the appointed hour Wilhelm was fetched and led in cautiously. The manner in which the Baroness came toward him in a small drawing room reminded him for an instant of earlier, happier times. She took him to the room of the Countess, where a questioning and investigation began. He presented his plan with the greatest possible ardor and enthusiasm so that the ladies wholeheartedly agreed, and our readers will allow us to make them, too, familiar with it in brief.

Chapter 6

In a pastoral setting children were to open the work with a dance which represented the game where one player runs around and tries to win another's place in the circle. After this they were to offer a variety of merriments and finally, to a recurring round dance, sing a song directed at praising loyalty. Then the old harpist was to come forward with Mignon and offer his song for their delight. Several countrymen were to assemble, the old man sing various songs in praise of peace, tranquillity, and joy, and then Mignon perform her egg dance. In this innocent joy they are interrupted by martial music, and the party is attacked by a troop of soldiers. The men defend themselves and are overcome, the girls flee and are brought back. Everything seems to be ruined in the tumult until finally a person, concerning whose role he was still uncertain, enters, and the news that the commander of the army is not far away restores calm to the scene. Here the character of the hero is depicted with the most beautiful traits, safety proclaimed amidst weapons, and arrogance and violence constrained. A general ceremony in honor of the generous commander is celebrated.

The ladies were quite satisfied with the plan, only they insisted there had to be something allegorical in the work in order to make it pleasing to the Count. Wilhelm proposed having the leader of the soldiers be characterized as the spirit of discord and violence, and finally having Minerva come to put him in chains, to bring news of the arrival of the hero, and to sing his praise. This proposal was accepted whole-heartedly and Wilhelm was urged to write the work without delay and to put it into verse. The Baroness assumed responsibility for subsequently persuading the Count that it was with some modification the plan he had provided. Only she insisted that during the celebration which was to close the piece it was necessary that his bust and emblazoned names had to appear, because otherwise all negotiations would be futile.

Wilhelm, who in his mind had already imagined how handsomely he would praise his hero through the mouth of Minerva, yielded only with the greatest reluctance on this point. He considered how the roles might be assigned and the necessary figures obtained, and respectfully took leave of the ladies, who dismissed him most amiably. The Baroness, who assured him he was incomparable, escorted him to the small stairway, where she bade him good night with a handshake.

Inspired by her fair glances and the genuine interest she showed in the matter, his plan, which had been reawakened through his description, again sprang to life. He spent the greatest part of the night and the following morning on it in order to set not only the songs but also the dialogue nicely into verse. Thus he was almost finished when he was called to the new palace, where he heard that the nobility, who were just having breakfast, wished to speak to him. He stepped into the hall, the Baroness again came toward him first and, under the pretense of wishing him a good morning, she whispered to him, "Say nothing about your work other than what is asked."

"I hear you're quite industrious," the Count called to him, "and working on the prolog we wish to give in honor of the Prince. I'm told you'll introduce a Minerva into it. It will be necessary to establish in good time how the goddess is to be dressed so that we don't put her in the wrong costume. For this reason I'm having brought from my library all the books in which there's a picture of her."

At just this moment some servants stepped into the hall with large baskets of books in every format. Montfaucon's *Antiquity Explicated and Represented in Figures*[47] and mythological texts were opened and the figures compared. This did not suffice: the Count's excellent memory recalled all the Minervas who chanced to appear on title pages, in vignettes, on medals or wherever. The Secretary had to procure one book after the other from the library, so that ultimately the Count was sitting surrounded by a pile of books. Finally, when no more occurred to him, he called out with a laugh, "I'd bet there's not another Minerva in the whole library, and this might well be the first time a collection of books has had to dispense so completely with the image of its protective goddess." The entire party was delighted with

---

[47] Bernard de Montfaucon, *L'Antiquité expliquée et representée en figures*, 15 vols., Paris, 1719-1724.

this conceit, and especially Jarno, who had encouraged the Count to produce more and more books, laughed exaggeratedly. "Well," said the Count as he turned to Wilhelm, "a major question now is, which goddess do you mean, Minerva or Pallas, the goddess of war or that of the arts?"[48]

"Wouldn't it be most appropriate, Your Excellency," replied Wilhelm, "if one left that undecided and, because she does play a double role in mythology, have her appear here appropriately in a dual capacity. She announces a warrior, but only to calm the people; she praises a hero by stressing his humaneness; she overcomes violence and restores joy and calm to the people."

The Baroness, who was fearful Wilhelm might betray himself, quickly interjected the Countess's personal tailor, who had to give his opinion how such an antique garb could best be fashioned. This man, who was experienced in masques, knew how to take care of the matter quite easily. Since Madame Melina, in spite of her advanced pregnancy, had taken over the role of the heavenly virgin, he was directed to take her measurements and the Countess, albeit with some reluctance of her chambermaids, described the clothes from her wardrobe which were to be cut up for this. The Baroness was again able to draw Wilhelm skillfully aside and soon gave him to know she had taken care of the other matters. She was sending to him right away the director of the Count's household musicians so that the latter could compose the necessary pieces or find appropriate melodies in the music library.

Now everything was going as desired. The Count no longer inquired about the play, but was principally concerned with the banner which was to surprise the audience at the end of the piece. His imagination and the cleverness of his pastry chef together produced a truly pleasant concept, for on his travels he had seen the greatest festivities of this sort, had brought back many engravings and drawings, and knew in good taste what belonged in them. Meanwhile Wilhelm finished his work, assigned everyone his role, and the music director, who also understood dance, arranged the ballet, and everything was going as well as possible.

Only an unexpected obstacle appeared that threatened to create a bad gap. He had promised himself the greatest effect from Mignon's egg dance and thus was astonished when the child in her usual laconic manner refused to dance, assuring him she was now his and

[48] The Greek and Roman names for the one goddess whose principal identification developed differently in the two cultures, as the Count indicates.

would no longer go on the stage. He tried to move her through all manner of arguments and did not cease until she began to cry bitterly, at which he gave up his wish and had the old man appear alone and rewrote the scene somewhat.

Philine rejoiced openly at this, since she was one of the country maidens and sang a solo in the round dance and was supposed to supply the verses for the chorus. Things were going exactly as she wished: she had her own room, was always around the Countess, whom she amused with her monkeyshines, and daily received something for so doing. A dress for the play was also prepared for her, and because of her natural gift for imitation, she had soon observed in her association with the ladies what was appropriate for her and in a short time had acquired good manners and deportment. The Equerry's interest increased rather than decreased, and since the officers also focused their attentions on her and she found herself in so rich an element, it occurred to her to try playing the coquette and to gain some practice in exercising a certain respectable appearance. As cool and calculating as she was, it did not take a week until she knew the weaknesses of the entire household. Had she been a creature concerned with advancing herself, she easily could have fixed herself for life. But here, too, she made use of her advantage only to amuse herself, to have a good time, and to be impertinent whenever she noticed she could do so without risk.

The roles had been learned and a dress rehearsal was ordered. The Count wished to attend and his spouse began to worry how he would take it. The Baroness consulted Wilhelm secretly and the nearer the hour drew, the more disconcerted people became, for absolutely nothing at all remained of the Count's proposal. Jarno, who was just entering, was drawn into the secret. He enjoyed it heartily and was inclined to offer the ladies his good services. "It would be bad, dear lady," he said, "if you weren't able to work your way out of this matter by yourself, but in any event I'll be ready to step in."

The Baroness told how heretofore she had related the whole work to the Count, but only one passage at a time and not in any order, so that he was prepared for each part of it although he still thought it would coincide with his plan. "This evening at the rehearsal," she said, "I'll sit down next to him and seek to divert him. I've already spoken to the pastry chef to see to it that the final decoration comes out quite beautifully, but also that here and there something minor is lacking."

"I know a court," replied Jarno, "where we could use such busy and active friends as you are, dear lady. I shall order my servant to take up a position not far from you in the hall at the rehearsal. If your arts are no longer working, gesture to him and have him do something or fetch you something trivial. At this sign I'll call the Count out of the rehearsal and not let him return until Minerva enters and we'll soon have help from the illumination. For some days I've had something to reveal to him concerning his cousin that I've postponed for various reasons but will become quite urgent this evening. That will indeed distract him, and not in the most pleasant manner."

With some astonishment concerning the way people were treating the lord of the house, Wilhelm hastened to the troupe which was memorizing, singing, and preparing as well as possible. Some business prevented the Count from being at the beginning of the rehearsal, then the Baroness conversed with him. Jarno's help was not necessary at all since the Count was quite distracted in finding things to straighten out, to improve, and arrange. When Mme. Melina finally delivered her lines as he had intended and the illumination came off well, he declared himself completely satisfied. But when it was over and they moved on to the play, he seem to be getting doubts and noticing the rather great difference. At a signal Jarno now emerged from hiding, the evening passed, the news that the Prince was coming was confirmed, several people rode out to observe the advance guard which had set up camp in the vicinity. The house was filled with noise and movement, and our actors, who were not always served all too well by the unwilling servants, had to pass their time in waiting and rehearsing in the old palace without anyone paying attention to them.

Chapter 7

Besides the young officers who sometimes visited the old palace and its occupants, the troupe also enjoyed the often interesting presence of the Baron von C**, a cousin of the Baroness, who had already been so helpful to our hero. His love for German theater was quite definite. He gave due respect to the actor's profession and he treated even the least among them with a respect which delighted everyone. Nor was it any wonder when, as a connoisseur, devotee, and author himself, he honored those who provided him the most pleasant entertainment and those by whom his own works were truly brought to life, works through which he himself was to gain a reputation among the best minds of his homeland. He never grew tired of conversing with them, of talking about rules of the theater, about the best plays and the art of the author; and generally he was finally so kind as to draw a manuscript from his pocket at the end and to make everything discussed up to that point quite comprehensible through a striking example.

The heroes of his plays were extraordinary noblemen worthy of their prince's favor, of the greatest wealth, and the greatest good fortune, but who also were ready to renounce with the purest heart and clearest mind all these worldly possessions, who like children forgave every insult with unusual magnanimity, and who like wise men renounced every desire. We know from the preceding that our troupe did not enjoy being read to, and one can assume in advance about every actor that he will prefer to hear himself reading rather than anyone else. Thus it was a mark of their utmost respect that they listened to long plays of five acts and were able to suppress their yawning which usually threatened to erupt during the most solemn passages.

His stay among them was all the more pleasant and since he proved to be generous, knowing how to purchase a bauble for the actresses from every notions peddler, quite a few of whom appeared, and to acquire many a bottle of champagne for the actors, he was always very welcome. He would stay with them for half the day, have them declaim their roles and see to it that they also learned by heart many a passage from his works. This delight had not lasted long when they noticed there was talking in the palace about his all too close association with them, something Wilhelm had inferred earlier from some bitter remarks by Jarno. The Baron did not let himself be diverted, defended himself as well as he could, and whenever the others rode out on a hunt or retreated to the gaming tables, he always hastened to the place where an insurmountable passion drew him.

Finally the Prince had arrived. His generals, staff officers, and the remaining courtiers, who arrived at the same time, made the palace resemble a bee hive about to swarm. Everyone pressed forward to see this excellent Prince, and everyone admired his affability and condescension. Everyone was astonished to see in the hero and commander-in-chief simultaneously the most pleasant and most sociable courtier.

Following the order of the Count, everyone was to stay at his post: none of the actors was to allow himself to be seen because the Prince was to be surprised by the unexpected festivities. And so it truly was on that evening, and when he was led into the large, well lit hall decorated with its embroidered tapestries from the preceding century, he seemed to be not at all prepared for a play and even less so for a prolog in praise of himself. Everything went as well as possible, and after the play was ended, the troupe had to appear and be introduced individually to the Prince, who cleverly knew how to ask each a question and to say something pleasant. As the author, Wilhelm also had to come forward and likewise receive his share of approbation.

No one inquired especially about the prolog, and in a few days it was as if nothing of the sort had ever been performed, except that Jarno found occasion to praise it quite knowledgeably to Wilhelm. To the latter's great surprise and alienation, he added, "It's too bad you're playing with empty shells for empty shells." For several days this expression lay in Wilhelm's mind; he did not know how he should interpret it nor what he should learn from it.

Meanwhile the troupe performed every evening as well as it could with its resources and did everything possible to draw the attention of the audience to itself. Undeserved applause cheered them on, and in the old palace they now truly believed the large number of people who assembled here in these days actually had come on their account, that the great number of strangers had been drawn by their performances, and among themselves they confessed without hesitation that they were the focal point about and for which everything was happening.

Wilhelm alone observed the opposite to his great annoyance. For although the Prince sat in his chair, diligently following the first few performances from beginning to end, little by little he seemed to find ways to excuse himself. Precisely those whom Wilhelm in conversation had found to be the most understanding, with Jarno at their head, spent only fleeting moments in the theater hall and otherwise passed the time in the antechamber, gambling or seemingly conversing about more serious things. It annoyed Wilhelm to see the efforts he also had taken with the rehearsals so poorly rewarded, yet out of habit, boredom, and loyalty he continued doing exactly the same thing. The Baron was always eager to visit with them, to assure them of the great success they were having. In doing so he regretted that the Prince for his part was inclined exclusively to the French theater. A part of his people, however, with Jarno outstanding among them, gave the advantage to the monstrosities of the English stage.

Sometimes of a morning the Count and the Countess had one or another of the troupe summoned, at which time each of them caught sight of Philine swimming along in enviable favor and undeserved good fortune. In the morning as he prepared for the day the Count often had his favorite, the pedant, with him for hours, whom as we know from the preceding Book he had picked out quite by chance. This creature was gradually outfitted, even to having a pocket watch and snuffbox, and made presentable.

Meanwhile the Baroness had set her eye on Wilhelm. She was so condescending, pleasing, and kind to him he was in danger of losing his freedom. She was so pleasant, so cheerful, so helpful, and at last acted so familiar on a few occasions that he was on the verge of opening his heart to her in order to receive in exchange permission to forget his station and the distance between the two of them.

That this did not happen was the fault of none other than the Secretary, who here performed for our friend a great service or, if you will, a disservice. For when Wilhelm once in the joy of his heart extolled this splendid lady to the latter and could find no end to her praise, the latter replied, "I've already noticed how things stand, our dear Baroness has found another for her sty." This unfortunate figure of speech annoyed Wilhelm greatly since he well understood that it referred to the dangerous caresses of a Circe.[49] "Every stranger," the Secretary continued, "believes he's the first to enjoy this pleasant behavior and he's very wrong. For we've all been led down this path. She simply can't endure the thought of a man, whoever he may be, who hasn't devoted himself to her at least for a while, attached himself to her, and in yearning striven to win her."

The fortunate person who has just stepped into the gardens of the sorceress and is received by all the delights of an artificial spring and whose ear is attuned to the singing of the nightingales cannot be more surprised than to hear some transformed predecessor come grunting toward him. It made just this bad an impression on Wilhelm, who now paid closer attention to the Baroness's conduct and did not let her out of his sight in the theater or wherever he could observe her. Soon he saw quite plainly that the Secretary's bitterness might not be unjust. Just like an obedient schoolboy he immediately dropped this affair of the heart completely without deriving any advantage from her favor, and she did not understand why even despite her demonstrations of favor she suddenly was no longer able to arouse the slightest stirring in his soul.

The troupe was sometimes ordered to appear in toto before the nobility at table. They regarded this as the highest honor and failed to notice that at the same time huntsmen and servants brought in dogs, and horses were being shown in the courtyard.

Wilhelm had been told that, given the occasion, he might praise the Prince's favorite, Racine, and thus create a favorable impression of himself. He found an opportunity for this on one such afternoon when he had also been summoned and the Prince asked him if he also diligently read the works of the French dramatists, to which Wilhelm answered with a very enthusiastic "Yes." He didn't notice that the Prince, without waiting for an answer, was about to turn away and to someone else; rather he approached him and almost blocked his

---

[49] In Homer's *Odyssey* the enchantress who turned her victims into swine.

path while continuing to speak. Not only did he greatly esteem the French theater and read the great works with delight, to his great joy he had heard that the Prince did full justice to the talents of a Racine. "I can imagine," he continued, "how people of quality and nobility must value a writer who depicts the circumstances of their exalted circumstances so splendidly and accurately. Corneille has, if I may say so, depicted great men and Racine noble persons. Whenever I read his works I can imagine the poet who lives at a splendid court, has a great king before his eyes, associates with the elite, and penetrates secrets of mankind which take place behind exquisitely embroidered tapestries. When I study his *Britannicus* or his *Bérénice*,[50] it seems to me I'm truly at court and have been initiated into the great and petty happenings of these dwellings of our earthly gods. Through the eyes of a sensitive Frenchman I see kings, whom an entire nation reveres, and the courtiers, who are envied by many thousands, yet all as in nature with all their faults and sufferings. The tale that Racine is supposed to have worried himself to death because Louis XIV no longer respected him and expressed his dissatisfaction is for me a key to all his works; it is impossible that a poet of such great talent, whose life and death hung on the eyes of a king, should not also write plays worthy of the approval of a king and a prince."

Jarno had stepped up and was listening to our friend with great astonishment. The Prince, who had not answered and had only shown his approval with a pleased glance, turned aside, although Wilhelm, who still was unaware that it was improper to want to continue a conversation or exhaust a topic under such circumstances, would have liked to go on and show the Prince he had read his favorite writer with profit and emotion.

"Have you never seen a play by Shakespeare?" Jarno asked.

"No," said Wilhelm, "nor has what I've heard made me curious to become better acquainted with these strange and senseless monstrosities where probability and probity are so little spared."

"Then I'll advise you," said the former, "to make an attempt to do so. It can't hurt if a person sees even the unusual with his own eyes. I'll lend you a couple of volumes and you won't be able to spend your time any better than to drop everything immediately and, in the isolation of your old building, peer into the magic lantern of this unfamiliar world. It's a sin to waste your hours teaching these monkeys how to dress and these dogs how to dance. I make only one condition: that you not take offense at the form. The rest I can leave to your

[50] Tragedies by Racine from 1669 and 1670.

good instincts." The horses were standing before the door and Jarno mounted along with some cavaliers in order to take pleasure in the hunt. Wilhelm's eyes followed him sadly. He would have liked to discuss many a thing more with this man, who, even if brusque in manner, gave him new ideas, ideas that he needed.

Sometimes when a person is approaching a new development of his strengths, skills, and ideas, he comes into a difficulty, out of which a good friend easily could help him. He is like a hiker who falls into the water not far from his camp; if someone reaches in immediately and pulls him on land, then it's simply a question of having gotten wet, whereas, left to himself, he might fight his way to the opposite bank and thus have to make a long and difficult detour to get to his goal.

Wilhelm began to sense that the way of the world might be other than he had imagined. He saw at close range the important and momentous life of the high and the mighty and wondered at how they were able to elevate him slightly. An army on the march, a princely hero at its head, so many participating soldiers, so many crowding admirers heightened his imaginative powers. In this mood he received the promised books and in a short time, as one can well imagine, the flood of this great genius seized him and carried him toward an immense sea in which he quite soon completely forgot and lost himself.

Chapter 8

Meanwhile the good relationship between the Baron and our actors became somewhat skewed. His preference for some of them became more noticeable from day to day, and this necessarily had to annoy the others. He praised his favorites exclusively and thereby introduced jealousy and disharmony into the troupe. Melina, who in any case did not know how to handle controversies, found himself in a very unpleasant situation. Those who were praised accepted it without being especially grateful, and those who were demoted let their annoyance be noticed in many ways and knew how to make the presence of their once highly respected patron among them unpleasant in one way or another. It was indeed happy for them when a certain poem, whose author was unknown, caused a great stir in the palace. Up to this time people had always, though nicely, dwelt on the Baron's association with the actors; they had spread a number of stories about him that had adorned certain events and given them an amusing and interesting cast. Finally they began to say a kind of professional envy had arisen between the Baron and some of the actors, who imagined

themselves playwrights, and it was on this rumor the poem of which
we spoke was founded and which ran as follows:

> I, poor devil, Herr Baron,
> Do envy you your noble state,
> Both for your place so near the throne,
> And for your ample real estate,
> And there's your father's palace fine,
> And, too, his game preserve and wine.
>
> And you, Baron, must envy me,
> Poor devil, so I've come to guess,
> Because from childhood on, you see,
> Good Nature's deemed me one to bless.
> Light of heart and mind, I grew
> Quite poor, but not a fool like you.
>
> Now I would think, dear Herr Baron,
> We'd try to live with what we've got:
> Then you will stay your father's son
> And I'll remain my mother's tot.
> We'll have no envy and no hate,
> Nor covet one another's fate;
> You'll seek no seat on Mount Parnassus,
> Nor I one in the upper classes.

When people heard that the Prince was said to have laughed
heartily at the poem, no one dared to find it wicked, and the Count,
who was accustomed to joking with the Baron in his manner, took
this as an occasion to torment him woefully. People tried to think who
the author could be, and the Count, who didn't readily grant that anyone had more acuity, fell upon an idea which he was immediately
willing to swear to: It could only have been written by the pedant,
who was a very fine fellow and about whom he had noticed something like that for a long time. In order to truly enjoy the matter, he
had this actor called of a morning and the latter had to read the poem
aloud to him in his own style in the presence of the Countess, the
Baroness, and Jarno, for which he received much praise, applause,
and a present. The Count asked him if he didn't know some other poems from his former days, which the latter was clever enough to decline. In brief, the pedant acquired the reputation of a poet and a wit,
and, in the eyes of those who favored the Baron, that of a libeler and
horrible person. The Count applauded him more and more whichever
way he played his part so that the poor creature finally had a swelled

head, indeed, was almost crazy, and was thinking of having a room in the castle, like Philine.

Had this happened immediately, he might have avoided a great misfortune, for one evening when he was returning late to the old palace and groping blindly along the narrow way, he was suddenly attacked and held firmly while others flailed away quite vigorously. He was so pummeled in the dark that he almost remained lying there and only with effort climbed up to his comrades, who, no matter how indignant they pretended to be, felt a secret delight at this misfortune and could scarcely keep from laughing when they saw him so thoroughly thrashed and his new, brown coat dusty, stained, and white all over as though he had had a fight with millers.

When the Count learned of it, he erupted in an indescribable rage. He treated this deed as the greatest crime, equated it with a violated truce, and had his magistrate conduct a severe inquisition. The coat powdered white was to be a principal piece of evidence. Everything in the palace having anything to do with powder and flour was drawn into the investigation, but in vain.

The Baron swore upon his honor that even though this kind of joke displeased him greatly and the manner in which the Count, whom he had every reason to regard as his friend, had conducted himself had been very unpleasant, he nonetheless believed he had to move beyond it and that he had had no part in the misfortune which had befallen the poet or libeler, however one wished to call him. The other activities of the outsiders and the confusion in the house soon let the whole matter die, and the unfortunate favorite had to pay dearly for the pleasure of having adorned himself for a short while with another's plumage.

Our troupe, which performed regularly every evening and was very well cared for because of the attention of the Secretary, now began to make ever greater demands, the better things went for it. In a short time food, drink, servants, and quarters were not suitable for them, and they explained to their protector that he should care better for them and help them attain the pleasure and comfort he had promised them. Their complaints grew ever louder and the efforts of their friend ever more fruitless.

Meanwhile Wilhelm scarcely ever made an appearance any more. Shut in one of the remotest rooms, to which no one save Mignon and the harpist was permitted entry, he lived and moved in the world of Shakespeare so that he neither felt nor knew anything outside himself. People tell of sorcerers who use magic incantations to summon an enormous number of ghostly figures into their chamber. Their incantations are so powerful that the room is soon filled; the spirits, pushed to the edge of the magic circle, multiply about it and above the head of the sorcerer in a continuously churning transformation. Every corner is jammed full, every bit of molding occupied, eggs expand, and gigantic shapes shrink into mushrooms. Unfortunately the necromancer has forgotten the phrase with which he could make the flood of spirits ebb.

Wilhelm sat like this and while an equally great stir took place within him, there came alive a thousand emotions and capabilities of which he had had neither an idea nor a suspicion. Nothing could tear him out of this state, and he was very unhappy whenever someone dared to come to tell him of what was happening outside. He did not want to listen at all when someone brought him the news that a flogging was to take place in the palace courtyard: a boy was to be whipped who had been acting suspiciously as though he were about to steal something and also, because he was wearing the coat of a wig maker, had probably been among the assailants of the poet. To be sure, he denied it most stubbornly and on account of this they could not punish him formally. Before chasing him off they wanted to give him a lesson on account of his immaturity since he had loitered in the area for a few days as a vagabond, staying at night in the mills, and had finally leaned a ladder against the garden wall and climbed over it. Wilhelm did not want to hear about the whole affair until Mignon came in hastily and assured him the captive was the blonde boy who had had the fight with the Equerry and the latter, who had recognized him, was at the present the principal force behind his being treated so harshly.

Wilhelm hurriedly bestirred himself and found preparations already underway in the palace courtyard, for the Count had a very great love for ceremony even in matters of this sort. Wilhelm intervened and requested that they halt since he knew the boy and had various things to present first in the boy's behalf. He found it difficult to get his ideas heard and at last received permission to speak alone with the boy. The latter assured him he knew nothing at all of any attack in which an actor was said to have been mistreated. The reason he had scouted about the palace and crept into it at night had been to look up Philine, whose bedroom he had identified and certainly would have found, had he not been picked up on his way. Out of loyalty to the troupe and generosity toward Philine, Wilhelm did not want to reveal the situation. He spoke with the Equerry and requested that he use his knowledge of the persons and the house to mediate and have the boy set free. "Before I let this lad be mistreated," he said, "I'll reveal everything that occurred over at the inn and what drew him here in the night. For your own honor you'll do best to give this matter a different turn, if it's possible."

The Equerry reflected, gave his promise, and actually did so. A small story was invented, that the boy had belonged to the troupe, had run away from it, but had desired to find it again and to be re-admitted to it. For this reason he had thought up the means of paying a nocturnal call on some of those he knew liked him. Moreover there was testimony that he had conducted himself well otherwise; the ladies joined in, and he was released.

Wilhelm took him in, and from now on he was the third person in the odd family that Wilhelm had regarded as his own for some time. The old man and Mignon accepted him in their midst as if he were well-known to them and all three now joined in serving their friend and protector attentively and pleasing him.

Chapter 9

Day by day Philine learned better how to ingratiate herself with the ladies. When alone together, their conversation usually concerned the men who came and went, and Wilhelm was not the last with whom they were concerned. Philine soon noticed that he interested the Bar-oness. The latter was annoyed that for some time he had obstinately removed himself from her friendship and kindness; she could not un-derstand how he could dare to be so insensitive and sullen in the face of them. Since Philine was induced to tell and talk much about him, it was natural that she soon began to talk about his theatrical talents and desired nothing so much as having the ladies see him on the stage. She added as a secret that he in truth was an actor, had performed with her troupe, yet now, however, although she did not know from what whim, was determined to not act again. As soon as the ladies had discovered this important secret, there was nothing for which they wished and desired more ardently than to see him on the stage. They could not rest until Philine promised to undertake negotiations, for which she begged most fervently that they not betray that she had re-vealed it. Since he had gone out of her way for a long time and never spoke to her, she requested the Baroness to create an occasion for her to approach him. It was arranged that he would be summoned as though the ladies wished to talk with him; they would not be present at first and Philine would appear in the room instead of them. The Baroness was satisfied with the proposal and Philine even more so, for although she was serious in accommodating the ladies, for her it was much more a matter of working in her own behalf and of return-ing this unfriendly creature to better ways.

The plan was executed, and Wilhelm to his great astonishment found Philine in the room instead of the Baroness. She met him with a certain dignified openness which she had been practicing. First she joked with him about the good fortune which had pursued him and, as she had noticed, had brought him here. Then she upbraided him in a pleasant way for his conduct toward her, went on to break out in accusations, blaming herself for deserving how he treated her. She gave such an honest description of her condition, which she called her former one, admitted everything and added that she would have to hate herself if she did not feel that she could change and be worthy of his friendship.

Wilhelm was struck by this speech. He had too little experience of the world to know that it is specifically the quite frivolous and incorrigible who accuse themselves most energetically, acknowledge their flaws most openly and repent, although they do not have the slightest power within themselves to retreat from the path along which an omnipotent nature draws them. When she finally found him somewhat softened, she brought forth her request when she said to him that if he didn't take care of the theater, if he didn't perform in certain plays, they would not be able to survive another week. She put it to him as lightly and gracefully as she was able; however, she was not able to wrest a promise from him, and ultimately had to console herself with a general consent.

Chapter 10

Wilhelm had scarcely read a few plays by Shakespeare when the effect they had on him became so great that he was not able to continue with them. His whole soul began to stir. He sought an opportunity to speak with Jarno and could not thank him enough for the joy he had provided him. "I saw in advance," replied the latter, "that you would not remain insensitive to the splendors of the most extraordinary, most wonderful of all writers."

"Yes," Wilhelm cried out, "I can't recall that a book, a person, or any circumstance of my life ever had so great an effect on me as did the precious plays which I've become acquainted with through your generosity. They seem to be the work of a heavenly genius who draws near to men in order to let them become acquainted with him in the gentlest possible way. They are not fiction; a person believes he is standing before the opened, frightful books of fate through which the storm wind of the active life blows, tossing the pages this way and that with force. I am equally amazed at their strength and delicacy, at their violence and calm, and I'm so unsettled that I simply await with yearning the time when I'll find myself in a condition to read further."

"Bravo!" said Jarno as he extended his hand to our friend and shook his. "That's what I wanted, and the consequences I hope for will surely follow."

"I wish I could reveal to you," replied Wilhelm, "everything that's happening within me at present! Every premonition I've ever felt concerning humankind and its fate, which have accompanied me from youth on, though I was unaware of it, and through which the people whom I met in life and the events I and others were subjected to, gradually seemed as familiar as old acquaintances. These premonitions I find as if fulfilled and carried out in Shakespeare's plays. It seems as if he revealed all riddles to us without anyone's being able to say just what the word is for solving them. His people seem to be natural human beings, yet they are not. These most mysterious and fabricated people of nature behave before us in his works as if they were clocks whose dials and casings had been fashioned from crystal. As was intended, they indicate the course of the hours, yet one can at the same time recognize the gears and springs which drive them. The few glimpses I've had into Shakespeare's world encourage me more than anything else to move forward more quickly in the real world, to take part in the flood of fates which are imposed on it. One day, should I be so lucky, I would scoop a few gobletfuls from the mighty sea of True Nature and, like that great Englishman, bestow them upon the thirsting public of my homeland."

"How this attitude I find in you pleases me!" replied Jarno and laid his hand on the emotional young man's shoulder. "Don't abandon your plan, and hasten to make good use of the years which are granted to you. I haven't yet asked how you happened into this troupe for which you cannot have been born or trained. I do hope and observe that you yearn to be free of it. I know nothing of your family or its circumstances; think about what you want to confide to me. But I can tell you this much: The times of war in which we live can bring a quick change of fortune. If you choose to put your strength and talents in our service and don't shy away from work and, in time of need, danger, then I just now have an opportunity to put you in a position, which, if you hold it for a while, you shall not regret."

Wilhelm could not sufficiently express his gratitude and was willing to relate the entire story of his life to his friend and protector. "Just consider what I've told you," the latter said. "Give me your answer at an appropriate time and put your trust in me. I assure you, it's been incomprehensible to me how you could have made common cause with such people up till now. I've often observed with disgust and irritation how you, simply in order to live to some small extent, have had to hang your heart on a wandering minstrel and a foolish, hermaphroditic creature."

It was fortunate that Jarno hastened away after these words, otherwise our friend's dismay would have grown even greater in his presence. He had scarcely ever found anything so insufferable as to see those human beings who most interested him at this time treated so repugnantly, and this from the mouth of a man whom he esteemed, in whom he had good reason to have confidence. He grew furious to his very depths and hastened to find a quiet place. There he broke out in reproaches against himself for having been able for even one moment to not recognize and remember Jarno's hardhearted coldness which shone from his eyes and spoke in all his gestures. "No," he exclaimed, "you just imagine, you degenerate sophisticate, that you could be someone's friend! Everything you offer me isn't worth as much as the emotion that binds me to these unfortunates. What luck that I learned in time what I would have to expect from you!" He wrapped Mignon, who was just coming toward him, in his arms and called out, "No, nothing shall separate us, you good, little creature! What seems clever in this world is not capable of making me abandon you, nor forgetting what I owe you." The child, whose passionate caresses he customarily rejected, was delighted at this unexpected expression of tenderness and clung so to him that ultimately he was able to free himself only with force.

From this time on he paid more attention to Jarno's actions, of which he could not approve at all. Indeed many things occurred that displeased him completely. Thus, for example, he had a strong suspicion that Jarno had composed the poem about the Baron, for which the poor pedant had had to pay so dearly. In Wilhelm's presence he had even joked about this occurrence, and our friend regarded it as the mark of a seriously rotten heart to make fun of an innocent person whose suffering he himself had caused and not to think of compensation or making amends. Wilhelm would have liked to do this himself, for through a very odd accident he had come onto the trail of the perpetrators of that nocturnal attack. Up to this time it had been kept from him that some young officers spent whole nights merrily in the lower hall of the old castle with some of the actors and actresses. One morning, after rising early as was his habit, he came by chance into the room and found the young gentlemen about to begin preparing for the day in a very unusual fashion. They had grated chalk into a basin of water and were using a brush to spread the paste on their vests and leggings without first removing them, thereby restoring the neatness of their uniforms in the quickest possible manner. The schoolmaster's coat with its stains and white dust occurred to our fiend, who was surprised by these activities; his suspicion increased when he learned that several relatives of the Baron were among the group. He was about to inform the Count of this when the army's marching orders silenced every other concern.

Chapter 11

The more things went pleasantly for the troupe and the better the food and drink they received, the more their true nature revealed itself, and not to their advantage. In addition to complete room and board, they received a certain something each week. Since they needed nothing for the moment, they always had some money in their pockets and in their presumption scarcely knew how to behave. The prudent Melina used the bit of cash left for him to outfit himself decently. He bought some clothes from the Count's valet and was able to clothe himself quite smartly from head to foot.

Unfortunately for all of them, the army was compelled to move forward and leave the area. The Prince made preparations for departure and since he proved to be very generous in the castle, the Baroness managed to arrange things so that a golden watch was marked for Wilhelm, which to be sure was not of great value but was meant as a token of appreciation for the prolog that Wilhelm had written in honor of the Prince. The Baroness was able to bestow it on him herself and in so doing graciously establish the importance of her friendship. Jarno sent for him several times before the departure and looked him up, but he had firmly resolved to avoid the heartless man of the world. The Prince departed and the castle became empty.

Some of the troupe now actually had the thought they would be moved from the old castle to the new and be assigned better and more comfortable rooms. How greatly were they thus disappointed when it was announced to them that after a week had passed they were to move out of this paradise.

Philine did everything possible during this time to bring our hero onto the stage once again, but in vain. In lieu thereof she saw to it that he had to give some dramatic readings, at which he conducted himself quite well and reaffirmed the favor of the ladies. Upon leaving he received undeniable proof of this when they offered him a purse, which they had knit themselves, containing thirty Dukaten. A part of this sum had been assigned to him by the lord of the manor, to which, because it seemed too small, the ladies had added something from their own purse. He obstinately rejected this offer when it was made and finally Philine interceded, bowed coyly, and took the purse from the Baroness' hand. "I must thank you, ladies, in his name," she said, "and become his treasurer for the future. On our journey he so generously spent his money on us that I regard myself as obliged to look out for him now."

There was joking about this idea. The Countess was rummaging in her desk, and Philine, who had noted that she was not disinclined to Wilhelm and that sometimes a childlike desire to give away everything came over her, very easily and with humorous brazenness brought things to the point that the lady gave him in addition a gold case, a pretty ring, and some other nice things of value. At each of his refusals, Philine tucked them away with a teasing remark and greatly amused the ladies while she plundered them.

Wilhelm, for whom this was too much, took his leave in order to make his own arrangements for travel. Philine soon followed him into the castle where she found him in some embarrassment as to how he would pack his clothing and gear, for he had generously ceded his trunk to Madame Melina, whose wardrobe had increased greatly during her stay, thanks to the generosity of the nobles. When he turned his back, Philine immediately took the best items and with the help of the blonde, blue-eyed rascal, who stood at her every beck and call, carried most of his possessions into the new castle and sent word she would pack everything in her trunk. She could easily do this, for the Equerry had taken care of her not only through numerous gifts, but also by acquiring a splendid chest for her so that she could carry away everything most safely and soundly. Wilhelm, to whom no favor from her was welcome, confronted her with indignation, whereby he achieved nothing save being laughed at by her and threatened with an embrace if he did not calm himself. Thus he had to let the mad creature prevail and deem himself fortunate when she otherwise left him in peace.

The question now arose how they would travel, what route they would take, and how amid the dangerous military actions they could safely reach H**, to which they decided to continue their journey. The greater part of their concerns had already been lifted by the Count himself, for he had calculated exactly how far he could allow them to travel with his own people. He had laid out their itinerary from place to place and obtained a pass for them from the Prince that would let them pass safely through the rear guard. He explained this plan to the director and obtained his promise that it would be followed precisely.

The castle grew emptier and emptier, the day the Count had designated for his own departure arrived, and the troupe had to leave as well. This was hard for them, for they could remember no happier days in all their lives. However, since they all had received gifts and were traveling off with acceptably full purses, the greater part left in the hope of being able to acquire a similarly good life somewhere else. The Equerry tenderly said farewell to Philine, the Secretary amiably to all of them, and thus they again set off on a journey with no actual prospect of a place to stay, but with all the more certainty of their own superiority and of a worth that had very just claims to being respected everywhere.

Chapter 12

Since our readers in any case might have complained here or there about all too extensive detail, it would be irresponsible to entertain them again with all the adventures and events to which our troupe was exposed. Rather we shall leap over many a hill and many a valley, over or through which they were dragged in foul weather, and look in on them at an inn where they lodged in order to discuss new wagons and horses and to give themselves a treat. Each did this in his own fashion, and it was truly striking to observe how they again broke up into small groups at different tables and, according to their quite different tastes, had themselves served all sorts of boiled and roasted meats.

Right at the outset of the journey from the castle, Melina tried to make them understand that each was responsible for his own expenses on the road. To be sure, he had assumed the role of director up till now, but only in order to lend validity to the troupe; moreover, what he had received from the Count had been divided with each receiving his share. To pool their money now was not advisable. If each paid for himself, he would have the choice of how he wished to live. All were well satisfied with this arrangement since each remained master of his own wealth, and Melina very wisely abandoned the post of director in the moment it could have become a burden for him.

Meanwhile Wilhelm was in the best of spirits. By chance he had read in Shakespeare's *Henry IV* the story of how a prince spends a period of time in low or even bad company and, in spite of his noble nature, delights in their sensual crudity, indecency, and foolishness. Thus he had an ideal to which he could compare his present condition and this extraordinarily facilitated the self-deceit to which he felt drawn almost irresistibly. He began to consider his clothing and found that a short vest, over which one could throw a coat in case of need, was a far more appropriate outfit than the usual one. Thus he adopted one and, because he often went on foot during the journey, rather wide pants and a pair of laced boots. It wasn't long until he appeared with a sash wound about his torso, wearing it at first with the excuse that it kept his stomach warm. On the other hand, he freed his throat from the tyranny of a kerchief and had some strips of muslin attached to the shirt as ruffles, which, however, since they were cut rather wide, looked very much like a collar. A round hat with a brightly colored band and a feather brought this splendor to perfection. In sum he appeared in the figure such as we saw first with a number of Göttingen students imitating Hamlet and then with an entire nation at the command of their king.[51] Everyone found this outfit especially handsome and the ladies in particular assured him how well it suited him. Philine acted as though she were madly in love with it, which didn't hurt her in his opinion.

Our friend, who now treated the others in Prince Hal's manner according to how they conducted themselves, soon developed a taste for initiating and instigating some mad pranks and was of the most pleasant, liveliest, and most courteous humor. On several occasions they neglected their theatrical rehearsals, rapiers were rummaged up, they fenced and roughhoused, and with happy hearts enjoyed in full measure the acceptable wine they had found. All sorts of disorder resulted from this style of living. Philine lay in wait for her coy hero and my fair readers would have had to worry for the morals of their friend, had not a fortunate star turned his thoughts in a different direction.

Chapter 13

One of the favorite entertainments with which they amused themselves was an improvised play in which they imitated and caricatured their previous patrons and benefactors. Some of them had noted quite well the mannerisms of various respectable persons and their imitation of these was received to great applause by the rest of the troupe. From the secret archive of her experiences, Philine produced some special professions of love which had been delivered to her. When Wilhelm scolded her for this, the cleverest member of the troupe spoke up and responded, "They paid and fed us for our performance; I don't know how their conduct otherwise deserves any special consideration." These words were the signal at which each of them began to complain of how little respect they had been shown, how greatly they had been neglected. They made fun of the conduct of the upper

---

[51] Swedish students at the university in Göttingen affected such an outfit. In 1784 it won a competition sponsored by King Olaf III to find a national garb for Sweden.

classes even among themselves and, growing ever more bitter and unjust, of their pursuits which wasted so much time.

"You think highly of yourselves," replied Wilhelm, "and because there's much that's true in your observations, you don't notice the mistake you make by observing these persons and their actions from too low a viewpoint. I also can't say that I was particularly edified at the castle, yet I had the opportunity to correct certain ideas, for which I am indebted to knowledgeable friends. Persons who through their birth are placed in an elevated position in human society and for whom inherited wealth creates a perfect ease in their existence, who, if I may express myself so, are provided comfortably and generously with all the amenities of humanity, usually become accustomed to regarding these properties as that which is first and most important. They lose the concept of the worth of a humanity endowed by Nature alone. Not only their conduct toward their inferiors, but also their conduct among one another is measured by externals: they gladly allow each person to distinguish himself through his title, rank, wealth, clothes, and outfit, but not through his merits."

The entire troupe gave generous applause to these words and they began to relate various anecdotes which were meant to support his view most strongly.

"Don't scold them for this, much rather pity them, for they seldom experience a heightened sense of that happiness that we must recognize as the highest because it is taken from the inner riches of Nature. Only to us poor, who possess little or nothing, is it granted to enjoy the happiness of true friendship in rich measure. We can't lift up our loved ones through mercy, nor advance them through our favor, nor make them happy with gifts, for we have nothing but ourselves. We must yield our entire self and if it is to be of any value, assure our friend of its possession for ever. What happiness! What a pleasure for the giver and the receiver! What transcendental bliss this faith grants us! It gives to the transient circumstances of man, as it were, a heavenly certainty. This is what constitutes our entire happiness and is the principal capital of our wealth."

During these words Mignon had approached him, wound her slender arms about him, and remained standing with her small head beneath his breast. He laid his hand upon the child's head and continued. "How easy it is for a great man to win men's spirits and claim their hearts. A pleasant, relaxed, halfway human manner works wonders. And how many means does he have for firmly retaining these spirits once gained! Our lives are drabber, everything is much more difficult, and how natural it is that we place great value on it! What moving examples there are of loyal servants who sacrificed themselves for their masters! How beautifully Shakespeare described them for us! In such cases I see loyalty as the attempt of a noble soul to become the equal of a greater one. Through sustained fidelity and love, the servant becomes the equal of his master, who otherwise would be justified in regarding him as a purchased and despised slave. And thus these virtues are only for the lower classes. The comfort in being able to buy one's freedom easily is too great for man not to succumb to it. Indeed, in this sense I believe I can assert that a great man can surely have friends, but can't be a friend himself."

Mignon held him even more tightly.

"All right," replied a member of the troupe who was not exactly its finest, "we don't need their friendship and haven't ever asked for it, only they ought to understand more about the arts, which they claim to protect. When we were performing best, no one wanted to listen to us and generally they gave their attention and applause only to what was foolish and tasteless."

"If I eliminate what may have been malice or irony," replied Wilhelm, "then I think things go in art just as they do in love. How is the harried man of the world going to preserve the responsiveness which an artist must have if he is going to produce something perfect and which must envelop even the person who wishes to understand the work as the artist wishes and hopes? Believe me, my friends, talents are like virtue: one must practice them for their own sake or give them up entirely and indeed they both will not be recognized and rewarded except when they are pursued in private and almost fearfully like a dangerous secret.

"Meanwhile a fellow can die of hunger!" someone called from the corner.

"Not exactly," replied Wilhelm. "I've observed that as long as a person stays alive and busy, he'll always find food, even if it's not the most sumptuous. But what do you have to complain about? Just when things looked worst for us, weren't we unexpectedly taken in and treated well? And now, when we still lack nothing, does it occur to us to do something to keep in practice and to strive to some degree for a kind of perfection in our art? We're pursuing unrelated things and like school children we immediately get rid of anything that could remind us of our lessons."

"Indeed," said Philine, "that's true and undeniable. Do you hear it striking six? Let's pick out a play and perform it right here and now. Everyone must do his best as if he were standing before the largest audience."

They did not take long to decide, some whistled the music, everyone quickly recalled his role, they began and performed the play through with great attentiveness and beyond the expectations of everyone. Even Wilhelm, the audience, more than once could not keep from applauding and calling out "Bravo!" When they had ended, they all felt a great satisfaction, partially because of time well spent, partially because everyone could be exceptionally satisfied with himself. Wilhelm grew expansive in their praise, their conversation was relaxed and happy.

"You can see," our friend exclaimed, "how far we could come if we continued this practice, what satisfaction we'd feel in doing so. I've often compared musicians to actors. The former can not be more delighted than when they sit down to practice together. What pains they take to tune their instruments harmoniously, to express the strength or delicacy of a note as is appropriate to the voice assigned it. Only the most untalented would believe he was doing himself credit by an overly loud accompaniment to another's solo. Everyone is concerned with the composer's intention and for his part contributes everything he can, be that small or great, to express it. Shouldn't actors be able to attempt this among themselves, to find their greatest happiness and pleasure in pleasing one another, and to treasure applause only to the extent it would be granted to a tasteful performance that they had guaranteed among themselves, so to speak?

"All the pettiness that debases this noble art to the level of a trade will disappear, people will no longer fight about roles nor try to steal scenes, each will satisfy his part and be rewarded from even the slightest one. How happy the director of such an association would have to deem himself. He would have to know his business and make each person aware of his capabilities, assign himself only those roles he is capable of, assume no exclusive right to this or that type of roles, just as no one else would be allowed to. Everyone would end up where his nature led him and practice had confirmed him, and in this position he would be readily acknowledged by everyone.

"To be sure, among good people the republican form of government is the best and only one. If I had anything to say about such an arrangement, the director's office would be rotated and he would be assisted by a kind of small senate."

"What's keeping us from making a try at something like that right now?" they exclaimed. "We're all free men, we have no ties and no obligations. Let's form this ideal republic at least for the journey which awaits us!"

"It will be a nation on the move," someone said. "At least we won't have any border conflicts."

They got down to business immediately. Wilhelm was elected the first director, the senate was appointed with women having seats and a voice in it. Laws were proposed, rejected, and approved. Time passed unnoticed and they believed they had never spent it so pleasantly.

Chapter 14

It had been difficult in the small town to assemble as many horses as were necessary for transporting the troupe and its effects. Finally everything was ready, only a new obstacle appeared. A report came in that a body of marauding soldiers had been seen in the area through which their route led. This unexpected news made everyone wary even though the news was uncertain and ambiguous, and from the position of the armies it seemed almost impossible that a hostile corps could have slipped through. Everyone was busy describing to the troupe in lurid terms the danger which awaited them and suggesting a different route. Most of them were made quite fearful and when in accordance with the rules of the new republic the senate was convened to take counsel and to make a decision, they were almost unanimously of the opinion that they had to avoid such a misfortune and choose a different path.

Only Wilhelm was not so seized by fear that he would readily abandon a plan that had been conceived after much deliberation. Rather he tried to encourage them, and his arguments were manly and convincing. "It's still only a rumor," he said, "and we know how many of those arise in time of war. Many say that such a situation is highly improbable and almost impossible. Are we supposed to be guided in so important a matter by unconfirmed rumors? The route the Count gave us and for which our pass is valid is the shortest one, and on it we'll find the best roads. It leads us first to a respectable city where we'll either find a good troupe or appear ourselves and earn something. We'll avoid great difficulties and gain time and money. If we take the road recommended by a frightened populace, one I've inquired about in detail, it will lead us on so great a detour and involve us with such bad roads that I'm not sure we'd find our way out and reach our destination before bad weather arrives."

He said much more and presented the matter to them from so many advantageous aspects that their fear was reduced and their courage increased. "Perhaps it is a corps of the friendly army, in which case the pass we have will protect us sufficiently. If they are regular troops of the enemy, we'll also have little to worry about for I can't imagine what travelers have to do with a struggle among kings. If we're attacked by a troop of roaming rabble, it seems to me there are enough of us to teach them respect and to offer resistance that will surprise them."

This last speech easily won over the young actors. The ladies who found the proposal heroic and unusual also joined up, first of all Madame Melina, who in spite of her advanced pregnancy had not lost her innate spunk. Now the remaining men did not wish to be cowardly and there was no one who did not seem to approve these proposals wholeheartedly. They began to make arrangements for defending themselves in all eventualities They bought large hunting knives. Wilhelm acquired a saber and a pair of pistols. The young actor, whom we mentioned at the beginning of this Book and whom we shall call Laertes in the following, armed himself with a flintlock. Other old weapons were distributed among those remaining.

Thus they set off on their journey, although with some reluctance from the drivers. On the second day these men, who knew the area quite well, proposed a midday halt at a clearing in a hillside forest because although a village was near, it was situated poorly and they would also bypass a dangerous sunken road. In good weather they usually carried along fodder and halted at the indicated spot. Since the weather was fine, everyone readily accepted this proposal.

Wilhelm hastened ahead and the strange figure which he cut certainly would have taken aback anyone whom he met. In addition to the costume described above, there came a broad weapons belt over one shoulder that bore the saber. He had stuck a pair of pistols in his belt and thus he strode with quick and assured steps up into the forest. The troupe which accompanied him looked just as strange. Mignon ran behind him in her vest and likewise wore a hunting knife at her side, which at her passionate begging no one had been able to deny her when the troupe was arming itself. The blonde boy, who was also still with the troupe, carried Laertes' musket. The harpist preserved the most peaceable appearance; he stuck his long robe into his belt so that it would not interfere in his walking and he supported himself with a gnarled staff. His instrument had remained with the wagons.

After a climb that was not without difficulty, they easily found the indicated place, recognizing it by the beautiful beeches that surrounded and shaded it, by the spring which it held, and by its view into the distance. They took possession of it, rested in the shade, built a fire, and, singing, awaited the rest of the troupe. These gradually arrived and unanimously hailed the place, its surroundings, and the beautiful weather.

Chapter 15

If they had often had good and happy hours between four walls, here they were even more pleasant since the freedom of the sky and the beauty of the region elevated each spirit. No one could find anything more exquisite than spending one's life in so pleasant a spot. They envied the hunters, charcoal burners, and woodcutters whose professions tied them to these happy surroundings. Above all, however, they praised the wandering life of gypsies, who in blissful idleness were justified in enjoying all the adventurous delights of nature.

Meanwhile people had begun to boil potatoes, some pots stood by the fire and the troupe settled into various groups beneath the trees and by the shrubs. Their unusual clothing gave them a strange appearance and the weapons they carried with them only heightened this. The horses were being fed to one side, and if someone had taken the trouble to hide the coaches, the setting would have been perfect.

Wilhelm experienced an exquisite joy at the sight of this. He could imagine himself as leader of this party; he entertained himself with every aspect of this idea and developed it as poetically as possible. The mood of the troupe rose, they ate, drank, and rejoiced, and confessed to never having experienced more beautiful moments.

We cannot hide from the readers that this was the original scene, reproductions and imitations of which recently have been seen more often than enough in German theaters. The concept of sturdy vagabonds, noble robbers, generous gypsies, and all sorts of other idealized rabble owes its true origin to this setting which we have just depicted with some reluctance because it cannot help but be greatly annoying if one has no opportunity to make the public acquainted with the original before the copies have already removed all charm and novelty from the place.

With every moment their merriment grew. Wilhelm and Laertes reached for their rapiers and began to practice for the duel in which Hamlet reaches so tragic an end. They had proposed to perform the play among themselves, and the role of the Danish prince had been assigned to our friend. The others had formed a circle about them, they fought with great ardor and the interest of the observers grew with each thrust. Suddenly the troupe was thrown into great fear when from the nearby shrubbery a shot was heard and then a second one. When they looked around, they caught sight of armed men advancing toward the place where the horses were feeding not far from the heavily laden coaches.

A general scream arose from the women. Our heroes threw their rapiers away and reached for their sabers. They hastened toward the intruders and called for them to stop and explain what they were up to. When they were answered by a couple of shots from muskets, Wilhelm fired his pistols at the man who had climbed onto the wagon and was cutting the cords holding the baggage. He hit him since the man immediately fell down and Laertes also had not missed. They both drew their side arms and countered this boldness with flashing sabers as one group of the party charged toward them with curses and screaming, likewise firing some shots at them. Our young heroes conducted themselves valiantly; they called to their comrades, encouraging them to assist.

Soon, however, Wilhelm lost sight of this world and consciousness of what was happening. Wounded by a shot that struck him between breast and shoulder and benumbed by a cut that split his hat and penetrated almost to the skull, he fell to the ground and had to learn of the unfortunate end of the attack only later from the accounts of others.

When he again opened his eyes he found himself in a most unusual situation. The first thing he could make out through the mist that still obscured his view was Philine's face which bent down over his own. He was too weak to rise and when he braced himself to sit up, he found he had been lying in Philine's lap into which he sank back. She was sitting on the ground, had gently pressed against herself the head of the youth stretched before her, and created to the extent possible a gentle resting place within her arms. Mignon with unkempt bloody hair knelt at his feet, embracing them with many tears.

When Wilhelm looked at his bloodstained clothes, he asked with broken voice what had happened to him and the others. Philine asked him to remain calm. "The others are all in safety," she said. "No one but you and Laertes were wounded." She did not want to go on and simply begged him fervently to calm himself because she was afraid he might reopen his wounds, which were only lightly bound. He extended his hand to Mignon and inquired about the cause of the child's bloody hair. When this goodhearted creature saw him wounded and found nothing around her with which to stanch the blood, she had used her hair to stuff the wounds of her master and father but soon had had to abandon her vain attempt. Later he was bandaged with fungus and moss. Philine had given her neckerchief and apron for this.

Wilhelm noticed that Philine was sitting with her back against her trunk, which was still securely locked and apparently undamaged. He asked whether the others had also been so lucky as to retain their possessions. She answered this question with a shrug of her shoulders and a look onto the meadow where broken boxes, smashed chests, slashed valises, and a number of small implements lay scattered here and there. The site was devoid of people and the strange group we have described was alone in this solitude.

Wilhelm now learned more and more what he wanted to know. Those who could have provided opposition were easily frightened and overcome, a part of them fleeing, a part watching the attack with horror. The drivers had conducted themselves most bravely on account of the horses but finally were no longer able to defend themselves. Within a short time everything was completely plundered and dragged away. As soon as the fear for their lives was past the frightened travelers began to bewail their losses and hurried with all possible speed to the nearby village. They took the lightly wounded Laertes with them and rescued only a few scraps of their former treasures. The harpist had leaned his damaged instrument against a tree and also hastened to the village in order, if possible, to find a surgeon to aid his benefactor, who remained behind, having been left for dead.

Book 6

Chapter 1

OUR THREE UNFORTUNATE adventurers had remained hoping and waiting for a long time in the unusual situation in which we left them at the end of the preceding Book. No one hastened to their help, evening was coming on, Philine's indifference began to change into anxiety. Mignon ran back and forth and the child's impatience increased with each moment. Finally, when their wish was granted and people were drawing near, a new fright overcame them. They heard quite clearly a troop of horses coming up the road they had also taken. Their only thought was that it would be another party of uninvited guests, who were visiting the site of the skirmish to see what they might still glean. How pleasantly they were surprised when the first thing they caught sight of riding out of the bushes was a woman mounted on a gray, who was accompanied by an elderly gentleman and some cavaliers. Grooms and servants followed after.

Philine was wide-eyed in astonishment and was about to call and beg the fair Amazon for help when the latter turned her eyes toward the strange group in astonishment, immediately turned her mount, rode up, and came to a halt. She inquired keenly concerning the wounded man, whose rest in the lap of the frivolous Samaritan seemed to strike her as highly unusual.

"Is he your husband?" she asked Philine.

"He's only a good friend," the latter replied in a manner highly offensive to Wilhelm. He had fastened his eyes on the gentle, quiet, sympathetic face of the newcomer and believed he had never seen anything more charming. A large man's overcoat hid her figure from him. She had, so it seemed, borrowed this piece of clothing from one of her companions to counter the effect of the cool evening air.

Meanwhile the horsemen had also drawn nearer and some dismounted. The lady did likewise and asked with kind concern about all the circumstances of the attack the travelers had faced and about the wounds of the prostrate youth. Then she quickly turned about and walked with the old gentleman toward some wagons that came up the hill slowly and drew to a halt in the forest clearing.

After the young lady had stood a brief while by the door of one of the coaches and conversed with the newcomers, a squat man climbed out, whom she lead to our wounded hero. From the case he held and his leather instrument bag, one could soon recognize him to be a surgeon. His manner was brusque rather than captivating, yet his touch was light and his help welcome.

After careful probing, he explained there was no danger and that he would bandage the wounded man sufficiently to enable him to be carried to the nearest village. Everyone was concerned, the young lady most actively. "Just see," she said after she had walked back and forth a few times and had led up the old gentleman once again, "see what they've done to him. And he's suffering on our account!" The sufferer, who had overheard her, did not understand what she had meant. As if perturbed she walked back and forth. It seemed as though she could not tear her eyes away from the sight of the wounded man and yet as though she were afraid she might offend propriety if she were to stay at a time when they were, with some effort, beginning to undress him. The surgeon was just cutting open the left sleeve when the old gentleman came up and spoke of the necessity of resuming their route. Wilhelm had cast his eyes upon her and was so taken by her glances that he scarcely felt what was happening to him.

Philine had stood up in order to kiss the noblewoman's hand, and it was inwardly repugnant to our friend that so unchaste a creature should approach or indeed touch that noble nature. The lady asked Philine various things, which Wilhelm could not catch. Finally she turned to the old gentleman, who was still standing alongside in full composure, and said, "My dear uncle, may I be generous at your expense?" She immediately removed the overcoat and one saw she did so with the intent of giving it to the wounded and unclad man. Wilhelm, whom the healing glance of her eyes had held fast until now, was surprised by her beautiful figure when the overcoat was removed. She stepped closer to him and offered him the coat by gently spreading it over him. At this moment, when he wanted to open his mouth and bring forth a few words of gratitude, the forceful impression of her presence had such a strange effect on his already besieged senses that suddenly it seemed to him as though her head were surrounded by a halo of light which gradually spread about her entire image.

The surgeon moved him less gently when he struck the bullet which had not emerged and made preparations for removing it. The saint disappeared before the eyes of the fading man as he lost consciousness. When he came to, horsemen and vehicles, the fair lady and her escort had vanished.

Chapter 2

When our friend was bandaged and dressed, the surgeon hastened off just as a servant, whom the nobles had sent to the nearest village, came up with a number of peasants. From lopped off branches and interwoven brushwood they quickly prepared a litter, loaded the wounded man onto it, and gently carried him down the hill.

The harpist, who had also returned, helped them. The remaining people lugged Philine's heavy chest. She quietly followed carrying some bundles, and Mignon leaped before them or again to one side, peering with concern at her wounded protector. The latter lay quietly on his litter, wrapped in his warm greatcoat.

An electric warmth seemed to cross from the fine wool into his body, even providing him a most pleasant sensation. Even from his earliest childhood he could not recall so pleasant an impression as that which the beautiful possessor of the coat had made on him. He still saw the coat falling from her shoulders, her most noble figure standing radiantly before him, and his soul pursued the vanished woman into all regions of the earth.

Thus the procession arrived before the inn where most of the remaining troupe were, filled with despair at their losses. The single small parlor of the house was stuffed full with people. Some lay on straw, others had taken over the benches, some had squeezed behind the stove, and in a mean cubicle Frau Melina was awaiting her delivery, which fright and mistreatment threatened to hasten. When the new arrivals also wanted to enter and find room, a general grumbling arose. They were greeted with scorn and resentment, for people remembered only too well that on Wilhelm's advice and under his leadership they had undertaken the dangerous route and exposed themselves to this misfortune.

Everyone now put the blame on him for the miserable outcome. They opposed his entry at the door. They demanded that he seek a place elsewhere. To Philine they even said that it would do her no harm if she had to spend a night in the alley. And it might have turned out that way, had not the servant, who had received strict orders from his fair mistress to care for the abandoned people, mixed into the argument and summarily ended it.

With mighty curses and threats he assured them he would hurl them all out the door if they didn't squeeze together and make room for the new arrivals. They soon accommodated to this forceful threat. He prepared a bed for Wilhelm on a table, which he shoved into a corner. Philine had her chest placed next to it. Everyone made himself as small as possible, and the servant went away to see whether he couldn't find more comfortable quarters for the married couple (for which he took the two to be). Scarcely had he departed when the muttering again began to become audible and one reproach to follow the next. Everyone related what he had lost with references to the audacity which had caused them to surrender so much.

There was no lack of malicious joy in the wounds of our friend. There was no restraint shown in bitter scorn of Philine and in turning the manner in which she had saved her chest into a crime. From all kinds of allusions and invectives one could conclude that immediately after the defeat and plundering, she had consented to take a walk into the bushes with the leader of the group, who, in return, restored her possessions. Fun was had concerning the modest behavior and refusals that she had used to inflame the mustached leader and to extort so high a price from him. She did not answer, but simply clanked the large locks on her chest in order to reassure them of its presence, making them angrier and angrier, and to increase their anguish at their own losses.

Chapter 3

Although Wilhelm had grown weak from a serious loss of blood and severe pain, and had become gentle and passive after the appearance of the helpful angel, ultimately he could not repress his indignation at the hard and unjust comments that were continually restated by the unhappy troupe in the face of his silence. Finally he felt strong enough to sit up and make clear to them the indecency with which they tormented their friend and leader. Raising his bandaged eye to heaven and as he supporting himself with some effort, he began to speak.

"On account of the pain each of you must feel at your losses, I forgive you for insulting me when you should be pitying me, for resisting me and casting me from you at the first occasion when I might expect help from you. It never occurred to me to desire gratitude from you for any services or favors. Don't tempt me, don't compel me to go back and reconsider what I've done for you; this accounting would only be painful for me. Chance led me to you, circumstances and a secret inclination kept me among you. I've taken part in your work and in your pleasures. I've gladly supported you with my limited knowledge of the fair art which you practice, one in which I hope you will perfect yourselves and find happiness.

"If you now bitterly blame me for the misfortune that has befallen us, then you're not remembering that the original proposal to take this route came from others and was approved not by me alone, but by all of you. Had our journey reached a happy conclusion, each of you would praise himself for the good idea of suggesting this route, of preferring it. He would recall with joy our deliberations and his exercising his right to vote. Now you're making me solely responsible and forcing a guilt on me that I'd willingly accept if my inner consciousness didn't declare me innocent, if I couldn't appeal directly to yourselves as witnesses. If you have anything to say in reply, then present it properly and I'll be able to defend myself. If you have nothing factual to offer, then hold your peace and don't torment me now when I need rest."

Instead of any answer, the girls began anew to recite their losses amid tears. Melina was quite beside himself, for he had indeed sacrificed the most. He walked crazily back and forth in the narrow room, beat his head against the wall, cursed and reviled in a most unseemly manner, and when the midwife stepped out from the chamber and brought the news that his wife had delivered a stillborn child, he permitted himself the most violent outbursts of anger. In unanimous support of him, they howled, screamed, roared, and clamored.

Wilhelm, who was simultaneously seized by compassionate concern for their situation and by irritation at their base and petty manner of thinking, felt himself moved most deeply and, despite the weakness of his body, the entire strength of his soul came alive. He exclaimed, "I almost have to despise you, however lamentable you may be! No misfortune justifies us in burdening an innocent person with accusations. If I've had part in this misstep, then I've lost my share, too. I'm lying here wounded, and if the troupe has lost, then no small part of this loss is also mine. You, Herr Melina, owed me for whatever costumes were stolen, whatever sets were ruined, and I herewith declare you completely free of this obligation."

Melina professed little satisfaction with this declaration, for he remembered the beautiful clothes from the Count's wardrobe that looked so good on him, the fashionable buckles, the watch, the hats, the cash, and many another lovely thing that had been lost. The others, who were glancing with envy at Philine's chest, made the point quite rudely that he had not done badly by associating with this beauty and rescuing his possessions through her good fortune.

"Do you believe," he exclaimed, "I want to keep something apart and for myself as long as you are in want? And is this indeed the first time I've honestly shared things with you in time of need? Let someone open the chest and whatever is mine, I'll dispose for common need."

"It is *my* chest," said Philine, "and I won't open it until I choose to. The few rags you gave me to keep can't go far, even if they were sold to the most honest Jews. Think of yourself and about what your recovery can cost, about what you may encounter in a foreign land."

"Philine," replied Wilhelm, "you won't keep from me anything that's mine, and I know roughly how far it will go. To be sure, it's not much, but still enough to save us from our predicament. But within man there's more than just cash with which he can assist his friends. And whatever is any way left for me shall be devoted to those unfortunates who surely will regret their present conduct when they come to their senses. Indeed," he continued, "I feel you are in need and whatever I possess I shall give to you if you still have some confidence in me, if I still deserve it from the time when we were together! Accept this promise from me as consolation for this moment! Who will receive it in the name of all of you?"

Here he stretched out his hand and cried, "Yes, I say to you I shan't depart from here, shan't leave here until each person has gained twice or thrice what he lost, until you have completely forgotten the situation in which, through whoever's fault it may be, you now find yourselves and have exchanged it for a happier one." He extended his hand and no one wanted to take it. "I promise it once again," he exclaimed as he sank back onto his pillow.

Everything was quiet, they were ashamed but not consoled, and Philine sat on her chest, cracking open some nuts that she had found in her pocket.

Chapter 4

The servant came back with some people and made preparations for removing the wounded man. He had persuaded the local preacher to take in the stranger and to care for him. He had Philine's chest brought along and found it quite natural that she came along too. Mignon joined the group, the invalid was brought into the parsonage, and a wide double bed was assigned to him, which had long served as a bed for guests or special friends. Here they noticed that his wound had opened and bled heavily. New bandages had to be found. The sick man fell into a fever which grew worse the further the night advanced. Philine attended him loyally, and when exhaustion overcame her, the harpist relieved her. Mignon had fallen asleep in the corner with the best intention of keeping watch.

On the following morning, when the patient had recovered somewhat, he desired to speak with the servant, who, he was told, was only waiting for him to awaken before riding off. He learned from this person that the respectable people who had come to his aid had left their estates to avoid the turmoil of war and to move into safer regions. He mentioned the names of the elderly gentleman, his niece, and of the place where they planned to stay in the future. He explained to Wilhelm how the young lady had given him orders to see to the abandoned people. He had fetched a surgeon from the nearby town and now, as soon as he knew the sick man had been properly bandaged, he wished to mount and ride after his masters. The entrance of the surgeon interrupted the emotional expressions of gratitude Wilhelm had begun to deliver to the servant. The former found the wound to be not dangerous, the contusion on his head to be of no consequence; he only ordered expressly that the patient remain quiet and wait things out.

After the servant had ridden off, Philine, who came in immediately, related that he had left behind for her a purse with twenty Louisdor and had ordered her most earnestly to see to the patient. She accepted that all the more willingly when the stranger took her for Wilhelm's wife, in which role she now introduced herself to him. She immediately brought him tea and made all the arrangements appropriate to a nurse.

"Philine," said Wilhelm, "I'm already greatly indebted to you from this misfortune which befell us and I wouldn't want to see my indebtedness to you increased. I'm troubled as long as you're around me, for I don't know how I can repay you. Give me my things you've rescued in your chest; join the rest of the troupe; find different lodgings; accept my gratitude and the golden watch as a small token, but leave me. Your presence disturbs me more than you can believe."

She laughed to his face when he was done. "You're a fool," she said. "You'll never get smart. I know better what's good for you. I'm going to stay, I won't stir from the spot. I've never counted on men's gratitude and thus not on yours. And if I like you, how does that concern you?"

She had soon charmed the pastor and his family since she was always cheerful, gave a present to everyone, knew how to tailor her comments to each of them, and all the while did what she wanted to do.

Wilhelm did not suffer from this. The surgeon, an honest and skillful man, soon put him on the road to recovery. Little would be left for us to do in this regard if new cares had not arisen from other quarters and new worries threatened.

Chapter 5

Mignon had been very quiet for some days, and when she was questioned, she finally confessed that her right arm was dislocated. "You have your impulsiveness to thank for that," said Philine, who related how during the fighting the child had drawn her dagger when she saw her friend in danger, had bravely slashed away at the freebooters until finally one of them seized her by the arm and hurled her aside. They scolded her for not having revealed her injury earlier although they saw readily that it had happened in order not to make her gender known to the surgeon, who had always taken her for a boy. She was tended to and now had to wear her arm in a sling.

That was all the more unpleasant for her since the greatest part of his care and nursing had to be left to Philine, and the happy sinner found this all the more to her liking.

One morning, when Wilhelm awoke, he found himself in unusual proximity to her. In sleeping on his broad bed he had rolled completely to the far side. Philine lay stretched diagonally across the near side, apparently having fallen asleep on his bed while sitting and reading. A book had dropped from her hand; she had sunk back with her head near his breast, across which her blond, untied hair spread like a river. The disarray of sleep heightened her charms more than art or intent could. A childish, smiling peace hovered over her face. He looked at her for a while and seemed to be upbraiding himself for his pleasure in gazing at her. Indeed, we don't know whether he blessed or cursed his current situation which did not allow him even the slightest movement. He sought to make a small attempt but did it clumsily, for she soon stirred and as she awakened, he gently closed his eyes so as not to admit to her he had found her so. Meanwhile he could not refrain from gazing at her through half-closed eyelids as she straightened her hair and clothing and departed in order to inquire about breakfast.

At various times Wilhelm had had inquiries made concerning Frau Melina and the rest of the troupe, and his messenger had always been met rudely. "It's no wonder," said Philine, "for I hear the servant also brought them money. When it's been used up, they'll be around soon enough." And in fact Melina did come a few days later and with apparent coldness stated that he was thinking of departing with the troupe. Without much ado he demanded an advance from Wilhelm, which he would immediately repay as soon as they were together again in H**.

Wilhelm consented to the demand, and against her will Philine had to produce her purse. She grew irritated when Wilhelm demanded of her that she set off with the troupe, and Melina on the other hand assured them he would not take her along. Her even temper left her but a moment, for she quickly recovered and said jokingly, "I don't need either of you and I'll find my own way soon enough."

Gradually a few people came to bid Wilhelm farewell, and when he inquired about the carefree lad whom we first met in the guise of a wig maker, he learned that he had disappeared from the scene of the skirmish and had not been seen again. The departure of the troupe was delayed for a few days because first one thing, then another was lacking.

One morning Mignon brought to Wilhelm in his bed the news that Philine had departed in the night. She had neatly piled everything belonging to him in the adjoining room. In the house they were saying that when the post carriage passed this morning, she had had it stopped, loaded her chest on it, and left with it. He had cause to be happy at being free of her, nor did he reflect long about it. He was much more concerned with his thoughts and fancies which were occupying him more than ever in a most pleasant manner.

He continually recalled that event which had left such an indelible impression on his spirit. He saw the beautiful Amazon come riding out of the bushes, approach him, dismount, try to help, and walk back and forth. He saw the enveloping coat fall from her shoulders, her face and her figure glow and then disappear. His imagination repeated the scene a thousand times, a thousand times he recalled the sound of her sweet voice. Just as often did he envy Philine, who had kissed her hand, and just as often he would have regarded this story as a dream, a fairy tale, if the coat had not remained behind which guaranteed the certainty of this phenomenon.

The greatest care for this garment was combined with the most fervent desire to wear it. Every morning, as soon as he arose, he threw it about him and was concerned all day long that it might be stained or something else happen to it.

The troupe departed, and he let them go under the excuse that he must not yet dare venture to travel. In his heart, however, he was of a quite different mind.

The two had remained with him: the harpist, whom he needed, and Mignon, whom he could not do without.

Chapter 6

He had thought out a plan. First he wanted to search out the helpful nobles in order to express his gratitude. Then he would follow after the wandering troupe in order to obtain them, as promised, the best possible situations with his friend, the director in H**. His desire to see his rescuer once again grew with every day and he finally decided to begin his journey as soon as possible. He went to the pastor for advice as to where the place lay that the noble family had chosen for its seat during the war and whether one might not perhaps find some news concerning them. The preacher, who was well educated, leafed through Büsching's geography,[52] examined the map, checked genealogical handbooks, and could find neither the name of the place in all the areas of Lower Saxony nor a similar family name among the entire aristocracy of the Empire.

Wilhelm grew more and more restless the longer it lasted, and his restlessness finally changed into dismay when the harpist revealed to him that he had reason to believe the servant had concealed the true name of the family, for whatever reason, and given them a false one. The old man was assigned to follow their trail but this allowed them hope for only a few days. He returned and brought no satisfying news.

In the general turmoil of the war, people in the surrounding villages had paid scant attention to a few horsemen more or less. The party, so it seemed, had also covered a good stretch more that evening so that the old envoy could find no trace of them. Finally, because he was in danger of being taken for a Jew and a spy, he had to turn back and appear before his friend and master with no olive branch.[53] In order to remove all suspicion of negligence from himself, he gave a precise account of how he had followed his assignment. He sought in every way to ease Wilhelm's dejection, recalled in his mind what he had learned from that servant, and recounted every inference the latter's remarks had occasioned. Wilhelm was little edified by this because from all of it nothing of what he wished to know could be guessed or concluded. One single point was important to him, for guided by it he could interpret some puzzling remarks made by the vanished beauty.

[52] Anton Friedrich Büsching, *Neue Erdbeschreibung* (New Description of the Earth), 15 Parts, Hamburg, 1754-1792.

[53] Cf. Genesis, 8.

The thievish band actually had not lain in wait for the poor wandering troupe, but for the nobles, concerning whose train they had received news. Given the disposition of troops in that theater of war, in order to attack them at that particular spot they must have made highly unusual and forced marches if indeed they were truly soldiers, a point that was still in doubt. Fortunately for the respectable and rich, the common and poor arrived at the clearing first and suffered the fate that had been prepared for the former. This is what the words of the young lady referred to, which Wilhelm still remembered quite well. If he now could be content and happy that some provident spirit had destined him to be the sacrifice needed for saving a perfect mortal, then on the other hand he was near despair at not finding her, not seeing her again, and at least for the moment he had to abandon completely this beautiful hope.

Chapter 7

For some days Wilhelm felt Philine's absence; in her he had lost a loyal nurse and cheerful company and he was now no longer accustomed to being alone. Mignon sought to fill this gap as well as possible, for when that frivolous beauty with her efforts and kindnesses had, as it were, won the wounded man over, the small girl had withdrawn and remained quietly by herself. Now, however, when the field was again clear, the entire vitality with which she was devoted to our friend was revealed; she was eager to serve him and be cheerful to entertain him. And often whenever he wanted to read or think to himself, she interrupted him with questions such as whether he had parents and siblings and how it looked in his home. He began to reply and while he satisfied the child's request, during his narration concern was reawakened about the condition of his relatives, whom he had not seen for so long.

And now there stirred within him the old struggle. He berated himself and his unpardonable procrastination in not having written home and sent word of himself. He vowed to do it, and again put it off.

A return to his family was unthinkable. He had things to do in H**. Feeling himself still obligated to the poorly led troupe, he wanted to wait for a letter from Melina. He reflected, meditated, and found a hundred reasons for going to where his heart was driving him. And thus he neglected natural, innate duties by regarding arbitrary and self-imposed ones as sacred.

But many a thing might also be said to excuse him; we especially must not forget that he was quietly seeking the trail of Mariane, whom he hoped perhaps to meet in H**. For a long time we have not mentioned this strand which ran through his whole existence. He scarcely admitted to himself the secret yearning to find her again, to hold her in his arms, and to beg her to forgive his severity. His first dreams, his hopes reawakened within him from time to time, and the most passionate memories bound him once more to the theater, indeed even to our poor troupe. Only his mind had taken a different tack since the appearance of that angel who had disappeared too soon. To approach her, as he passionately wished to do, would mean stepping out of the circumstances in which he found himself, and a conflicting desire pulled him from one world into the other.

To divert his mind, to give his emotions a new turn, nothing was more effective than the writings of Shakespeare, to which he devoted himself more and more from day to day. Especially *Hamlet* had drawn his attention.

In the preceding Book we already saw him studying the role of the Prince. Naturally he began with the most powerful passages, the soliloquies, and those scenes where strength of the soul, exaltation, and vitality have free play and a free, noble spirit can reveal itself in passionate expressiveness. Also he was inclined to accept the burden of deep melancholy, and the practicing of the role entwined itself in his lonely life to the extent that finally he and Hamlet began to become a single person.

Finally, when he had worked through the individual passages sufficiently, he undertook the whole work in sequence, and then many of them no longer seemed to fit. First the character contradicted itself, then his statements contradicted each other, and our friend found it almost impossible to find one tone in which the role could be played with all its variations and shadings. He labored in vain for a long time in this labyrinth until he finally found a path on which he hoped to reach his goal. Now he went through the play simply with the intent of noting what of Hamlet's character before the death of his father might reveal itself as a track, and he soon believed he had found it.

Gently and nobly born, the royal flower grew up amid the direct influences of majesty. The concepts of what is right and of royal dignity, the feeling of what is good and proper and requisite to the high station of his birth developed simultaneously within him. He was a prince, a born prince, and wished to rule solely in order that the good man might be good without impediment. Pleasing of figure, by nature well-mannered, cordially courteous, the model of youth and the delight of the world, with no dominating passion whatever, his love for Ophelia was a quiet premonition of his needs, and his ardor in knightly exercises was heightened by the praise given to a rival. He

recognized the just and knew how to esteem the calm which an upright spirit enjoys at the honest bosom of a friend. Up to a certain
point he had learned to recognize and value the good and the beautiful in the arts and sciences. Vulgarity was repugnant to him, and if
hate could emerge in his tender soul then it was only just enough to
despise fickle, false, miserable courtiers and to play with them deri-
sively.

Calm in his being, simple in his deportment, neither comfortable in
idleness nor all too desirous of employment, half spoiled by academic
routine, more cheerful from whim than from the heart, a good companion, obliging, modest, concerned, and preferring to forget an insult
to himself before one made to that which is right, good, and honest.

After Wilhelm had assembled these traits and documented them
with passages, the concept grew much easier for him, only he could
see in advance that in the future he would have to treat a great part of
the passages differently from the way he had recited them up till now.

During his work evening had fallen, and unnoticed by him the image of the benevolent beauty again hovered before his spirit. He in-
dulged in sweet visions, and a yearning overcame him that he had
never before felt in his bosom.

Mignon and the old man had been singing to the harp for some
time in the next room. Finally an unfamiliar melody drew our friend's
attention; he listened as Mignon sang:

> Only he who's had to yearn
> Knows all that I now bear!
> As every joy I must spurn,
> No one with whom to share,
> My eyes to Heaven turn,
> Searching everywhere.
> When will my love return
> With love and care!
> Fresh pains within me burn,
> And soon I'll faint, I swear.
> Oh, whoever's had to yearn!
> Only he who's had to yearn
> Knows all that I now bear.

Chapter 8

The gentle tempting of his loving, protective spirit could not set our
friend on the right path. The uneasiness he felt was only increased by
the song. A secret fire stirred in his veins, within his soul distinct im-

ages alternated with vague ones, arousing an irresistible longing. First he longed for a steed, then to have wings, and only when it seemed impossible for him to stay did he look about to determine where he longed to go.

In the thread of his destiny so many knots had been tied that either had to become more entangled or finally be untied. Often when he heard a horse trotting or a carriage rolling, he quickly peered out the window with the hope it would be someone who would pay him a visit and even if by chance bring him news, certainty, and joy! He invented a hundred stories how his brother-in-law Werner could travel into this region and surprise him, how Mariane might perhaps appear. The sound of every postman's horn (for their route ran through the village) roused him. Most probable though was that Melina would be sending him news of his fate, and he was most pleasantly occupied with the thought that the servant might return and reveal to him the whereabouts of the splendid beauty. Although he was hardly aware of it, it was this last thought that held him most firmly in his mean lodgings.

One pleasant vision followed the other until his spirit was guided by a sequence of images and observations to a topic that grew ever more repugnant and unbearable the more closely he examined it. It was the memory of his unfortunate period as commander of the troops which pained him. For although he had said almost everything he had to say on the evening of that evil day, he still could not deny his own guilt and had to assign it to himself in every way. He had called for their confidence, guided the will of those who were reluctant, and, led by inexperience and rashness, had taken the lead. All had followed him in confidence and a danger had befallen them that they had not been able to overcome. Spoken and silent accusations pursued him, and when he had promised the misguided troupe after their painful losses not to abandon them until he had replaced everything they had lost with interest, this had been a new audacity through which he had presumed to take a general, shared misfortune onto his shoulders alone, and it was perhaps not only excitement, caprice, or the dilemma of the moment that compelled him. That generous offer of his hand, which no one had been willing to accept, was only a mere formality compared to the oath his heart had taken. He thought of means of being useful and helpful to them and, as manifold as these were, they were still insufficient to remove from his spirit the pressure that lay heavily on him in hours of melancholy.

His thoughts continued to revolve in this wondrous circle and perhaps, like a person held in a spell, he would have remained within it if a letter from Melina had not torn him out of his reveries and urged him to come to H**. This poor man found himself in a distressful situation, for the director wanted nothing to do with him and his people. If something still could be arranged, it could happen only through Wilhelm's presence. Thus he set out with his two companions, and the strange trio soon arrived in that vital and bustling community, where new and unusual events awaited them.

Wilhelm hastened to call on his old friend Serlo (for that is what we will call the director). The latter received him with open arms and called to him from a distance, "My dear Meister, is that you? Am I seeing you again?"

"Quiet," replied Wilhelm as he embraced him, "I'm now called Geselle and that's the only name I've used till now."

"Good, my friend," said Serlo as he observed the newcomers. "You've changed little, if at all. Is your love for the noblest art still so strong and vital? I'm so happy at your arrival I almost forgot what good reason I have to complain to you."

"How so?" responded Wilhelm, who had a rough idea of where his remark was leading.

"You're not dealing with me like a good fellow," said Serlo. "In your last letter you treated me like a grand lord to whom one in good conscience can recommend useless people. You haven't paused to consider that we must earn our daily bread. Your Melina and his people are truly good for nothing."

Wilhelm was about to speak in their defense, but Serlo began to give so merciless a description of them that our friend was quite content when a young woman entered the room, interrupting the conversation, and was immediately introduced by his friend as his sister Aurelie. This admirable young woman, a widow, received him most cordially and her conversation was so pleasant that he did not once notice the pronounced trait of grief that had marked her intelligent face. They spoke of the newest plays and of current taste. One topic led to the next and Wilhelm did not fail to find an occasion to present to them his Hamlet which had so occupied him. Serlo assured him he would gladly have played the role of Polonius and said to his sister, "You'll surely assume Ophelia?" The smile with which he said this displeased Wilhelm, for it seemed to have something insulting about it.

Aurelie answered calmly and coldly, "Why not?"

Wilhelm now began in his fashion to grow quite loquacious and very didactic concerning how he wanted to have his Hamlet played. He presented in detail his findings, which we saw him busily pursuing in the preceding Chapter. He took great pains to make his views acceptable, no matter how much Serlo sought to cast doubts upon his hypothesis. "All right," the latter finally said, "we'll grant you everything. What more do you want to explain with it?"

"A great deal! Everything!" replied Wilhelm. "Imagine a prince as I've described him, whose father dies unexpectedly. Ambition and a desire to rule are not the passions that move him. He had gone along with being the son of a king; now he sees himself compelled for the first time to pay more attention to the distance separating king and subject. The right to the crown was not hereditary, yet a longer life of his father would have strengthened the claims of an only son and destined him to be the future king. On the other hand, he feels himself so poor in grace, in property, so alien to that which he had regarded as his possession from childhood on. It is here his spirit takes its first melancholy turn: he no longer feels himself to be more than any nobleman; he pretends to be everyone's servant. Not courtly, not condescending, no, fallen and in need.

"He looks back on his previous condition as a vanished dream. In vain his uncle tries to cheer him, to show him his situation from a different viewpoint, but the sense of his nothingness remains with him.

"The second blow that struck him hurt him more deeply, bowed him lower. This is the marriage of his mother. When his father died, his mother remained for him, her tender, faithful son. If he honored the heroic figure of that great departed man, he could do so in the company of a surviving, noble, faithful mother. Now he also loses the latter, and in a manner worse than death. The reliable image a well trained child gladly paints its parents disappears. There is no help from the dead man and no reliance on the living woman. She's another female! She too is now included in the general designation of 'frailty' applied to her sex.

"Now he feels quite defeated for the first time, now for the first time orphaned, and no earthly fortune is capable of restoring to him what he has lost. He is not melancholy, not pensive by nature; this melancholy, this pensiveness become a heavy burden for him. That's the way we see him enter. I don't believe I exaggerate at all."

Serlo looked at his sister and said, "Did I give you a false picture of our friend? He's off to a good start, he'll tell us a great deal more and talk us into accepting much of it."

Wilhelm swore most solemnly that he didn't want to talk them into anything, but to convince them, and he asked for a moment's patience. "Imagine vividly this youth, this son of a prince, visualize his situation, and then observe him when he learns his father's figure has appeared. Stand by him in the frightful night when the venerable spirit appears before him! A monstrous horror seizes him, he speaks to the miraculous figure, sees it gesture to him, follows, listens — and what does he hear? The most frightful accusation against his uncle! A call to revenge and the urgent repeated plea: 'Remember me!' And when the spirit has vanished, whom do we see standing before us? A young hero panting for revenge? A born prince who feels happy to have been challenged twice and thrice to face the usurper of his crown? No! Astonishment and melancholy come over him; he vows not to forget his departed father. He grows bitter at the smiling villains and sighs,

> The time is out of joint; o cursed spite,
> That ever I was born to set it right!

"In these words, it seems to me, lies the key to Hamlet's whole conduct, and it's clear to me what Shakespeare wanted to depict: a great deed imposed upon a soul that was not capable of performing it.

"And this I find splendidly carried out in the play. Here an oak tree is planted in a precious vase that should only have borne lovely flowers; the roots expand and the vase is destroyed.

"A beautiful, pure, noble, highly moral nature, but one lacking the toughness of mind that makes the hero, perishes beneath a burden which it can neither bear nor reject. Every duty is sacred to him, but this one is too difficult. The impossible is asked of him, not that which is impossible, but that which is impossible for him! However he twists, turns, torments himself, advances or retreats, he is always reminded, always reminds himself and ultimately almost loses sight of his goal, without ever having regained happiness."

Chapter 9

Their conversation was interrupted by several persons who gradually joined them. These were musicians and actors whose various views agreed in that each lived entirely according to his own thinking.

Philibert, a splendid young clarinetist, stepped in, filled with indignation that the public had not paid justice to his friend, an excellent cellist in his estimation. "That is my friend," he exclaimed, "and no intrigue is going to rule his life." He himself did not wish to produce another note if the cellist were not also heard and paid.

Tarconi, a trained composer, and some actors increased the group, and since each was accustomed to speaking only of himself, the conversation soon grew diffuse, except that the shifts in the dialogues seemed all the more unusual. Finally Horatio, the beloved violinist, entered. The size and beauty of his figure delighted everyone who saw him, and the gentleness of his nature, combined with a masculine dignity, opened all hearts to him. When he took up his instrument, one might pardon Raphael for having presented his Apollo with a violin instead of a lyre. Withdrawn into himself, he was of few words, his whole soul seemed simply to hover over the strings in order to awaken the spirit which was asleep within them and to invite it to a secret conversation with his own. The hearts of his listeners melted at this dialog, which he alone with a few of the initiated understood completely, and even the reverberation of the harmony that filled him completely could make them happy.

Melina finally entered, by nature and clothing the poorest figure, looking as though the best he might be able to do would be to take notes concerning the life of the others, their cleverness and bad manners, their arrogance and discontent, their follies and weaknesses.

But Aurelie seemed to take little part in all that transpired; rather she finally led our friend into a side room and as she gazed at the star-filled sky, she said to him, "You have many more observations for us about Hamlet, but I don't want to rob my brother of the good things you still have to present. Let's leave the Prince and speak to me about Ophelia."

"There's not much to be said about her," Wilhelm replied, "since with only a few traits her figure is completed by the master's hand.

"Ripe, sweet sensuality! Her inclination to the Prince, to whose hand she may lay claim, is so completely left to itself that father and brother both are fearful and warn her. Propriety, like the light crepe at her bosom, cannot hide the stirrings of her heart and much rather becomes its betrayer. Her imagination is inflamed, in quiet modesty she breathes desire and love. When the accommodating goddess Opportunity shakes the tree, the fruit will fall."

"And now," said Aurelie, "when she sees herself abandoned, rejected, scorned, the noblest transformed to the basest in the soul of her demented beloved and he offers her the bitter cup of sorrows instead of the sweet goblet of love?"

"Her heart breaks," replied Wilhelm, "the whole framework of her being is disjointed, her father's death is added to this, and the whole beautiful edifice collapses completely."

Wilhelm had not noticed the emotion with which Aurelie had spoken her last words. Whenever the conversation was about art, he thought only of the work and not of the effect it has on people, each of whom senses and relives his own pain and joy in the fate of another and in the images of the artist.

Aurelie still stood holding her head and with her eyes, which filled with tears, turned heavenward. She had repressed her suffering for a long time until finally she no longer could hide it. She grasped the hands of the astonished man. "Forgive me," she exclaimed, "forgive a tormented heart! Society restricts and constrains me; I have to try to hide my true self from my merciless brother. Your presence has released all the constraints. My friend," she cried, "I've known you only for a moment, and you're already my confidant!" She could scarcely speak and sank onto his shoulder. "Don't think the worse of me," she said sobbing, "for baring myself to you so quickly, for being so weak! Be and remain my friend! I deserve it." He spoke to her in utmost kindness, but in vain! Her tears flowed and choked off her words.

At this moment someone opened the door. Quite unwelcome, Serlo stepped in and, quite unexpectedly, Philine, whom he led by the hand! "Here's your friend," he said to her, pointing at Wilhelm. "He'll be happy to greet you."

"How do I come to find you here?" Wilhelm replied in astonishment.

In a modest, restrained manner she approached him, bade him welcome, and praised the generosity of Serlo, who had taken her into his splendid troupe on hope and without her having deserved it. She behaved most cordially to Wilhelm, but kept a respectful distance. This pretense lasted only as long as the other two were present. Aurelie departed in order to hide her suffering, and Serlo was called away. Philine first checked the doors quite thoroughly to make sure they were gone and then jumped about in the room as if demented. She sat on the floor, almost choking with laughter. Then she leaped up, flattered our friend and rejoiced unrestrainedly at how clever she had been to have gone ahead, scouted out the terrain, and found herself a nest.

"Life's rather colorful here," she said, "just the way I like it. Aurelie had an unhappy love affair with Baron von J**, who is said to be young, rich, handsome, and smart, and he left her a souvenir, unless I'm very mistaken. If it's his image, the papa must be a darling. She has a boy with her who's about three years old and fair as the sun. I usually can't stand children, but this lad is a delight. I figured it out: the death of her husband, the new acquaintance, it all fits together.

"The friend has now gone his way and hasn't seen her for a year. That's made her distraught and inconsolable. The fool! The brother has a dancer in his troupe with whom he's familiar, several more in the city on whom he calls, and now I'm on his list. The fool! About the others," she looked at the door, "you shall hear tomorrow. But just a brief word about Philine, whom you know: The archfool! She's in love with you!" She swore it was true and assured him with curses that it all made an excellent joke. She begged Wilhelm fervently to fall in love with Aurelie, then the fun would really begin. "She'll be running after her faithless lover, you after her, I after you, and her brother after me! If that doesn't provide us fun for half a year, then I'll die in the first episode of the novel this lovers' quadrangle produces." She begged him not to ruin the plot and to show her the respect she intended to earn through her public conduct.

Chapter 10

The next morning Wilhelm thought he would call on Madame Melina but did not find her at home. He asked about the other members of the wandering troupe, but they were not to be found. Finally he learned Philine had invited them all to breakfast, where he found them quite relaxed and cheerful. The clever girl had called them together, treated them to chocolate, and let them know their prospects were still not closed. Through her influence she hoped to convince Serlo how advantageous it would be for him to join such skillful people to his troupe. They listened attentively to her comments, sipped one cup after another, and found the girl not at all as contemptible as she had appeared a few weeks ago. Even after she had dismissed them, they continued to speak well of her and found it to their advantage to leave certain frivolous little stories untold.

"Do you believe," said Wilhelm, who had remained alone with Philine, "Serlo can decide to keep all of them or even some?"

"By no means," replied Philine. "Nor is that any concern of mine. I wish they were gone, the sooner, the better, and I'll see how I can get rid of them. But a different concern does worry me. Oh, if you could just decide to join us, to take up an art for which you were born, and which would surely bring you honor and ample reward!"

"Don't even think of it," replied Wilhelm. "I hope you haven't revealed that I've already been on the stage."

"How can you attribute such an indiscretion to me!" the latter replied.

"Good," he said, "I'll rely on that, for I've about made up my mind to resume using my true name and call on my father's friends."

"Don't be in a hurry," said Philine, and the two parted.

Wilhelm had requested of Serlo permission to attend the rehearsal, which the latter had denied him, directing him rather to the performance itself. "You must become acquainted with us when we're at our best, before we allow you to learn our tricks."

With great satisfaction he attended the play the following evening. It was the first time he had seen theater in such perfection. Actors with splendid talents, fortunate instincts, energy, and a high concept of their art, who, even if they were not all equal, nonetheless sustained, supported, and inspired each other by turn. Serlo showed himself to great advantage. Whenever he came on the stage, whenever he opened his mouth, one had to be astonished at his humor and vitality; one could feel his inner contentment with his being, a sense of which spread throughout the audience. An extraordinary practicing of his art had made him skillful at expressing the finest nuances of the roles with utmost ease.

His sister, Aurelie, was no less skillful and received even greater applause, since she stirred the spirits of the audience, whom he was only able to delight. But I shall refrain from talking further about her and the others. We shall see their actions and their acting, and the reader will be able to judge for himself.

The following morning Aurelie asked to see our friend. He hastened to her and found her lying on the sofa. She seemed to be suffering from a headache and fever. Her eye brightened when she saw him entering. "Forgive me!" she exclaimed. "The trust you inspire has made me weak. I can no longer keep to myself the secret, the suffering, that until now has given me strength and consolation. Without knowing it, you have untied the bonds of silence and now, without wanting to, you will have to participate in the battle I'm waging against myself." Wilhelm answered her amiably and obligingly and assured her that her image and her suffering had constantly hovered before him during the night, that he was asking for her confidence, and that he would devote himself to her as a friend.

While he was saying this, his eyes were drawn to the boy, who was sitting before her on the floor and busy with all sorts of toys. As Philine had reported, he was perhaps three years old, and only now did Wilhelm understand the simile that normally less than elegant, frivolous girl used when she likened the child's beauty to that of the sun. The most beautiful, golden locks curled about his large, blue eyes and full face; dark, slightly arched eyebrows were traced on his dazzling white forehead; and a pronounced glow of health shone upon his cheeks.

"Sit down by me," said Aurelie. "You're looking at that happy child with astonishment. Certainly I accepted him with joy and I'm raising him with care. Only in him I also sense the degree of my suffering because only rarely do I feel the value of such a gift. Permit me," she continued, "to talk now about myself and my fate, for it's very important to me that you not misunderstand me. I thought I had a few unhurried moments free, that's why I summoned you. You're here and I've lost the thread of my thoughts.

"You'll say, 'One more abandoned creature in the world!' You're a man and thinking, "How she's carrying on about a necessary evil, one surer than death: a man's infidelity! The fool!" Oh, my friend, if my fate were usual, I would gladly endure a common misfortune, but it is extraordinary. Why can't I say this to you while talking into a mirror, why can't I have someone else tell it to you! Oh, had I been seduced, surprised, and then abandoned, like Ariadne, then there would still be comfort in my despair. I'm in a much worse way, I deceived and betrayed myself while knowing better, this is what I can never forgive myself."

"With attitudes such as your own, you can never be entirely unhappy," replied her friend.

"And do you know to whom I owe these attitudes?" asked Aurelie. "To the worst possible training through which a girl was ever ruined, to the worst example by which one can lead the mind and instincts astray. After the early death of my mother, I spent the most delicate years of my development with an aunt who made it a law to disrespect the law of respectability. Blindly she abandoned herself to every inclination, whether she might be in command of its object or be its slave, so long as she could forget herself in wild abandon.

"We children, whose true vision of innocence let everything appear pure and clear, what sort of ideas were we compelled to form of the male sex? How dull, pushy, impudent, and clumsy each one was whom she enticed; how sated, arrogant, and tasteless each one who had satisfied his desires. Thus I saw this woman for months being degraded at the command of the most horrible men. What encounters she had to undergo, with what audacity she was able to accept her fate, and indeed with what style to bear her disgraceful fetters!

"Thus did I become acquainted with your sex, my friend, and how purely I hated it when I saw otherwise decent men lose every vestige of goodness in this relationship to my own sex.

"An elderly man who treated me as a daughter completely opened my eyes. I also became acquainted with my own sex and, truly, as a girl of sixteen, was wiser than I am now, when I scarcely understand myself. Why are we so wise when we are young? So wise in order to grow ever more foolish!"

The boy became noisy and Aurelie grew impatient. She rang a bell, and an old woman came in to take him away. "Do you still have a toothache?" Aurelie asked the woman, who had bound up her face.

"Still almost unbearable," the latter replied in a muffled voice as she picked up the boy, who seemed to go along willingly, and took him off.

Scarcely had the child been removed when Aurelie began to weep bitterly. "I can't do anything but cry and complain," she exclaimed, "and I'm ashamed to lie here before you like a poor worm. I've lost

my presence of mind and I can't go on with my story. You were supposed to hear from me how my love for art lifted me up, how I first
hoped for everything from my nation and then again despaired of it."
She hesitated and fell silent. Her friend, who didn't care to speak in
platitudes but had nothing else to say, held her hand and looked at
her for a while. Then in his embarrassment he picked up a book lying
on a small table before him; it was the works of Shakespeare, opened
to *Hamlet*.

Serlo, who just stepped into the door with a question concerning
the welfare of his sister, glanced into the book our friend was holding
and cried out, "Do I find you again studying your Hamlet? That's perfect! Some doubts have occurred to me which seem to diminish the
canonical respect you'd so like to give to the work. How is it with
your plot? Especially with the last two acts after Hamlet has spoken
with his mother? It simply doesn't work. The English themselves have
admitted as much."

Wilhelm replied, "It's quite possible some elements of the nation
that has produced such masterworks fail to recognize even the best
part of it. But that can't keep us from seeing with our own eyes and
being just. Far from believing the plot of this play is to be criticized, I
am much more of the mind that no greater one has ever been conceived. Indeed, it wasn't thought up, it simply is."

"How do you hope to prove that?" asked Serlo.

"I'll not prove a thing," said Wilhelm. "I'll simply present to you
how I understand it."

Aurelie raised up from her pillow and propped herself up with her
hand. She looked at our friend, who continued to speak with the
greatest confidence in the correctness of his views.

"It does please us, it flatters us greatly whenever we see a hero
who acts on his own, who loves and hates when his heart commands
him to, who undertakes and carries out actions, turning aside all obstacles and achieving some great goal. Historians and poets have led
us to believe that so proud a fate can befall man. Our play teaches
otherwise. Here the hero has no plan, but the play has one. Here we
don't have a trivial thought of revenge through which a misdeed is
punished. No, a monstrous deed occurs that rolls forward with all its
consequences, sweeping the innocent along with it. It seems to want
to avoid the abyss prepared for it, yet plunges into it just when it
thinks it has run its course. For it's characteristic of the monstrous
deed that it spreads much evil among the innocent, just as the good
act spreads much good among the undeserving, without the origina-
tors of either being punished or rewarded. Here how miraculous! Pur-
gatory sends its spirit to demand revenge, but in vain! All circum-

stances converge and pursue vengeance, but in vain! Neither mortals nor spirits succeed in carrying out that which was reserved for Fate alone. The hour of judgment comes. The evil man falls with the good! One family is mowed away, and another steps in."

After a pause in which they looked at one another, Serlo spoke. "You pay no special compliment to Providence when you exalt your poet, and then in honor of him you seem to ascribe to him ends and means he never thought of, which others would ascribe to Providence."

Chapter 11

"May I also," said Aurelie, "pose a question? I've looked through Ophelia's role again and feel up to performing it under certain conditions. But tell me, couldn't one let the mad woman sing other songs that could be fragments of ballads, but not such ambiguous and filthy lyrics? What's the purpose of that?"

"My dear friend," replied Wilhelm, "I can't concede one iota, for here too lies great expressiveness. We see what the good child is concerned with in her heart. Secretly the sounds of lasciviousness echoed within her heart, and like a foolish nurse, she sought to sing her sensuality to rest with ditties which necessarily made it more wakeful. She lived quietly unto herself, scarcely hiding her yearning and desires. Now, when she lost command of herself and her heart hovers on her tongue, this tongue becomes her betrayer, and in the innocence of madness she takes delight before king and queen in the echo of her songs of loneliness made naughty by her love: about the girl who is won, the girl who sneaks to her young man, and so forth."

He had not yet finished talking when before his eyes there occurred a strange scene which he could in no way explain.

Serlo had walked up and down in the room a few times and had imperceptibly drawn near to Aurelie's night stand. Suddenly he reached quickly for something lying upon it and hurried towards the door with his booty. Aurelie, who noticed, arose and hurled herself in his way, grabbed him with unbelievable emotion, and was adroit enough to grasp one end of the stolen object. They struggled and scuffled quite intently, he laughing, she growing more earnest. They turned and twisted about, and when Wilhelm hastened to calm and separate them, he suddenly saw Aurelie leap to one side with a naked dagger in her hand and Serlo half angrily throw down the scabbard that had been left to him. Wilhelm stepped back in astonishment, and his perplexed look seemed to ask for the cause why such a singular struggle could arise between them over such a strange household item.

"You shall be the judge between us," said Serlo. "What is she doing with this sharp steel? Have a look at it. This dagger is fit for no actress. As pointed and sharp as any knife or needle, what is this joke for? Emotional as she is, one day she's accidentally going to hurt herself. I have a deep hatred of such oddities. A serious thought in this direction is insane, and a toy this dangerous is in poor taste."

"I have it back!" cried Aurelie, raising the naked blade. "I'll now take better care of my true friend. Forgive me," she exclaimed as she kissed the blade, "for neglecting you so!"

Serlo seemed to become seriously angry.

"Take it as you wish, Brother," she continued, "I find you unjust. Do you know what a precious talisman has been granted to me in this form, what solace and counsel I find in it in bad times? Must everything that looks dangerous be harmful?"

"Remarks like those, which are without reason, can drive me mad," Serlo said and left the room in repressed fury. Aurelie returned the dagger to its scabbard, which she lifted from the floor, and pocketed it. "Let's continue our conversation where my unhappy brother interrupted it," she interjected when Wilhelm introduced some questions concerning the odd struggle.

"I can't do anything if you describe the good Ophelia so, for it may have been the poet's intent, but I can pity her sooner than empathize with her. And permit me to say that, just as we were interrupted, I was concerned with an observation for which, my friend, you've given me occasion in this short time. With amazement I've noted in you the great and correct insight with which you judge literature, and particularly dramatic literature. The deepest abysses are not hidden from you, you notice the finest nuances. Without having known the objects in real life, you recognize them for what they are in their images. There seems to lie within you a foretaste of the whole world which is stirred and developed through harmonious contact with poesy. For truly," she continued, "nothing enters you from without! I have scarcely seen anyone who so completely misjudges the people with whom he lives as you do. Permit me to say, if a person hears you explain your Shakespeare, he believes you just emerged from the counsel of the gods, who were discussing making men in their own image. When I see you dealing with people, I see in you the first child born as an adult in all of Creation, who with unusual surprise and delighted good cheer addresses lions and monkeys, sheep and elephants as being of his own kind, simply because they exist and move."

"I'll admit my schoolboyish nature and ask your forgiveness," he replied. "From childhood I've always looked more within than without, and thus it's quite natural that I've become acquainted with people up to a certain point without understanding them in the slightest."

"Indeed," said Aurelie, "in the beginning I thought you were making fun of us when you said so many good things about the people you met at our place. Your splendid Tarconi is nothing more and nothing less than a pedant and a loudmouth as well. The friendship between Philbert and Celio is a simple farce: the latter, a mediocre musician and a bad human makes the former believe what he wishes. He caters to his whims and desires only in order that the energetic, universally welcome, talented young artist will drag him along with him and share all his advantages with him. And what a miserable pack the entire troupe is that you recommended to my brother! I can sooner pardon you for having been deceived by Horatio. This splendid Apollo, this dignity, this bearing seems to proclaim something, and one can not be supposed to think that in its entirety this would be a lifeless lump of clay, had the violin bow not been invented to elicit some sounds from it."

Wilhelm stood before her, ashamed; no one had ever drawn him so clear a picture of himself. He did not answer; rather he thought back and reflected about himself. It was as if a fog were lifting before his eyes.

"You mustn't be downcast at this," cried Aurelie. "It's a fine quality for a young poet and artist, and you are both, even if you don't wish to present yourself as such. This ignorance and innocence is like the sheath that surrounds and nourishes a bud; it's sad enough when we're forced to come out prematurely. Certainly it's good if we aren't always well acquainted with those for whom we labor.

"That's the way it was for me, too, when I appeared on the stage with the highest opinion of my nation. Weren't the Germans everything! Couldn't they become whatever they wanted! I spoke to this nation, above which a small scaffolding raised me and from which I was divided by a row of lamps, whose glow and smoke prevented me from distinguishing clearly the objects before me. How welcome was the sound of applause that resounded up to me, and what a precious thing that gift was, offered to me unanimously by so many hands. For a long time I lulled myself with the thought. As I affected them, so my audience influenced me; I and my public had the best relationship and we were in perfect harmony with one another! And in the retinue of my public I always beheld my nation, with everything noble and good!

"Unfortunately it was not merely the actress who interested a large portion of the theatergoers; they made further demands on this young, vivacious girl. Many wanted me to share the emotions I had aroused in them, but unfortunately I wasn't at all interested in that. I hoped to elevate their minds! I didn't make the slightest claim to what they called their heart, so one after another became a burden to me. Every class, age, and character, each made an attempt in his own fashion, and I sent each of them off in my own fashion. Nothing was more annoying to me than my not being able to shut myself in my room like any other decent girl and thus spare myself no end of trouble.

"The men now presented themselves in the light I was accustomed to at my aunt's. Here they would have appeared despicable again, had I not been able to find their foibles and follies amusing. Since I couldn't help seeing them at the theater and also in our house, I decided to wait them all out. My old, valuable friend helped me resolutely with this. If you consider that from the tasteless shop clerk and the conceited merchant's son to the shrewdly calculating sophisticate, the brave soldier, and the imperious prince, they in time all came my way, the one wanting to begin his novel, the next trying to write a new chapter for his, then you'll have to concede that in any case I might believe I've experienced my nation rather well.

"The fantastically attired student, the humbly awkward scholar, the smug, mincing canon, the primly attentive man of business, the ignorant baron, the amiable, suave courtier, the young cleric going astray, the casual man of wealth, as well as the most speculative, adaptable merchant, I've had the pleasure of seeing them all maneuver, and, by Heaven, there were few among them who would have been capable of arousing a mutual interest within me. On the contrary, I was extremely annoyed to garner from the fools individually and with maximum pomposity and boredom the approbation which had so pleased me en masse and which I had gladly claimed in toto. I now began cordially to despise them all, and it was as if the entire nation had deliberately sought to prostitute itself before me through its ambassadors. On the whole they appeared so clumsy to me, so poorly educated, so ill informed, so devoid of a pleasant nature, so tasteless, that I then often said, no German can buckle a shoe unless he's learned how from a foreigner.

"You see how blindly depressed I was, and the longer it lasted, the worse my illness became. I could have hanged myself, but I went to the other extreme: I married, or much rather, I let myself be married. My brother, who had taken over the theater, wanted to have an assistant, and my old friend wanted to know I was provided for before he died. Their choice fell to a young man who was not offensive to me.

He lacked everything my brother possessed: genius, life, spirit, and an impulsive nature. But he also possessed what the other lacked: a love of order, diligence, a precious gift for administration and for managing money.

"He became my husband, though I don't know how; we lived together, though I hardly know why. Suffice it to say matters went well, we took in a lot, the result of my brother's cleverness; we made ends meet, and this we owed to my husband. I no longer thought about the world and my nation. I had nothing to share with the world, and I despised my nation or, much more the case, I didn't think about it. Whenever I acted, I did so in order to live, and whenever I opened my mouth, it happened because I wasn't permitted to remain silent, because I had made an entrance in order to speak.

"But I mustn't paint things too black! Actually I had consented completely in my brother's intentions, who was concerned about applause and money (for, just between us, he likes to hear himself praised and he spends a great deal). I now no longer acted according to my feelings or convictions, but as he directed, and when I had earned his approval, I was satisfied. Money came in, he could live according to his whim, and we had good days with him.

"Meanwhile I had fallen into a professional rut, I passed my days without joy, without participating, my marriage was childless and lasted only a short time. My husband was sickly and, apart from caring for him when his strength was fading, I lived in general indifference. Then I made an acquaintance with whom a new life began for me, a new and quicker one, for it will remove me from the scene earlier."

She was silent for a while, then she continued: "All of a sudden my talkative mood has ended, and I don't trust myself to open my mouth again! Let me rest a little; then if we are not disturbed, you'll not depart without learning in more detail what you already know. Meanwhile call in Mignon and hear what she wants."

During Aurelie's narrative, the child had been in the room a few times. When she noticed they lowered their voices when she was there, she had gone off and was sitting in the parlor and waiting.

When she was summoned back, she brought along a book which was soon recognized by its shape and binding as a small geographical atlas. At the pastor's on their journey, she had seen maps for the first time and with great astonishment. She had informed herself, as well as she could, through a hundred questions. Her unusual desire to learn seemed to have become much more active through this new knowledge. She begged Wilhelm fervently to buy her the book, she had left her silver buckles as security for it, and because it had grown too late this evening, she wanted to redeem them early tomorrow morning. He gave his consent. She now opened the book and began partly to recite what she knew, partly to pose in her fashion the oddest questions. They could see that despite her great efforts, things were very difficult for her. The same was true of her handwriting, over which she had so struggled. She still spoke very broken German, and only when she opened her mouth to sing, whenever she played the zither did she seem to make use of the only medium through which she could unlock and reveal her innermost feelings.

Since we are speaking of her, we must also mention the embarrassing situation into which she recently had put our friend. At every opportunity when he arrived or departed, said "Good morning!" or "Good night!," she embraced him so firmly within her arms and kissed him with such ardor that he often grew worried and fearful at the emotion of this emerging personality. This pulsing vitality in her nature increased, and her whole being stirred in restless silence. Often when she seemed to be standing idly by, one noticed she was clenching her teeth or gnashing them quietly. She always had to have something in her hands, a towel that she twisted, a string that she wound, and never with the casual expression of playing, but only as though thereby a strong inner shock were being averted.

Since on this occasion there seemed no end to her questions, Aurelie grew impatient, being in the mood to hope to continue a conversation with our friend on a subject that concerned her greatly. This was made clear enough to the youngster, and when that did no good, she was sent away.

"I must tell you," said Aurelie, "the rest of my story, now or never. If my dearly beloved, unjust friend were but a few miles from here, I would say you should mount your horse, make his acquaintance on whatever pretext, and when you return, you will have pardoned and pitied me. Just at the critical time when I was concerned about my husband's last days, I became acquainted with him. He had returned from travels, and his traveling companion had departed.

"He met me with a casual dignity, with an open good nature, spoke about me and my situation, my acting, so that his first conversation immediately made me attentive. His judgments were sound and never derogatory, trenchant without being heartless; if occasionally he was hard, it wasn't offensive, and his playfulness was also pleasing. He seemed to be accustomed to good luck with women, which interested me. He was in no way flattering and pushy, which made me trusting.

"He associated with few people, was usually on horseback, visiting his many acquaintances in the area; when he returned, he dismounted at my place, treated my ever failing husband with genuine concern, brought comfort to the sufferer through a skillful doctor, and since he was always interested in everything that concerned me, he also let me share in his affairs. He told me how he as a second son had always felt devoted to the military life for which he felt an irresistible attraction, how through the death of his elder brother he had been compelled to submit to his family's wishes. He had to travel and concern himself with things that interested him little. Enough, he hid nothing from me, he revealed his entire soul to me, his history, his talents, his emotions, everything attracted me, everything, everything drew me to him.

"In the midst of this, I lost my husband more or less as I had found him, and the worry for everything fell entirely upon me after his death. My brother wanted only to act and live, and not to worry. I was extremely busy; I studied my roles more intently than ever and acted as I had long ago, and indeed with a quite different strength and vitality. I didn't always act as well as possible when I knew my noble friend was in the theater; sometimes he secretly overheard me and you can imagine how pleasant his unexpected approval was to me. Certainly I'm a strange creature! Whenever I played a role it always seemed to me as if I were praising him, for that was the mood of my heart, whatever the words may have been. If I knew he was in the audience, I was ashamed to act and speak with full force as though I didn't want to praise him straight to his face. If he was absent, then I had free play and I held nothing back. Also as if by a miracle my relationship to the public and to the entire nation had changed. Suddenly it again appeared to me in the most favorable light. I can't tell you how astonished I was, and it's still inconceivable to me how such a change in perception can take place within us.

"How foolish you were, I often said to myself, back when the nation displeased you simply because it is a nation. A mass of human beings among whom a number of abilities and strengths are distributed without their actually having a common purpose, without their being individually interesting. And precisely because of this they turn into a single element upon which an exemplary person can exert influence. I rejoiced in their having been born in order to be led; I loved them on account of that, for I believed I had found their leader.

"Lothar had always presented the Germans to me from the aspect of their bravery and assured me there was no braver nation in the world if it were properly led. This struck me and I was ashamed I had never thought of this primary characteristic. Now I quickly began to improve my way of thinking, I no longer asked about education, about style, and let the coarse and unsightly crust please me for the sake of the splendid core. Now I declaimed as if inspired, mediocre verses turned to gold on my lips, and had a poet assisted me, I would have achieved miraculous effects. Thus did your young widow live for months. He could not do without me, I was very unhappy whenever he stayed away. He showed me letters from his relatives, from his splendid sister, he was informed about every detail of my circumstances, a more perfect, heartfelt unity has never been conceived, the name of love was not mentioned.

"He departed and returned, returned and departed. And now, my friend, it is high time that you also leave."

Chapter 12

Our friend now stood as an intimate between the brother and sister, who were equally important to him and each of whom captured, nourished, and occupied a half of his being. Aurelie's fate moved him deeply, but without arousing any tenderness for her. Her passionate understanding called his good nature back from its childish intoxication and led him out of his ideal world into the real one. He was astonished when he became aware of himself, as it were, for the first time and through comparison with others was shown where he belonged.

He also could find no more desirable teacher and guide for his favorite art than Serlo, who not only appeared to great advantage in the theater, as if he were in his true element, but also had thought about the art he had practiced from earliest youth. He was in the best sense of the word born to the stage: as a child he had played to the public's great satisfaction the harlequin who crawls out of the egg or emerges from a cloud as well as the darling chimney sweep's assistant, carrying his little white ladder. As a youth he had directed his mischievous talents at the monotony of the other actors and was able to imitate each of them in voice and manner and gestures so perfectly that each, even if he saw himself mocked, had to laugh. A splendid memory came to his assistance, he knew entire plays by heart, and his natural talent captured every expression, save the pathetic and the heartfelt. Restlessness and a fear of the consequences of some frivolous pranks drove him away from his family when he was scarcely fourteen years old. He was never at a loss in finding his way, and before high and low, before ordinary people and connoisseurs he dared to present an unheard-of entertainment by performing entire tragedies and comedies all by himself. He knew how to improvise a theater in any room or any garden, and without the illusion of scenery he entertained and delighted the observer through his successful delivery. He imitated all exaggerated characters admirably and likewise the voices of women and children to the point of deceiving every ear. Probably no one has ever presented the caricature of a Jewish rabbi so well. The strange drive, the sensual, repulsive eagerness, the mad gestures, the confused mumbling, the shrill screaming, the effeminate movements and spasmodic tensings, the eccentricity of senile confusion he had captured so splendidly and reproduced in such sharp focus that this bit of poor taste could amuse even the most fastidious person for a quarter of an hour. He had the kindness to introduce over time all such tricks of the trade to our friend, who took extraordinary delight in them. Although it was all far removed from his own style, it was his first introduction to the true dramatic sense and spirit, and he was able to derive precepts and examples from it for himself.

This would have all been fine had not Melina and his people sometimes appeared as evil spirits in the background. These unfortunates, who were starting to feel true want, trusted Philine's words for a while. They had not yet given up entirely on getting work through her, only now they admonished Wilhelm more sharply that he should contribute his share. He had sought to persuade his friend Serlo, but no one persuaded the latter to anything that was not to his advantage; rather he gradually tried to make it clear to our friend how wonderful it would be if he would make up his mind to go into theater. His arguments grew more forceful after the discovery, which Philine secretly revealed to him, that Wilhelm had already performed once, and thus it was all the more probable his passion for the stage could be used to capture him.

After Wilhelm had spent an entire afternoon in this fashion with Serlo, he hastened to Aurelie, whom he found resting on her bed. She seemed quiet.

"Do you still think you'll be able to go on tomorrow?" he asked.

"Oh, yes," she replied emphatically, "you know there's nothing preventing me. If I only knew a way to reject the applause from the parterre. They mean well, but they'll kill me yet. The day before yesterday I thought my heart would burst. Formerly I could bear it if I pleased myself, had studied my lines and prepared well, and the welcome sign that it had been successful echoed from every corner. But now! I don't say what I want to, nor in the manner I want to. I'm torn along, I grow confused, and my acting makes a far greater impression. The applause grows louder, and I think, 'If you only knew what delights you! You're bestowing your best wishes to the deepest suffering of my soul !' "

"This morning I studied, rehearsed, practiced, and am now tired and broken. Tomorrow it starts again, tomorrow evening there's another performance, and that's how I drag myself along, getting up and going to bed. Everything's drawing a never ending circle about me; then all sorts of pitiful consolations appear. I reject them and curse them. I will not surrender! Why should that be necessary? What has condemned me? Perhaps it could be otherwise! I simply must pay the price for being a German. It's characteristic of the Germans that they take everything seriously and that everything weighs heavily upon them."

"Yes, my friend, if only you wouldn't take it so hard!"

"It's hard enough!" she interrupted him.

"Is nothing left for you," he replied, "your better days, your health, your art? If you lost an estate through no fault of your own, must you throw everything else after it? Is that, too, necessary?"

She was silent for a few moments, then she began anew. "I know well it's nothing but a waste of time, love's nothing but a waste of time! What I could have done! Should have done! It's all turned to nothing, nothing at all! I'm a poor, lovesick creature, nothing but lovesick! Have compassion with me, for, God knows, I'm a poor creature." And after a pause she exclaimed, "You're accustomed to having everyone throw themselves at you. No, you can't feel it, there's no man who can appreciate the worth of a woman who knows how to respect herself. Among all the holy angels, among all the images of bliss which a good-natured heart can create for itself, there is nothing sweeter than the soul of a woman surrendering herself. If we deserve to be called women, we are cold, proud, dignified, clearheaded, and clever, but now all this — ! I want to despair, quite deliberately despair! There's not to be a drop of blood within me that will go unpunished, not one fiber I won't mortify.

"Smile! Laugh at this theatrical display of emotion!"

Wilhelm felt far removed from any inclination to laugh. He was most deeply tormented by the frightening, half natural, half compulsive state of his friend. He also felt the torture of her unfortunate strain, his brain was deranged, and his blood coursed feverishly.

She had risen and was walking back and forth in the room. "I tell myself," she exclaimed, "why I shouldn't love him. I also know he's not worthy of it. I turn my mind this way and that, I keep busy. Often I'll take up a role even though I won't have to act it, I rehearse the old ones, in detail and ever more intensely, and rehearse and rehearse. My friend, my confidant, what horrible work it is to forcibly escape oneself!

"My reason suffers, my brain is so racked, and in order to save myself from madness, I again abandon myself to the feeling that I love him. Yes, I love him! I love him!" she cried amid a flood of tears. "I love him! And so I want to die!"

He took her by the hand and begged her most insistently not to agitate herself. "Oh," he said, "how strange it is that men are denied not only so much that is impossible, but also so much that is possible! You weren't destined to find a loyal heart, which would have brought you bliss. I was destined to bind my entire happiness to an unfortunate woman, whom the burden of my loyalty dragged to the ground like a reed, and perhaps even shattered." He had confided his story about Mariane to Aurelie and thus could allude to it.

She looked fixedly into his eyes and asked, "Can you say you have never deceived a woman, you've never tried to incline one to your wishes with silly compliments, wicked gallantry, and vows to lure the heart?"

"I can," said Wilhelm, "and without boasting. My life was very simple, and I've very seldom been tempted to try temptation. And what a warning, my beautiful, my noble friend, is given me by the sad condition in which I find you! Accept my vow, one quite appropriate to the nature of my heart, whose clarity has been restored by the state in which you've set me! I will resist every fleeting inclination and retain even the serious ones within my bosom. No woman shall ever receive a profession of love from my lips unless I can devote my entire life to her!"

She looked at him with a wild indifference and stepped back a few paces as he extended his hand for the oath.

"It's not important at all," she said. "So many women's tears more or less won't cause the sea to rise. But," she continued as she turned around, "one woman among a thousand, that's surely something! One honest man among a thousand, that's acceptable! Do you know what you're promising?"

"I know," replied Wilhelm smiling and extending his hand. "I'll accept it," she replied. Wilhelm still had his hand outstretched, she made a movement with her right hand, and he thought she would take his. Instead she reached quickly into her pocket, whipped out the dagger as swift as lightning, and drew its point and cutting edge lightly across his hand. He withdrew it quickly, but the blood was already showing.

"One has to give you men a sharp reminder if you're to notice," she exclaimed with a satisfaction that quickly changed into a flurry of activity. She took her handkerchief and wrapped his hand in it in order to stem the flowing blood. "Forgive a half-crazed woman," she exclaimed, "and don't regret these few drops of blood. They've brought me back to myself and on my knees I'll beg you for forgiveness. I will heal you, that's my concern."

She hastened to her cupboard, fetched linen, adhesive tape, and instruments, stanched the blood, and examined the wound carefully. The cut ran through the ball directly beneath the thumb, divided the life line, and ran out beneath the little finger. She bandaged him silently and withdrew into herself with a pensive gravity. He asked several times, "Best of women, how could you wound your friend?"

"Hush!" she replied as she laid her finger on his mouth. "Hush!"

Chapter 13

Serlo, for whom nothing would have been better than having Wilhelm in his troupe, had learned from him who the business friends were in the city with whom his father was connected. As soon as he knew this, he managed to inquire quickly as to what news might have arrived concerning the Meister household. In return he was told that some time ago letters had arrived that announced the death of the elder Meister. His widow, it was believed, was scarcely going to wait out the year of mourning in order to marry an old and much loved friend. The son-in-law Werner had taken over the business completely, and the eldest son had disappeared during a trip. People thought that since he had shown unusual interests from childhood and had found little joy in the business, he had become a soldier in the newly erupted war, hoping to find his fortune along this path.

Serlo regarded this news as very favorable to his purposes. He hastened with it to Aurelie and let her know clearly he was pursuing his plan for her sake too. "My dear Brother," she said with a deep sigh, "I wish you all the best in your endeavors and am convinced you would make a very good conquest with this young man. But as for me, I don't want anyone taking me into consideration. I'm no longer among the number of those who hope, and whoever counts on me will probably find himself quite deceived."

"Hope," replied Serlo, "is the most precious heritage of the living, and even if they wanted to, they probably could not divest themselves of it. If you are to be healed, my good woman, this friend is the only one able to do it."

"Brother," she replied, "you have an evil habit of saying things that one might better be silent about and leave to time." He smiled and asked whether she wished to bring the news to Wilhelm or leave it up to him. She asked him to do it.

Some days passed before Serlo found an opportunity to inform our friend about the fate of his family. In the meantime, not a day passed when the latter had not grown closer to Aurelie. The necessity of having her tend his dressings, her care, her melancholy, and her good nature won her the most amiable inclinations of his heart, and she found her burden greatly eased in his company.

She had prepared from black taffeta a rather elegant covering for his hand. "I hope," she said seriously, "you'll soon be healed, but I think you'll bear the mark of this wound all your life. You are honest, my friend, but what man doesn't need a constant reminder? Should your good spirit leave you and, contrary to your oath, you dare to extend your hand to tempt a woman to whom you hadn't given your heart, then look at this scar and pull your hand back while there's still time."

Serlo seized the first opportunity to give our friend without great preparation the report about the state of his family, and we can imagine how strongly it struck Wilhelm. Without letting him recover, Serlo forcefully repeated his offer. "You can now do it without hesitation," he added. "Because your family has survived their worry at your being amid the dangers of war, it will serve as a double or triple consolation for them to see you engaged in so pleasant and pleasing a profession."

Wilhelm did not have much to counter him except that this step seemed insuperable. His heart was so inclined, but a nameless something was opposing his desire.

Serlo besieged him in every way. He offered him considerable earnings, indeed finally even a share of the profits, and when this all proved to no avail, he came out with the strongest argument, which he had saved to the last. "There's no better way for you to recognize my desire to win you for the theater than when I also offer to engage your entire troupe at the same time and thereby free you from an onerous obligation."

"And how," Wilhelm replied half indignantly, "will that make the people you've so greatly despised until now any better?"

"They won't get any better," answered Serlo, "but it's the only way they can be of use to me. I'll lay my plan before you, and you'll see it can't be carried out without you. You know the actor who plays the romantic lead for me; although he has a handsome figure and a pleasant voice, he's far removed from the perfection one may wish for in such roles. He lacks a certain fire, an emphasis, for which a soulful, yet pleasant nature is no substitute. Apart from not being satisfied with him, I've had to engage his wife and his entire entourage. If I can get rid of him, then the others can also go, and then I can more or less use your troupe or incorporate it.

"The wife of my principal lover plays the roles of the mother, the queen, or the like. Madame Melina perhaps would do them no worse, and perhaps better. His brother would be replaced by your so-called

Laertes, who at least gives hope of becoming much better. At the same time a young woman is leaving, whose place Philine can fill. In any case I'll be sending others away, in whose roles it's not important whether they're acted a bit better or worse. The pedant and all of them will find a place. Melina is to become the wardrobe manager and fight off the moths.

"You can see I'm not contradicting myself if I'm now willing to hire those whom I once seriously opposed. Remove yourself from the plan and you'll find not even the slightest part of it can be carried out. Consider my proposals and think of what an essential service you'd be performing through such a decision — for yourself, for us, for the abandoned troupe, and for the public.

"One word more," said Serlo as he held the door in his hand. "If you can't decide now then perhaps you'll do so within two weeks. I have a well-founded hope that a young woman will step onto my stage, who till now has never trod one, but, like you, has quietly and patiently practiced our art. The most beautiful, most imposing figure, a splendid voice, a pure, precise enunciation, such bearing! Everything one can wish for. I'm not saying this so that you'll fall in love with her. I'm saying it simply to convince you that we're not totally unworthy of you. And things will certainly improve greatly, once you count yourself as one of us."

Chapter 14

It is a property of the human soul that it recovers most quickly when it has been most sorely depressed.

To those burdens that lay upon our friend and, so to speak, had gradually crushed him, there now was joined the death of his father and the fate of his family, which so constricted his spirit that he had to seek an outlet somewhere. Remorse and sorrow at the loss of the good, old man, whose existence had been interwoven with his own from his earliest years, the partial alienation from his mother, little interest in the business of his brother-in-law, his own mistakes and his own history, everything twisted and turned up and down, becoming jumbled more than once. Finally he sensed the whole strength of his youth, he shook himself and with a free, courageous mien faced the present, behind which happy images of the future were gathering.

"Here I stand," he said to himself, "not at the crossroads, but at my destination, not daring to take the final step, not daring to seize the prize.

"Indeed, if ever a profession, a calling, was clear and emphatic, then it's this one. Everything happened as if by chance and without my contributing to it, and yet it's all just as I had conceived it earlier, just as I had proposed it. Very strange! A person seems to be familiar with nothing so much as his hopes and wishes, which he has long preserved and nourished in his heart, and, nevertheless, when they once confront him, when they, as it were, force themselves upon him, he doesn't recognize them and pulls back. Everything I ever dreamed of before that unhappy night separated me from Mariane now stands before me and offers itself to me. I wanted to flee to this place and I've gently been led here. I wanted to find a position with Serlo, now he's seeking me and offering me conditions I couldn't expect as a beginner. Was it merely love for Mariane which chained me to the theater? Or was it the love for art that bound me more firmly to her? Was that prospect, that outlet welcome only to an unsettled, restless youth who wanted to continue a life that the circumstances of the bourgeois world didn't permit? Or was it all different, purer, worthier? And if these were once your attitudes, what has caused you to change them? And isn't this step now much more to be approved when it has no secondary motivation that someone might question?"

He once more considered all the circumstances that invited, excited, and drove him, and he finally found he was compelled to take this step. That he could keep Mignon with him, that he would not have to cast out his harpist seemed to be important grounds for his decision.

And yet, as customarily occurs in such cases, when the full weight of conviction has been placed in one pan of the scale, the entire counterweight suddenly hurls itself into the other and hinders the decision. But this too turned out to be advantageous in the matter at hand. "The first time I stepped onto the stage," he said to himself, "I was surprised and carried away, even though it was only an accidental sampling. Now, when it's to last for life, I have the time and leisure to consider and weigh everything."

As he was wrestling with these observations, the door opened and unexpectedly Aurelie, Philine, and Serlo entered. It was Philine's idea, which Serlo gladly followed and by which Aurelie, as it were, let herself be drawn along, although she completely saw through its author in spite of her dissimulation and hated her with all her heart. They greeted him most amiably, and Philine said jokingly, "We've come to hear your assent."

Wilhelm wanted to say something in reply.

"A 'Yes'," she said, "or not a word. We'll gladly permit you to remain silent, but if you choose to speak, then let it be to make us all happy."

"I have no right," said Aurelie, "to ask you for so important a favor, but if I did, I'd use it to give greater emphasis to the various factors that influence your decision. Thus, if it's possible, a 'Yes'."

"A 'Yes'!" said Serlo, "One little word! Indecision's good for nothing, it's the worst waste of time! Once you've made up your mind, the rest will take care of itself."

"A little 'Yes'," Philine coaxed him.

"Then 'Yes'," replied Wilhelm.

Aurelie took his still bandaged right hand in restrainedly genuine joy. Philine seized the left one and, bending down, quickly directed his hand to her lips and planted a loud kiss on it, which he could not avert. Serlo embraced him warmly and heartily. He could not respond to them, for he stood as if benumbed in their midst and fell into silent reflection. His thoughts wandered here and there, and suddenly the forest clearing again filled his imagination. On a gray horse the Amazon came riding out of the bushes, approached him, dismounted, her solicitude compelled her to move here and there, she stopped, the garment fell from her shoulders and covered the wounded man. Her face and her figure again grew radiant — and disappeared.

The End.

In 1910 a Zurich pupil showed his teacher a family heirloom, an eighteenth century manuscript that the latter identified as the long lost first version of Goethe's *Wilhelm Meister's Apprenticeship* (1796). During Goethe's first visit to Switzerland (1775), he had met Barbara Schulthess in Zurich. Either at that time or in their subsequent correspondence she asked to examine his novel in progress. As was not unusual in that day, first she and then her daughter made copies of the work before returning it, thus preserving a work that Goethe, in effect, suppressed.

At the center of *Wilhelm Meisters theatralische Sendung* (*Wilhelm Meister's Theatrical Calling*) stands the theater. In following its youthful protagonist, we are systematically exposed to its many manifestations which characterize its development: from marionettes and child's play through acrobatics, vaudeville and circus down to court theater and, ultimately, modern theater reflecting middle-class, urban life. His work on the novel was interrupted by his journey to Italy in the late 1780s, and after returning to Weimar he abandoned the *Calling* while preserving much of its material and poetry in the *Apprenticeship,* where the medium remains the theater while the focus has shifted to the maturation of young Wilhelm.

The *Calling* is no mere early version of the *Apprenticeship*. It provides much material not found in the *Appren-*